The Information Society

Digital Media and Society Series

The Information Society

Robert Hassan

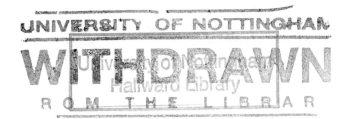

polity

First published in 2008 by Polity Press

Polity Press
65 Bridge Street
Cambridge CB2 1UR, UK

Polity Press
350 Main Street
Malden, MA 02148, USA

ISBN-13: 978-0-7456-4179-9
ISBN-13: 978-0-7456-4180-5 (pb)

1005552399

A catalogue record for this book is available from the British Library.

Typeset in 10.25 on 13 pt FF Scala
by Servis Filmsetting Ltd, Stockport, Cheshire
Printed and bound in Great Britain by Biddles Ltd, Kings Lynn, Norfolk

For further information on Polity, visit our website: www.polity.co.uk

Contents

Preface

We live in an information society. This much is clear; indeed, this much is acutely palpable. It surrounds us and we are a part of it. We 'know' this society insofar as it constitutes a growing reality that is reshaping the world and what it means to be an individual, a worker, and a member of the public within it. Information technologies based upon computer logic have networked our world, shrinking it to the point where it is possible to be constantly in touch with others, no matter where they are or what the time is. The extent of this connectivity is historically unprecedented and it is something that is growing in complexity and utility every minute of every day. How do we make sense of it?

Most of us are by now pretty comfortable with the Internet, for example. We use it to shop, to be entertained and to find out information on the widest possible range of subjects. But why is it 'there'? And what made it technologically (and politically) possible? Mobile phones, similarly, are a ubiquitous device used by seemingly everyone and are evident when walking on a city street, or travelling on public transport, from New Delhi to Sydney and from Montevideo to London. Mobile phones were first developed in the 1940s, but what caused the technology to lie undeveloped and uncommercialized until the 1990s when they exploded as a social and cultural phenomenon, to the point where half of humanity now owns or has access to one?

The information society (and the networkable applications and gadgets that comprise it) is also now a central component of how we earn a living. From the florist's shop on the street corner to the executive office on the top floor, being a part of the network society is becoming more and more a necessity instead of a flight of fancy. The florists will use it to find the best prices from wholesalers and to advertise their wares; and the executives of the multinational will use digital connectivity for more or less the same reasons. We take all this for granted now, with barely a thought given to the process. Moreover, through practice and through trial and error we are becoming competent and often expert with these growing arrays of technical applications and gadgets, and through this learning process we simultaneously stitch ourselves deeper into the fabric of the information society. It becomes part of us and vice versa.

But what does it all mean? What has been gained, and has anything been lost? Is the world a more efficient, smarter and better-organized place? Perhaps most centrally, much of the rhetoric of the information society is oriented towards placing an emphasis upon the notion that information technologies 'empower' the individual. As Bill Gates, founder of Microsoft, put it, computers are 'the most empowering tool we've ever created' (Grossman, 2004). How true is this? Do you feel 'empowered' by the acquisition of a new computer upgrade, or a faster processor, or a more multifunctional mobile phone?

These questions and more are becoming increasingly salient, and so this book is intended as an introductory guide to this new and radical society. We can begin by agreeing that it is impossible to look at the information society as some kind of punctual event – as if it is something that simply 'happened' in conjunction with sudden and unexpected advances in computer technology. The reality is, to employ a phrase by Fredric Jameson, that our technological present has 'a before and after time that only gradually reveal themselves' (2001). It has a history (or histories) that are traceable through an interpretive framework of political economy that makes connections to the relevant social, political, economic and technological structures and institutions. The strands of history stretch back to the beginnings of the Industrial Revolution, and have, along their course, 'moments' of great historical import with, for example, the development of the factory assembly line which first produced the Model T car in the USA in 1914. This moment set in train a whole productive logic that swept the world. The post-Second World War context of Cold War rivalry between the USA and the USSR is another moment of profound importance in terms of the development of computer science. More recently, the great economic and social changes that came in the wake of the global economic crises of the mid-1970s set in train yet more strands of logic and paths of historical development that led to the construction of our networked and digital planet; an information society driven by a particularly virulent economic reorganization of industrial and social relations on a world scale.

For the purposes of understanding these interrelated dynamics, it seems to me that we can construct our framework of analysis through three interdependent processes that have influenced and shaped our contemporary world in a most profound way. These will be defined and analysed in the main text, but let me preface them briefly.

The first is neoliberal globalization. This is the foremost economic dynamic that has, since the late 1970s, spread throughout the world to the point where, for the first time in history, an economic system has no serious challengers (Klein, 2007). It is a logic that has become the 'basic grammar' that informs our understanding of how the world operates (Anderson, 2007: 6). Second, and flowing directly from neoliberal globalization, is the information technology revolution. In the 1960s and 1970s the economic imperatives of an emergent globalization began to dramatically supercharge basic research into computers that had, until that time, been largely within the purview of military research and university lab tinkering – and brought it into the commercial realm. The third results from the effects of the first two. Principally, this has been the 'speeding-up' of time and the 'shrinking' of space. Again, I shall explain these in more detail in the chapters, but it seems to me that much flows from this 'time–space compression' (Harvey, 1989: 241).

Many of us, I think, can relate to the shrinking of space. For example, we are now able to communicate with people far more easily than was possible only a couple of decades ago. New computer-based technologies such as the 'voice over the internet protocol' (VoIP), called Skype, links me (for free) to people who might live in different countries or different continents. With only a couple of keystrokes I can now see the faces of friends or family or colleagues and feel 'in touch' in a way that is unprecedented on a mass scale. This is but a small revolutionary dimension of a broader revolutionary process.

The 'speeding-up' of time takes a bit more imagination to recognize. How can we speed up the clock, which is a rigid form of time? Well, we can't but we *can* experience the acceleration of time if we recognize that the clock is simply a technology to measure duration, and that our experience of the duration of time (forget the clock) can become more intense. For example, we feel the intensification of duration through 'multitasking' or the packing of more tasks into an hour or a day than we used to. And it is information technology that allows (or forces) us to do this. We can browse on eBay while a split screen shows us the arrival of emails, and we can do these tasks while listening to a voicemail on our mobile phone, at the same time as feeding a child or writing an essay and listening to music streaming from the computer. Multitasking is a juggling act that is becoming integral to everyday life (Kenyon, 2008). This 'speeding-up', as we will see, has differing articulations in work, in leisure, in family life and so on. Moreover, it is a pressure to act and be 'efficient', 'productive' and 'connected' that inserts itself into almost every realm of life. And this has potentially momentous consequences for our cognitive ability to understand the reality of our world and the nature of the information society under the aegis of neoliberal globalization. As we will also see, this process increasingly compels us to live more in the present – where the past seems less relevant to us and where the future, as it reveals itself, does so in the form of sometimes nasty and unanticipated developments. And so, at one level of analysis, the dream of the information society that we see in the TV ads for the enabling Microsoft Vista, or exciting Apple iPhone, are sometimes (oftentimes) lined with the nightmares of living in an insecure world of no guarantees, of the constant changing of careers, of a volatile and irrational stock market whose effects permeate everything, and the increasing expectation to be 'flexible' and adaptable to these constantly changing situations. We need to remember, though, that this brave new world is made possible by the same networkable technologies that give us Facebook or YouTube or the personal blog.

The book will proceed by examining the various claims made for the information society – those of the boosters who visualize a world of dreams, and those of the more critical and reflexively oriented who see a world of nightmares – and try to judge them on their merits through the interpretive framework that will guide us. What makes this perspective somewhat different from a number of other very laudable books, such as Terry Flew's *New Media: An Introduction* (2003), is that instead of being primarily descriptive, 'laying it all out' so to speak, it attempts to introduce a new dimension into our understanding of the dreams and the nightmares of the information society. The book argues that not only is it necessary to have some conception of the intellectual, political, economic and technological dynamics that make the information technology a reality, but we need also to be cognizant of what constitutes our understanding of this reality, and that is information itself – more particularly, our production and our consumption of it.

Here the narrative of *speed and acceleration*, stemming from ever-faster computer speeds and network speeds, that runs through the book becomes both important and revealing. The perspective presents us with an intellectual (as well as political and social) dilemma, the answer to which depends upon how we understand the nature of computing in a neoliberalized world. It is a dilemma we can see illustrated in the approaches to information and information technology from two highly respected figures in their field, individuals we will have cause to consider more in this book. First is J. C. R. Licklider, acknowledged as one of the intellectual 'fathers' of the Internet. He was all for computers. In an influential essay published in 1960, titled 'Man–Computer Symbiosis', Licklider observed that in the 'symbiotic partnership' between men and computers, humans will set the parameters within which computers will do the work, to 'prepare the way for insights and decisions in technical and scientific thinking . . . [and that] preliminary analyses indicate that the symbiotic partnership will perform intellectual operations much more effectively than man alone can perform them'. Computers would be the servants of humanity, in other words, doing our bidding in the production of 'intellectual operations' (better than we are able to – but with us still in control), in the formation of the emerging 'knowledge society' that was already being anticipated (Machlup, 1962). A counter to this perspective comes from Herbert Simon, a pioneer in computer-based artificial intelligence, expert in cognitive psychology, and Nobel Prize winner for his work in economics. In 1971, in response to the growing amounts of computer-based information being generated that we were increasingly expected to consume, he seemed to lose his earlier enthusiasm for the possibilities held out by computerization. He began to argue that information takes up our attention span, and obviously too much of it may be a problem in terms of what we now call 'information overload'. The information society today produces information in volumes that are infinitely larger than those produced in 1971. Computers may be able to 'perform intellectual operations better than man alone', as Licklider put it. But can they – in the context of a world that neither Licklider nor Simon could have imagined – 'prepare the way for insights' not only in the fields of science and technology, but into the human condition in a highly computerized and high-speed world, an information society?

What follows is, I hope, an accessible and comprehensible guide through these competing perspectives and resultant dilemmas.

1

The Information Society Today: The Acceleration of Just About Everything

> We live in a moment of history where change is so speeded up that we begin to see the present only when it is already disappearing.
>
> R. D. Laing, *The Politics of Experience*

In this introductory chapter I want to sketch out the broad contours of the information society. It is a necessary step, I think, because 'information' in its digital form constitutes an unconscious backdrop to the lives of many, if not most, of us. It has migrated, in a very short space of time, from being novel and radical, to somewhat demotic – if not invisible. Indeed, this latter, naturalized, state is what Generations X and Y have been born into, and so it is doubly important to make these implicit relations with information technologies more *explicit* – the better to hold them up to understanding and analysis.

For example, the networking of society, the interconnecting of people, processes, applications, work tasks and leisure pursuits, has led to a globalized society, a 'one-world' context where causes and effects can reverberate throughout the entire system. This is a society where digital information is, at its root, ideological. That is to say, it was developed not as a neutral concept and neutral technology – but as 'an ideology that is inextricably linked to the computer' (Kumar, 1995: 7). And the computer, as we shall see in later chapters, is itself a technology that is suffused with its own political, military and industrial imperatives that evolved in the context of the Cold War era of the 1950s and 1960s. However, today, and in respect of this general introductory overview, I note here only that digital information, along with its originary logic, permeates culture and society to an unprecedented degree. It brings with it what I have termed the 'network effect' that is expressed as an increasingly strong compulsion to be a part of the information society; it is a compulsion linked to the needs of a neoliberal global economy that demands connectedness; requires that we synchronize to its ever-quickening tempo, a tempo that produces positive and negative effects; and insists (as part of what might be called digital information's 'ideological effect') that such connectedness is also efficient and productive – and can even be fun and allow us to express our 'individuality'. The contours of the information society, then, beyond its implicit everydayness, are revealed as contradictory. On the one hand there is a definite compulsion – a logic that is difficult to escape or avoid – that is about working 'smarter' and faster, and all the stresses and strains that this can bring. And on the other hand there is, undoubtedly, the 'fun' element: the new multifunctional mobile phone, the thrill at finding an item on eBay, or the pleasure of Skyping friends or relatives in far-off places, or expressing yourself through a personal blog. The first intellectual move to make, therefore, is to 'denaturalize' the information society, to *define* it and judge it as a humanly constructed process that is shaped by the everyday conflicts and struggles in our society that, in their turn, are reflective of larger (and more portentous) political and economic dynamics.

The network effect

To inform a young person, say, a ten-year-old (the age of my eldest), that we live in an information society would be almost meaningless. My son Theo is not stupid, but to state something like this to him would be akin to saying we live in time and space. At one level this would be a profound observation, but then again we are born into time and space and move through them with hardly a thought, so second nature have they become. 'What's to know?' might be his incredulous reply. For the typical ten-year-old in a developed country (and increasingly in many developing countries too), connectivity and access to networks are simply part of what life is. We live in and live by pervasive and rapid 'flows' of digital information (Castells, 1996). Why did this come about? How did we individually and collectively become so *au fait* and casual with information technologies and the world they create? Are we really so? And anyway, do we really want to be? And do we have any real choice in the matter? We shall discuss these questions in some detail in the subsequent chapters, but a quick schematic sketch from the point of view of computer scientists – as opposed to social scientists – gives some useful background.

In their celebrated 1996 paper, 'The Coming Age of Calm Technology', Xerox engineers Mark Weiser and John Seely Brown forwarded the idea of 'ubiquitous computing'. They saw this as the third stage of computer evolution. The first stage was the 'mainframe era', which saw the arrival of bulky, hot and slow 'data processing' or 'defence calculator' computers that in the 1950s and 1960s took up the space of a couple of large rooms. They were devised and built by corporations such as IBM and were used mainly for military research into thermonuclear weapons. Second was the 'personal computer (PC) era', beginning in the early 1980s, that was the result of innovation in micro-processing technology that was able to put a standalone (non-networked) computer on an office or home desktop. After that came what the authors called the 'transition phase' that began in the 1990s with the growth and increasing sophistication of the Internet and computer networks in businesses, in the universities, and in what Howard Rheingold (1993) called 'virtual communities'. Weiser and Seely Brown distinguish this transition as one of 'distributed computing'. This third phase they calculated to occur over the years 2005–20 and it would be distinguished by what they term 'ubiquitous computing'. Here the Internet and embedded microprocessors in everything from garments and mobile phones, and from bus tickets to refrigerators, will push an awesome and invasive computing power into the background, just below the horizon of our consciousness, to emit its 'calming' effect. Through attention to the design of 'calm technologies', the authors argue, the era of ubiquitous computing – which we have already entered – will herald a radically new age. It is to be an era of perfect 'man–computer symbiosis' that Internet pioneer J. C. R. Licklider had already dreamed of in the early 1960s, where 'men will set the goals, formulate the hypotheses, determine the criteria and perform the evaluations [and] computing machines will do the routinizable work' (1960). Clearly taking their cue from Licklider, Weiser and Seely Brown predict that ubiquitous computing and 'calm technologies' will create an information society where people 'remain serene and in control' (Weiser and Seely Brown, 1996).

We need only look around to know that computing is certainly ubiquitous, but whether or not it is 'calm', unobtrusive and enables us to free up our lives for higher things, as these technological utopians predict, will be a major focus of this work.

For good or ill, computers are all around us, enveloping us in an *information ecology* that is comprised of networks, systems, processes, technologies and people – and they are not about to go away or become any less prevalent. Ten-year-olds, teenagers and adults inhabit this information society, and it pervades almost everything that we do. Our everyday working lives that take place in jobs in manufacturing industries or in the provision of services have either been radically transformed through computerization or have evaporated into obsolescence. Millions of us do new jobs in new industries that did not exist in our fairly recent past. The nature of business itself has changed due to the transformative effects of computerization. For example, the primary goal for large corporations, and for many smaller businesses too, is – as Jeremy Rifkin puts it – to become 'weightless' (2000: 30–55). That is to say, to get away from the ownership of fixed assets such as factories, machines, fleets of trucks and so forth that dominated the productive forces of an earlier age. In this so-called 'new economy', intangible assets, above all *ideas*, are 'more powerful than controlling space and physical capital' (Rifkin: 55). Ideas, moreover, are eminently suited to computerization, to be transformed into processable information through binary logic. Indeed it is ideas that make Microsoft, or Apple, or Google what they are – huge informational entities that are comprised of few or relatively few fixed assets. The comprehensiveness of this process means that the need for weightlessness is not confined to high-tech companies either. More traditional industries, those that still have comparatively high percentages of fixed assets such as plant and machinery, also use information technologies to their utmost capacity to speed up production, make production and distribution more flexible, and be more able to respond to changing customer demand. Automobile manufacturers, for example, the quintessence of the 'old economy' mode, are now awash with flexible computerized systems that make the car factory an utterly different business to what it was only twenty-five years ago.

In the information society, the age-old and modernist conception of there being some kind of bifurcation between private life and work life has been made as redundant as the 3.5-inch floppy disc. Flexible working systems, the proliferation of part-time and casual working, and the increased working load that many now have to bear, mean that the once-distinct and regularized times for work and rest have become blurred – if not eliminated altogether (Schor, 1993). Networked computers, mobile phones, PDAs, wireless laptops and so on mean that we are far more mobile and no longer so tied to the office desk or designated workplace. But they also mean that our work is able to follow us wherever we go. Being 'always on', as the network advertisers like to remind us, is an allegedly wonderful thing that allows us to ride the cusp of the high-tech wave. But it also means that the student who works part-time is made available at short notice to a boss who suddenly needs more staff for a couple of hours; and means that the office worker is made available to read and act upon a report that will be emailed to her at home at 10 o'clock on a Friday evening, with a response due by 9 o'clock Monday morning. There is today a distinct pressure that compels the individual within the network society to be connected and 'always on'. And so if you want a decent job and a career, or to start up a business of almost any sort, you will need to be a willing and connected 'node' in the networked economy. The result has been that there are fewer and fewer refuges in time and space where you can be outside the pull of the network effect, to resist the virtual life and to experience another reality.

The pressure to be connected exists at almost every level. In the developed economies it is now almost impossible to go through high school and university, for example, without what would not so long ago have been considered advanced computer user skills. Not only that, but students must also be able to access networks and be online for considerable amounts of time if they want to progress through the curriculum. Universities have taken up the challenges of the information society with alacrity and are amongst the most computer-filled places in the world. Indeed these institutions, especially in the Anglo-American economies, see themselves as progressively more 'weightless' businesses that exist largely to deliver pedagogy to its 'customers' or 'clients' through flexible computerized systems (Currie, 1998; Hassan, 2003; Bates, 2004). The Internet has even become a way for the elite universities such as Yale and MIT – who set such reputational store by their 'traditions' – to go global and decidedly non-traditional. Both these universities have put course materials online for free, with Yale going one better by uploading video lectures in 2006. This acts as a global branding and marketing exercise for these and the other universities who will doubtless emulate them. By offering access to free material, the hope is that users will then want to get the Yale or MIT degree by becoming actual online students and paying for the privilege. In the information society where the 'user pays' principle dominates, the keenly contested 'student market' thus truly becomes universal through such hi-tech practices. No longer do you need to go to the physical university to get a degree – the university, even the biggest, most prestigious and traditional of them, will come to you (at a price). We see that the logic of acceleration imposes itself here, too, with degrees becoming 'virtual' and 'flexible' and 'fast-tracked'. A typical example of the marketing of the alleged attractions of gaining a three-year degree in two years comes from the website of a UK university that claims this compressed degree will 'accelerate your career: [allowing you to] gain a real advantage by entering the job market a year earlier. You'll save money and get on the career ladder sooner' (University of Northampton, 2007). Note that the emphasis is not on learning, or the acquisition of knowledge, but on efficiency, and getting into the workforce sooner so as to save time and money.

Possibly it is in the realm of entertainment that the orbital pull of information technologies has been most apparent and habit-changing. For example, television executives have been increasingly vexed by the fact that viewers are switching off and logging on instead. Time spent online has what is termed a 'hydraulic' effect in that it diverts from time spent on other pursuits (Markoff, 2004). And while online increasing millions consume and contribute to the growing 'flows' of information that make up the information ecology. We do this, for example, by generating billions of emails every day. Add to this the uncountable text messages, voice calls, video conversations, picture sending and so on, and you get some idea of the 'hydraulic' gravitation towards online activity. For those who spend extended periods online, outside of the formal work situation, we need to look to the video gamers, the growing millions of users who are the simultaneous consumers and creators of an entertainment industry said by Bill Gates in 2003 to be bigger than the movie industry. Indeed, accountancy firm PricewaterhouseCoopers predicted that the industry (game consoles and software sales) would expand from $21.2 to $35.8 billion from 2003–7 (PWC, 2005). The market, moreover, has enormous room for further expansion as the network society spreads and deepens. For example, the number of users in China went from around zero in 2000 to 14 million by 2005; and industry leaders Microsoft, Nintendo and Sony are deliberately seeking to expand the global market out from its young male demographic (Joseph, 2005). It is a strategy that seems to be working, probably to the further consternation of TV industry executives. For example, journalist and media theorist Aleks Krotosi observes that in South Korea, for example, 'practically every street in Seoul has an Internet café – a "PC Bang" – where kids and OAPs game side by side' (2006). Moreover, online games, or what are called 'massively multiplayer online role-playing games' (MMORPG), are exploding in popularity. One game, *Lineage*, held the record for the largest number of players for a few years until the current mother of all MMORPGs, *World of Warcraft*, was released in 2004 and attracted up to 7 million users worldwide. As Krotosi notes, however, *Lineage* is still hugely popular in South Korea, with 4 million users, which is reportedly more than the total number of TV viewers (Krotosi, 2006).

Add to this the immense popularity of video-enabled mobile phones, DVDs, iPods, PlayStations, Xboxes, GameCubes, Wiis and the rest, and it becomes clear that in the information society entertainment is a dominant 'hydraulic' force on the time people spend online; time that is progressively more screen-based, digitally transmitted, and comes through networkable devices.

This mass migration to digital forms at work and in leisure brings us to the nub of the 'network effect'. We see an example of this when, say, your best friend buys a mobile phone. The action exerts a certain social pressure, a pressure which, depending on the circumstances, either gently cajoles you into buying one yourself at some stage, or compels you into getting one the very next day. Those who have a mobile and reflect upon their reasons for purchasing it can easily understand this phenomenon; and marketers have understood this dynamic for a long time. In the information society taken as a cultural and economic totality, however, there is another kind of network effect at play. That is to say, to be part of the information society and to be affected by its pressure and its imperatives, you don't even need to be connected – you only have to live and work in a modern or modernizing economy. It is important to recognize that so deeply and powerfully has the information society transformed our world that it moves us as workers and as consumers in ways we hardly register, except often as a form of stress. Even if we don't sit at a networked computer screen, or walk around with a mobile phone clamped to one ear, as millions of people do, these others who are ostensibly 'unconnected' are nonetheless linked to vast networked flows of information that create momentum and speed, to produce what Hartmut Rosa has termed a generalized 'social acceleration' (2003). In other words, as the social world gets faster, its centripetal force (the network effect) draws us all in whether we are connected or not.

Let me explain this idea a bit more through an example. It is still common for mail sent through traditional means to take days or weeks, but now such time lags for communication seem anachronistic, from a very different world indeed. Letter writing is in decline mostly because 'society' now deems it too slow, and this will affect the unconnected through the closure of many post offices, the disappearance of uneconomic postboxes, the increasing cost of postage and so on. The network effect thus presents us with a choice: which is either to get connected and speed up your mode of communication – or be left behind. To ignore the network effect is to miss out on what might be important information, to lose out on opportunities or to be ignorant of changes that can affect us in our everyday lives. In the information society, to be in a position of unconnectedness is to run the risk of sinking rapidly from the social, economic and cultural radar.

We experience the network effect at the level of the individual, but it is felt too in institutions and industries that must also constantly adapt and synchronize – or die. This is clearly evident in 'old' media such as television, newspapers and radio. These media have had to speed up in the frantic quest for relevancy in the information age. Any TV show worth screening (and many that are not) will now have its own website where viewers can email each other about it, give feedback on what they like or dislike, and so on. Indeed, through podcasting and digital streaming, television content is migrating online in a big way. The BBC, for example, podcasts much of its audio content from its radio stations, thereby keeping listeners connected as if they were still listening to 'old media' radio. In late 2007 the BBC also launched its iPlayer which allows internet users to view BBC video content for up to seven days after it went to air – again allowing 'old media' players to not only keep people watching their content, but also take a lead in some ways, in respect of the shaping of how people use the Internet.

Newspapers saw the writing on the wall at least a decade ago and went online in a big way. Good examples are the British-based *Guardian* and the *New York Times*. Both are profitable enterprises, offering a combination of free and paid-for articles. For instance the *Guardian* through its *Guardian Unlimited* site gives much of its content away for free. And for a fee it gives the functionality to print the paper as it appears on the newsstands, enabling the reader to get the 'morning' paper in any part of the world at any time. The squeezing of time and space through information networks means that, for example, someone in Australia is able to read the London morning edition of the *Guardian* before most Londoners are out of bed. Through its blogs, the *Guardian* allows a globalized readership to immediately comment on op-ed pieces by being able to directly email the author and/or enter into a debate with other respondents. Radio too has gone online with most large commercial stations, and even small subscription-supported stations, offering streaming audio of their content, having separate web pages of their programmes which feature their popular hosts, and so on. In media and in business more generally, and at the level of both the individual and society, the pressure of the network effect to become part of the network logic is ever more compelling, bringing with it an acceleration of economy, culture and society.

The speed effect of the network effect

The network effect means that old media speeds up, communication speeds up, economies speed up and life speeds up. And this fast pace of life, as we shall see in chapter 6, has its benefits and its costs. But before we get to that discussion, I want to preface it – indeed preface the whole book – with a sharper idea of speed and what it means in the context of the information society, and how it is able to produce both dreams and nightmares for those who are part of it. Speed is built into the logic of computers. The perceived need to process information faster, it could be said, is their *raison d'être*. And speed can be good or bad, depending on the circumstances. We can enjoy instant communication with friends or loved ones over great distances and this is unambiguously good; but, as any stage magician knows, speed also blurs perception and dulls acuity. It can confuse and muddle our thinking, and the pressure of speed can cause us to act too quickly (or not quickly enough) – with results that may be decidedly bad. Think of reading that op-ed just mentioned from the *Guardian*, hot off the press so to speak on your computer. Reading on, fifteen hundred or so words later, you come across the author's email address, and are invited to submit comments to the blog that will go online almost immediately. You are enraged by the piece and fire off a response quickly (because you can, and because the network effect prods you on), and suddenly it is finished. You press the 'send' button. Seconds later, your email has flashed through and your comments are uploaded for all the world to see. And then you read it and think: I spoke too soon. I should have said this; did not really mean that; or could have expressed this point more clearly; that sentence makes me sound like a bigot. Too late. The dream of instant communication and information sharing has become the nightmare of personal embarrassment and public (global public!) ignominy. The best you can hope for is that no one will recognize your username, or that you will be ignored completely. A moment of red-faced embarrassment may be all that will transpire, but as we will see below, the pressure of speed may have a much more disastrous effect.

Speed and illusion

The speed effect of the network effect can also create an illusion. The illusion in the above example may be that, notwithstanding the potential global audience your words have, no one will ever give your reply a second thought. It could be that for all the alleged potential of computerized communication, you might as well have not bothered. But let us look at the issue of speed and illusion a bit more closely. A lot of books begin their chapters with quotations. This one, as you will have noted, is no different in this regard. It's a serviceable way to get the reader's head into a certain space, to think down this or that line of reasoning, and to act as a kind of *mise en scène* for the narrative that is about to unfold. Inserting a quotation has also, by the way, been an appropriately self-effacing way of conveying to the reader your extensive range of learning. Therefore, something judiciously chosen from Plato's *Republic* would imply that I had read it, and that my thesis or argument is suitably profound and is supported by the immense intellectual tradition of 2,000 years of Platonic learning in Western civilization.

In truth the above quote was picked, more or less at random, from a Google search function that trawls its directories for quotations downloaded from the Internet. It took not the two or three days it might take to read a book – but less than two minutes. Nonetheless, the quote is a fairly good one; it's apt and it fits with what I want to say in this opening chapter. Incidentally, Laing's book *The Politics of Experience* has in fact taken up a bit of space on my bookshelf for a long time, but has been completely unexplored since the day I brought it home from a second-hand bookseller. I have it before me now and discover inside its pages a tram ticket dated 13.11.89. I have no idea if I purchased the ticket or some previous owner did. However, precisely how I came by these particular words, floating in cyberspace, disconnected from the rest of Laing's writing, is illustrative of what I want to write about in this book. The very *ease* with which I could pluck it from the digital ether is in itself nothing short of astonishing if we pause for a while and reflect upon this fact, a fact we now routinely take for granted. And so a major aim of this book, thinking about you the reader, is that it is intended, in a very modest way, to be a 'pause' for reflection within the maelstrom of technological transformation.

This short digression is also intended to highlight the fact that the information society is a society in constant flux and change. It moves at an ever-quickening pace and causes the ties that bind us to the old, to the traditional and to the known, to easily slip their moorings. In such instability, illusions are easy to create, as I showed with the example of the quotation. I didn't need to read the book, or even reach to my bookshelf to flip through its index. It was readily to hand in cyberspace and accessible through a few keystrokes on my computer. Moreover, what is available to me in the 'network of networks' is being added to, massively, every hour and every day of the year. Hundreds of billions of web pages containing almost every conceivable idea and utterance and image are now within my reach. Similarly, the information creating and gathering technologies that sustain these networks and flows of information are being improved and made more efficient and powerful every hour and every day of the year.

In the midst of ongoing change, everything is constantly new. But what is disturbing about this is that we have quickly become used to novelty; we are soon jaded by the next generation of this or that phone or computer, or digital gadget. We become jaded because the fruits of the information society are ultimately unfulfilling. The illusion is laid bare for only a short time, however, until the next new thing briefly distracts us and beguiles us. The speed of the action, in the construction of the seemingly 'new', disguises what is essentially an empty gesture. It is the illusion, in other words, that constitutes the reality of the information society.

A caveat needs to be inserted at this point. To say that the information society constructs illusions – and it could be argued that many of us know this at some level of intuition, such as when the computer is found to be too slow, or the iPod malfunctions too easily, or when the new software just complicates things even more – is not the same as saying that what is being projected in the rapid flickering of the screen and in the flows of digital networks is necessarily and always *false*. Illusion and reality exist side by side; they intermingle and interchange. Your illusion may be my reality and vice versa. It would follow that if truth constructs reality, then especially in our postmodern world, we need to always keep in mind that *truth is provisional* (Lyotard, 1979). As a community and society we need implicitly or explicitly to agree that something is true – such as the once widely held belief that plastic was a cheap, flexible and durable substance that would transform the way we live. It did. But new knowledge (new context, new understanding) showed that it is made from a finite and constantly more problematic source (oil) and it does not easily degrade, and is destined to stay inert in landfill as waste for hundreds of years. Truth then can become a chimera when the context that sustains that truth changes. As Helga Nowotny noted in the context of knowledge production: 'new knowledge arises under changed conditions of creation and in changed structures of organization' (1994: 87).

To try to make some sense of this rather tricky conundrum in the context of the information society we need first to ask: what is the illusion of cyberspace meant to portray and, second, when (and for whom) does the illusion (the dream) attain reality?

A digital dream

Not long ago I was at an academic conference in the UK where a range of speakers, from universities, from governments and from businesses, gave their views on how to engage with the future. Ways to think about time obviously formed a core theme of the conference. I gave a paper which argued, in short, that liberal democracy as a political practice functioned at a particular pace and cannot be overly rushed, and so therefore is unable in many ways to function properly (democratically) in our high-speed information society. At the parallel sessions, where I attended to hear papers, there was always the same person who seemed to be attracted to the same ones as me. I could see from the obligatory name badge that he was not an academic from a university, but a corporate employee, an American living in Paris and working as a consultant on future strategies for a high-tech multinational. He dressed immaculately, in contrast to most of those present. An expensive watch complemented his crisp shirt, silk tie and dark business suit. He looked poised, confident and relaxed. He sat at the front row of each session with a tiny Sony laptop on his knees and typed on it at high speed, using all his fingers in the manner of a super-efficient typist. He never looked up while the speaker gave his or her paper, just typed. After each presentation, he would close his laptop and quickly raise his hand as he lifted his head from his computer, all in one seamless motion. He was always first in with the questions and they were always calmly put, incisive and to the point, ensuring that he finished with his own counter-point as well (he never seemed to agree with the academics). He came to hear my paper and I could see him as I spoke – head down as usual, clicking away thoughts that were immediately fixed on to his computer's hard drive. When I finished speaking his hand shot up even while the mandatory ripple of applause was going round the room. He asked, as I anticipated, about my argument regarding 'social acceleration', about how and why information technologies have speeded up society to an unprecedented degree.

I must have given him an unsatisfactory answer because afterwards, at a tea break, I noticed him softly clicking his mobile phone shut and making a straight line towards me with a broad smile on his face. He was an affable and supremely smart fellow, and I could see as he made his way towards me that I needed to come up with better answers this time. Over the following twenty-five minutes he didn't actually ask any questions at all. He simply argued his case that 'social acceler-ation' was a myth. Time today in our postmodern, information society was actually going *slower* and it was information tech-nologies that were causing this to happen – the polar opposite of my proposition. His position was actually one I'd heard before, and a version of it is well put by Jeremy Stein in a col-lection, *Timespace* (2001: 106–19). For my American inter-locutor, however, the really radical speed-up in time and space occurred not for him and his generation, but for his great-grandparents who had moved from Russia during the early part of the twentieth century. For his forebears and for every-one else in the USA at that time, the introduction of the tele-graph, the motor car and the railroad were the epitome of what Marx (and he knew his Marx) called 'all that is solid melts into air' – meaning that it was *their* world that had been completely transformed. It was they who truly experienced the temporal rupture from the pace of the countryside, to the drive of the mechanized city; theirs was a world out of their control with larger forces than they could comprehend, overwhelming them until they gradually learned to adapt and synchronize to the new pace of life, to twentieth-century modernity. *This* was what 'speeding-up' was all about, he maintained.

He, on the other hand, was in the process of constantly *evolving with* the information society. For example, the call he had been making previously was to his five-year-old daughter who was sitting on a swing in a Paris playground. What could be more life-affirming, positive and convenient? Where was the so-called 'disorientation' that the network society was supposed to induce? Information technologies conferred control and autonomy upon him, he insisted. As far as he was concerned, life would be impossible without ICTs, as would the company that employed him. But this did not mean he was a slave to them. He told me he could switch them all off and go hiking, which he regularly did; he loved his job as he dealt with ideas and communication, and real people, and he made a lot of money and he had a wonderful family who were all bilingual. Life was good. The pressure of work he could deal with because he was in control; he controlled its pace and never felt harried or rushed. What was all the fuss about?

A digital nightmare

There is an immensely popular computer game called *The Legend of Mir 3* that online players from around the world can get involved in. Like many in the gaming world it is of the fantasy genre, full of heroes, mysteries, castles, monsters and gods. Its website defines it as:

> a massive online multiplayer role-playing game based in a mysterious Oriental-style world. In *The Legend of Mir* you can be a powerful warrior and develope (sic) your ability in close combat, a skilled wizard with a whole set of spells or a mystic Taoist provided with inner spiritual powers. (Legend of Mir, 2007)

Again, as with many of these games, combat is the thing. In the different 'quests', you fight enemies and in defeating them become stronger and gain trophies and weapons, and graduate up the levels of expertise. Characters are represented by 'avatars', which in virtual-reality games are icons (symbols or pictorial images) that represent the user. Avatars are important. For serious gamers, they represent 'real' things that vitally affect their online status and their online persona, such as whether they are heroic, or wise, or have attained a high level of combat proficiency. Swords are of course important avatars in such virtual-reality games, as would be, say, a laser-power gun in a more futuristic game. Some swords in *Legend of Mir* are 'wooden' and others 'metal', and their skilful and 'honourable' use can propel the user up the various levels. Indeed, just as with a commodity or thing in real life, these avatars can be bought and sold, so a novice with a lot of real money can purchase a prized sword to help her progress – or at least gain some online status. Avatars can be bought and sold online between users at an agreed market price on websites such as eBay. As one seller noted in his/her eBay auction for a female warrior avatar for the *Legend of Mir*, the buyers 'are paying for the time it takes me to earn this char[acter] and items involved'.

The weaving of the evanescence of virtual reality into the concreteness of real life – the spending of real money to buy virtual things – is testimony to the power of the dream in online gaming. However, virtual dreams can and do have nightmarish real-life consequences. In mid-2005 the gaming blogosphere buzzed with the news that a gamer in China, a Mr Qiu Chengwei, killed another gamer, Mr Zhu Caoyuan, in a dispute over a 'dragon sabre' that is a virtual sword for use in the *Legend of Mir*. Mr Qiu loaned his sword to Mr Zhu, who allegedly sold it to a third party. BBC News Online reported, curiously in its 'technology' section, that: 'Qiu Chengwei stabbed Zhu Caoyuan in the chest when he found out he had sold his virtual sword for 7,200 Yuan (£473)' (BBC, 2005). The *China Daily Online* reported on the same day that Mr Qiu had been sentenced to death, a penalty that could be 'commuted to life in prison if he behaves well in jail, and no other crimes relating to him are uncovered' (*China Daily*, 2005).

The virtual dream of heroism, of warrior status and online respect shattered into a real-life nightmare for Mr Qiu and for the family of the victim of his stabbing. The power of the information society to colonize the lives of individuals and so to shape and help determine their thoughts and actions could not be clearer than in the case of Mr Qiu. The contrast between cyber dream and digital nightmare, indeed, could not be more marked than that between Mr Qiu and my conference colleague. For one, the information society is replete with powerful resources that enhance one's control over online and offline life. Personal self-confidence and success in career and family life are the result of a low-key and positive relationship with information technologies. For the other, the network effect has had much more drastic consequences. An essentially solitary pursuit builds up a virtual world of importance where it is no longer clear where reality begins and ends. Where morality begins and ends becomes fatally blurred too. The commonplace of virtual death crosses over for a single instant into the death of a real individual, to change forever the lives of all those involved. The reality of the nightmare begins to assert itself for Mr Qiu when his digital dreaming is no longer possible in a Chinese jail cell that is presumably not modem or wi-fi connected.

Digital dream and cyber nightmare have been contrasted here in two real-life, but nonetheless *singular,* instances. What could they represent in our pursuit of a coherent understanding of the information society? In his book *Mediated: How the Media Shape Your World* (2005), Thomas de Zengotita argues that to live in the information society is to dwell in a world of purported choice, a veritable 'field of options' made plentiful by capitalism where being connected means that almost anything is possible. Crucial in this respect is our attitude to the choices offered. Optimally, this 'stance' is a reflective position that gives context to what is represented to us as consumers in the digital age. On this question of choice, de Zengotita writes that:

> On one hand it's a party, a feast, an array of possible experiences more fabulous than monarchs of the past could even dream of . . . On the other hand, an environment of

representations yields an aura of surface – as in 'surf'. It is a world of effects . . . We are at the center of all the attention, but there is thinness to things, a smoothness, a muffled quality. (2005: 15)

A few things to ask to begin with are: how do we know what we want? And when we choose, what is the consistency of the 'realness' constructed within the information society? And, in the process of choosing, do we really choose or are we confronted by a *fait accompli*, by the illusion of choice? I am not in a position to judge the 'realness' of my conference colleague's life within the information society – only he can really do that. Similarly, Mr Qiu's prison cell is real, but I am in no position to pronounce upon the texture of his previous online life, an undoubtedly complex and ultimately fraught relationship between reality and virtuality.

What my examples did illustrate, however, were the opposite ends of a continuum that we must now try to place in some kind of contextual and analytical framework. To construct an analytical framework is by necessity to take an intellectual stance. This comprises a series of biases and intellectual proclivities that arrange the materials I use and shape the way I make sense of the world. It would be disingenuous for me to admit otherwise in a book that draws together some fairly commonly agreed salient perspectives on the information society and organizes them into some kind of narratable whole. The only alternative in a strictly 'neutral' rendering of these perspectives would be to simply *describe* them in isolation with no analytical commentary based upon a worked-out position. This would be an exercise in futility and make the process of *understanding* the information society an impossibility. What I present over the following chapters then is an unavoidably biased perspective. If nothing else, this gives you the reader a foothold in the process of comprehension, a story to take or leave, or to take bits and leave bits. This in itself would have been a success, because even to reject the book's argument is to place yourself in opposition through worked-out biases of your own. What I hope the book will achieve most of all is the urge to find out more, to support or critique, preferably to do both at the same time, thereby adding to our general social understanding of the information society and what it means.

Speed, time and social life

Close readers will have spotted some proclivities already. Principal amongst these would be my conviction that if we understand what the *speed of information technologies* means in our society, then we have an insight into the nature of the information systems that surround us. Speed and time, as we shall see, makes an understanding of the information society both more difficult and easier. More difficult, because in simple terms if society moves more quickly, if we as individuals literally have less and less time to spare, then we are less able to reflect adequately upon our position; on why we do the things we do and why our society seems to be the way that it is. On the other hand, if we have a conceptual key to use, and if we take the time to consider and reflect – to work against the prevailing logic of speed in business, in academia and life more generally – then certain things may become more apparent.

I wrote that the quotation by R. D. Laing at the beginning of this chapter took me a couple of minutes to locate and choose. And so it did. However, what my eye sought out in a semi-unconscious act of elimination in the selection of this particular quotation was the term 'speeded-up'. And when I reread it and thought about it more, the sense of it seemed to be an idea worth discussing further. Let us return for a moment, though, to de Zengotita's *Mediated*. Consider, in the context of speed, what he terms an 'enviroment of representations' in the words cited above. Information technologies mediate the world – bringing (re-presenting) the world to us – in a maelstrom of fast-moving images, signs and symbols, creating what I earlier termed an information ecology. The ever-increasing speed of information technologies creates a blurring effect where

concrete reality and virtual reality become difficult to distinguish. The speed of daily life creates what de Zengotita
describes as a 'numbness' that begins to invade our sense-
making capacities and our perception of coherence about the
reality of the world. He goes on to observe that 'our state of
numbness' is constituted by being:

> swamped by routine activities. The old-fashioned superficial-
> ity of routine blends seamlessly with the new superficiality,
> the surface quality of ubiquitous representation – and this
> hybrid accelerates constantly, as you take on more and more.
> (. . .) The result is a simulation of reality convincing enough
> to pass for the original, for most of us, most of the time. It is
> only when the ultimate reality descends on us in the form of
> a tragic accident, illness, death or a miraculous recovery, the
> birth of a child – only then does that simulation stand
> revealed for what it is. (2005: 186)

Laing's quote suggests that as time unfolds, and as the present recedes into the past, only then do we have the proper perspective on what happens in the 'now'. The present is too full
of life's complex 'reality' demanding our immediate attention,
that only when the present becomes the past do we have time
to consider what the present means (or meant). Laing's words
were written in 1967 and so I cannot impute to his words the
consequences of the information technology revolution, nor
can I suggest that this is what he meant by 'speeded-up'. What
I *can* argue – and this will be conducted in more detail in chapter 6 – is that life today, due first and foremost to the effects of
ICTs, has indeed 'speeded up', and has accelerated to a degree
much greater than Laing could ever have imagined at that
time. Moreover, it is important to note that as a psychoanalyst
he did not argue a social theory of speed per se – but a psychi-
atric theory of perception. However, if we think about *social*
acceleration as emanating from a technological basis, then
speed and perception become part of the same process. We can
see this as a blurring of perception or 'numbness' where the
'now' does not inexorably recede into the past to supply a

perceptual vantage-point from which you can then make sense of the world, as Laing would have it. It stays with you.

A broad definition of the information society

To end this introductory chapter, I want to define the information society so as to present it more clearly as an object of analysis. Too often and for too long, politicians, info pundits and the media more generally have referred to the 'information society' in the implied or explicit context of 'we are all on the Internet now' or 'almost everyone has a mobile phone'. As will be apparent by now, I take it to be infinitely more than these trite and narrowly focused statements suggest.

At its broadest level of conceptualization we can begin by saying that the information society is the successor to the industrial society. Information, in the form of ideas, concepts, innovation and run-of-the-mill data on every imaginable subject – and replicated as digital bits and bytes through computerization – has replaced labour and the relatively static logic of fixed plant and machinery as the central organizing force of society. The *modern* industrial society of relatively ordered and organized dynamics has been transformed, essentially since the 1970s, into a *postmodern* information society where disorganization and fragmentation are its salient characteristics (Lash and Urry, 1987; Jameson, 1991; Kumar, 1995). Not so long ago, in sociology, in political theory and so on, the term 'industrial society' related mainly to the world of work, and to the 'modes of production' such as Fordism that gave this society its particular shape and form. By contrast, the information society (or as Manuel Castells (1996) has termed it, the *informational* society) has been powerfully connected to the idea of a *paradigm shift*, that is to say, to the insertion of fundamental change across every sphere of life. Daniel Bell, as we shall see in the next chapter, saw the function of information and the role of 'information workers' as being the core elements of what he termed the 'post-industrial society' (1973).

Bell's thinking on the centrality of information has been borne out in many ways, but he did not envisage the all-transforming power of computerization. The transformative nature of computers was recognized in the work of the late Rob Kling, for example, Director of the Center for Social Informatics at Indiana University in the USA. Kling viewed computers as 'enabling' technologies that not only created new, information-based industries such as the Microsofts and Intels of this world, but they have also completely transformed old industries and institutions (Kling, 1998). 'Old' industries such as steel production and automobile manufacture (those that did not succumb to the shock of 1970s–80s economic restructuring, that is) became essentially 'renewed' through computerization, automation and the use of flexible processes and flexible employees. These and other dominant industries such as manufacturing and construction now show only the barest resemblance to their recent ancestors of the post-Second World War era.

The logical evolution of this process was the *networking* of industries across sectors and across space. Manuel Castells's analysis of this emerging information order has not yet been surpassed for both his clarity and in his establishing the central ideas through which we make sense of it. On the networking process, for example, he writes that:

> Networks constitute the new social morphology of our societies, and the diffusion of networking logic substantially modifies the operation and outcomes in processes of production, experience, power, and culture. While the networking form of social organization has existed in other times and spaces, the new information technology paradigm provides the material basis for its pervasive expansion throughout the entire social structure. (1996: 469)

Castells here uses what may appear to some as fairly high-flown language. The phrase 'entire social structure', for example, may seem something of an exaggeration, and indeed it is always prudent to recognize that there will always be forms of social, cultural and economic life where the power of information and the sprawling reach of networks have been relatively slight. However, these realms are diminishing as the information society spreads and deepens. The concept of the network effect that we have just discussed, for instance, gives some indication of how, without exaggeration, the 'entire social structure' may be affected. But let me give a more specific example. As Terry Flew (2003: 24–5) reminds us, the al-Qaeda attacks on the USA on September 11, 2001, could not have been conceived, organized and carried out without the use of sophisticated communication technologies. Mobile phones, email, satellite phones, Internet websites and media such as the al-Jazeera television station allowed for the networked 'flow' of ideas of perceived injustices towards Arabs, and Muslims more generally, to have their devastating consequences. These network technologies continue to be the basis and mainstay of the 'cyber jihad' that is able and willing to conduct operations throughout the world. Conversely, these terror attacks by aggrieved Islamic groups have triggered an equally networked response by the Western powers in the form of intelligence sharing and political and military actions. A result of this is that no part of the world has been unaffected by this deadly interaction that takes place in both the virtual and real worlds. And, as a visit to almost any international airport will reveal, governments across the world have legislated against the so-called 'war on terror' in ways that can potentially affect everyone. One can argue then that in the case of the September 11 event, the effects of information technologies do indeed reverberate (through networks) across 'the entire social structure'.

It is necessary to understand in this definition of the information society that it is the computer and computer networks that make globalization technologically possible. As we shall see in chapter 2, ICTs are both the cause and consequence of globalization. Versions and visions of globalization have been described since at least the time of Marx and Engels. However, it is only through information technologies that the prophecy of a truly global economic system has become reality. The theory of a single economic system becoming hegemonic and pervasive through computer logic is only part of the story. Just as ICTs have been the cause and consequence of the convergence of formerly disparate capitalist industries since the 1970s, so too have ICTs enabled the logic of a market-based economy to incorporate and dominate the social, the cultural and the political realms as well – but this is to get ahead of the narrative slightly.

Let us end this brief sketch of what I see to be the primary factors involved in the construction of the information society by pointing to table 1.1, showing a schematic representation of what I have been describing from the perspectives of both advocates and critics of the process. It becomes clear from this table that the perceived effects of ICTs go deep and wide, and that interpretations of these are commonly expressed at both ends of the spectrum: the dream and the nightmare scenario, so to speak.

To take point 1 of table 1.1 as an example: in the 1970s, it was widely predicted by the advocates of new information technologies that the class-based strife that had plagued capitalism would be greatly reduced in the new economic order of post-Fordism. 'Knowledge workers' would be more autonomous and more empowered by ICTs, and as consumers they would be more able to negotiate the evolving information systems and structures that they themselves would be helping to construct. The old dualities of capital and labour, of bosses and workers, would be flattened out in a new approach to work and to economic relations. The highly influential business commentator Peter Drucker envisaged such a scenario when he wrote that:

> The leading social groups of the knowledge society will be the 'knowledge workers' – knowledge executives who know how to allocate knowledge to productive use; knowledge professionals; knowledge employees. Practically all these

Table 1.1 Perspectives on the Information Society

	Advocates	Critics
1. Economic relations	More skilled workforce, flattened hierarchies, empowered consumers, more profitable businesses	Economic dualism, deskilling of middle classes, 'information proletariat'
2. Employment	More leisure time, more knowledge-based jobs, greater efficiencies and flexibilities	Trades and skills lost to ICTs, 'downsizing' by employers, and widespread job insecurity
3. ICTs and democracy	Two-way, decentralized political communication, emergence of 'electronic democracy'	Neoliberal domination, widespread political apathy, growth of state corporate surveillance
4. Global dimension	'Global village' and the 'technological leapfrogging' of Third World countries, i.e., China, India	Domination by corporate capitalism, exacerbation of global inequality in development of economic power
5. Information and culture	Vast expansion of access to information, the centrality of the Internet, 'networked communities'	'Information without meaning', loss of 'real' community, dominance of Anglo-American cultural imperialism
6. Space and time	End to 'tyranny of distance', rational coordination of global business, time-savings of ICTs	'Tyranny of the moment', lack of reflective 'slow' time, superficial and hurried cultural forms

Source: Adapted from Lyon (1988) and Flew (2003)

knowledge people will be employed in organizations. Yet unlike the employees under capitalism they both own the 'means of production' and the 'tools of production' – the former through their pension funds which are rapidly emerging in all the developed countries as the only real owners, the latter because knowledge workers own their knowledge and take it with them whereever they go. (Drucker, 1993: 7)

If there is any agreement on the nature of the information society, it would probably be that constant and accelerating change is what characterizes it most of all. Now, how do we see

Drucker's comments from the perspective of hindsight? Does the passage of time vindicate his generally positive ideas, or does it lend credence to the more critical approach? Well, there is no doubt that many knowledge workers have indeed been 'empowered'. But it depends upon *what kind of knowledge worker* and what kinds of knowledge he or she possesses. For example, there is strong empirical evidence that suggests that the most powerful and world-shaping form of knowledge in the information society is financial information. It is digital information and is stored, shared, created, hidden and proliferated through computers. It is a process that has been termed 'financialization' and it closely follows the logic of ubiquitous computing in that, as Robin Blackburn notes:

> It [financialization] permeates everyday life, with more products that arise for the commodification of the life course such as student debt or personal pensions, as well as the marketing of credit cards or the arrangement of mortgages. The individual is encouraged to think of himself or herself as a two-legged cost and profit centre, with financial concerns anxious to help them manage their income and outgoings, the debts and credit, by supplying their services and selling them their products. (2006: 39)

For most of us, the financialization of everyday life is something that happens *to* us. However, knowledge workers with the kind of expertise that makes this process happen are able to develop profoundly valuable knowledge that shapes the parameters of change in the globalized and networked economy. These are Drucker's 'knowledge executives', whom he distinguishes from your average computer programmer, university academic or administration worker. Such workers have grown from a virtually negligible number in the 1970s and 1980s to become a significant stratum in global business. These are the entrepreneurs who have used their ideas and their expertise – alongside another new economy instrument, 'venture capitalism' – to become powerful and wealthy in the information society. They work feverishly in the context of the acceleration of information flows, where the trick is to know when is the 'right' time to buy, share, create or produce information. The fact that 'timely' access to knowledge and the ability to manipulate it is a key function for success in the information society is reflected in the research of the business community itself. In 2005, for example, Merrill Lynch reported that the number of high-net-worth individuals (HNWIs) – people having a net worth of at least US $1 million, excluding their primary residence – increased by 7.3 per cent to 8.3 million, an overall increase of 600,000 worldwide over the 2004–5 period (Merrill Lynch, 2005). Economic growth and market capitalization (that is, the size of a corporation measured as a reflection of its stock price) have been identified in the report as the main drivers of this wealth increase. Stock prices, especially, are crucial in the high-speed information society, and can be said, indeed, to be the main factor deciding whether the global economy grows or not. And what drives the stock market is knowledge and information. To have *primary* access to the kinds of information that determine stocks and shares, to be able to use this within a select community of 'knowledge executives' in business, and be able to transfer this knowledge and information into 'new' forms of knowledge that can then be sold, is to be on the inside track of the information economy.

To this extent Drucker has been proved correct. But there are other realities that stem from what these people do with their privileged knowledge. Consider the blithe reference to 'pension funds' as the 'real owners' of the 'means of production'. Consider it in the context of the idea that pension funds and the growth in importance of the finance (financialization) process in general have been the economic power behind what Robert Boyer (2000) has termed a 'finance-led post-Fordism'. And consider now that the financial markets, as drivers of the world economy, are exceptionally volatile and inherently unstable (Stiglitz, 2002). Indeed, the collapse of the now-notorious (and ironically named) Long-Term Capital Management (LTCM) was evidence of how immense crashes of 'virtual' corporations affect the real lives of millions of people as they take their savings and pensions with them into liquidation. LTCM began trading in 1994 and had a Board of Directors stuffed with clever people such as Myron Scholes and Robert C. Merton, who shared the 1997 Nobel Prize for Economics. It vaporized as a business entity in 1998 after losing 4.6 billion dollars in the space of four months (Mackenzie, 2006). Then of course there is the Enron Corporation, 'a case study in financialization' which was another virtual, knowledge- and information-based entity named as 'America's Most Innovative Company' by *Fortune* magazine. Enron crashed and burned, taking with it into oblivion the savings of its investors, amounting to some 62 billion dollars, and ending the employment of over 20,000 individuals (Fox, 2003: 2–4; Froud and Williams, 2003).

This typifies the argument that Drucker's 'real owners' are in fact wheelers and dealers in what Susan Strange (1986) called 'casino capitalism'. They have no real sense of control, or power, or autonomy in the way that this influential champion of the capitalist, globalized and networked system envisages. Seen in a more critical perspective, these 'knowledge executives' may be argued to create little that is tangible or enduring. They stand on permanently shifting sands that threaten to envelop those whose money they use when either the numbers no longer look good to the market, or when the market's inherent volatility simply overcomes them – usually for reasons they did not anticipate, despite their knowledge and expertise.

It is these kinds of questions and these kinds of contrasts, within the context of an accelerating information society, that much of the rest of the book will be taken up with. The intent is that the dreams and nightmares of our digital world can become part of a rational and coherent narrative that makes sense of the seeming chaos and apparent unpredictability of life that can earn the individual billions or bring low a major corporation. A framework of temporality which these dreams and nightmares can be set against is, of course, no solution.

Indeed, it does not even presume to supply answers to the questions posited. What this book will provide, though, is a selection of pathways to further questions, to a wider literature that brings the horizons of understanding rather nearer to hand. Whether you see this world to be comprised of cyber dreams or digital nightmares (or a bit of both) is up to you. However, I think it unarguable that the information society is a world where collective and personal autonomy, in any real and abiding sense, has been gradually diminishing in the wake of an accelerating economy, culture and society that we can barely keep up with. This is my particular bias. I also think that reading and reflective thinking are ways to exert control over time, to slow down the 'constant present' (Purser, 2000) and lead to forms of understanding – power and knowledge of a specifically political kind – that can act as the basis for agency in the real world.

2

The Coming of the Information Society

American efficiency is that indomitable force which neither
knows nor recognizes obstacles; which continues on a task
once started until it is finished, even if it is a minor task; and
without which serious constructive work is impossible.

Hughes, 2004: 251

Speed is everything. It is the indispensable ingredient of
competitiveness.

Jack Welch, former CEO of General Electric Corporation,
in *Jack Welch Speaks* (2001)

The capitalist 'mode of production' and the role of speed

The first question we need to consider is: how did it come to be
that the societies that emerged out of the post-1970s era con-
tracted a severe case of what Doug Henwood (1995) calls 'info
fetishism'? To put it another way, what is it that motivated the
widespread conviction that computers and computerization
are the solution to just about every problem that confronts us,
and that the faster they are made to run, the better we all will be
for it?

To help answer these questions, we need to understand something about how economies work (or sometimes don't work). In
the late 1700s Adam Smith, Chair of Moral Philosophy at
Glasgow University, was one of the first modern thinkers to construct a theory of what we now call 'economics'. In his *The
Wealth of Nations* (1776) he elaborated upon the processes of
'supply and demand' and how self-interest, or what we would

later call 'individualism', would, if left to its own devices, eventually work in the interests of everybody. Smith was concerned to show that market processes were guided by an 'invisible hand' that, if unrestricted, led to a natural equilibrium. His central point was that trade and production needed to be free from government and other institutional meddling or encroachment so as to find their natural levels. Smith also pointed out that a 'division of labour' in society was the key to unlocking its productive potential. Here, tasks were divided up into an assembly-line process involving many people, as opposed to one or two persons completing the whole job – the dominant method in previous guild and craft-based production systems. In his famed discussion of the pin factory, for example, Smith was able to show how the new-fangled manufacturing processes of a nascent capitalist system that functioned through a division of labour were able to achieve astronomical gains in productivity. He calculated that if one man was to try to make a pin himself he could perhaps make twenty per day. Visiting an actual factory where eighteen individuals were assigned specific tasks such as drawing, cutting, sharpening, etc., Smith observed that 4,800 pins were produced in the same time (Smith, 1776/1965: 69).

Smith wrote at the time of the European Enlightenment, when the decline of the power of religious authority compelled thinkers to pose new explanations for the nature of the momentous social changes that were taking place. A term used for the evolving and cumulative method that sought to understand the processes of an increasing rational and industrializing Europe (and North America) was political economy. This was an intellectual framework for a new way of considering society and it concerned itself primarily with the causes and effects of aggregate economic activity. The political economy theorizing of men such as Smith, David Hume and Adam Ferguson of the so-called 'Scottish Enlightenment' began to view the evolution of human society as developing in a historical process. This was along a steady progressive trajectory wherein both the individual and society were constantly improving. Indeed 'improvement', especially in agriculture, was something of a catchphrase of the time, indicating the attitude of 'change for the better' across all realms of life. They developed what has become known as the 'stages' theory where, over historical time, societies moved progressively through stages of development. These were hunting, pastoralism, feudalism and (now) commerce. The role of production was key to allowing one stage to 'progress' from one to the next. Enlightenment contemporaries viewed the transition from feudal agriculture to capitalist industry as particularly revolutionary. Given that historiography and political economy were nascent disciplines at this time, the works of these philosophers may be seen as little more than bold speculation. However, they developed a tremendously influential set of ideas that shaped much subsequent thinking concerning what it meant to be modern. Indeed, 'modern' came to be the generic Enlightenment term for a humanity seen to be freed from the shackles of religion and superstition, and set upon a course of progressive improvement of all its social, economic, political and cultural conditions (Berman, 1981).

To align oneself during the Industrial Revolution with the optimistic theory of progress tended to help assuage issues of what industrialism actually entailed. Liberal intellectuals, politicians, and laissez-faire capitalists were often able to convince themselves that what Friedrich Engels (1987) described as the 'dark satanic mills' of the English factories he visited, from 1842 to 1844, were but a necessary (and temporary) circumstance of progress and improvement. The slave-labour conditions, the exploitation of children and the terrible death and injury rates could thus be almost justifiable as the birth pangs of a new world.

Not everyone thought so at the time. Notwithstanding the fact that the division of labour and the factory system more generally was certainly more productive and efficient, they were also perceived by some as alienating and dehumanizing processes. So-called 'radicals' such as Marx and Engels, and 'reformers' such as Robert Owen, sought to better the conditions of the emerging working class through, on the one hand, catalysing worker militancy, and, on the other, through paternalistic reform by 'enlightened' capitalists and politicians.

Radicals and reformers may have disliked the terrible conditions of the early factory system, but the *materialism* of Enlightenment political economy, that is to say, the stress on those same productive forces of society, as being the engine of growth and progress, was viewed as a tremendously important and necessary aspect of it. Karl Marx, of course, has been the most influential proponent of what has been termed 'historical materialism'. Marx accepted, and further developed, the idea of a materialist conception of history and that capitalism represented the latest stage in human social development. The difference, as Marx saw it, was not that capitalist commerce was the final stage in history, where the role of the individual pursuing his or her own inclinations would (by default) contribute to the common good; capitalism and its productive base represented for him the *penultimate stage* that created the material means for capitalism itself to be transcended and for communism to be realized. Marx argued that capitalism's own contradictions of exploitation and the creation of antagonistic classes would create, ultimately, the basis for a socialist revolution where the working class would come to power and accomplish its historic mission (Marx, 1975).

Setting aside questions of socialism and 'stages', in the perspective of a general political economy analysis, capitalist industrialism was indisputably the dominant mode of production in the modernizing societies of the eighteenth and nineteenth centuries. It was a process dominated by machines and factories and was geared constantly towards speed, flexibility and efficiency. It was also a process motivated (to a greater or lesser extent throughout history) by *competition* in the context of a free-market system. According to this theory, the 'productive forces' of capitalism, i.e., the machines, and forms of industrial organization, are bound to continually 'progress' and 'improve' because of the pressure of competition. New techniques, new equipment and new ways of producing things need to be constantly introduced, or the system begins to stagnate and economic and social crisis ensue.

Capitalism and the 'need for speed'

It is necessary at this point in the discussion of the dynamics of capitalism to slightly interrupt the loose chronology of the narrative so as to introduce the idea that, as a mode of production, capitalism has what might be termed a 'need for speed' at its core. This is important if we are to understand the nature of the information society that emerged from industrial society. This 'need', as we shall see in later chapters, has been delimited by technological capacities, and by political/ideological imperatives since the Industrial Revolution began. With the rise of the information society, however, it is my argument that computerization has unleashed the technological restraints, and neoliberal globalization has unfettered the political and ideological boundaries that surrounded a previously more 'organized' form of capitalism (Lash and Urry, 1987).

The 'need for speed' is not an innate human propensity. Some of us may be addicted to cars, or to motorcycles or speedboats, but this obsession may represent a reflection of elements of our modern, and now postmodern, cultures. Partly, it may be a more deep-seated thrill at the thought of we mere humans somehow defying the laws of physics. However, most of us, I venture, would prefer not to drive at 170 mph down a highway even if it were legal. And most of us, I would further suggest, would not volunteer to become expert multitaskers – that is to say, people who dash from one thing to the next in a perpetual motion, working faster all the time, and in more concentrated bouts – if presented with a genuine choice in the matter. As I see it, the 'need for speed' comes not from any entrenched psychological need, but from the social system of capitalism as it has evolved since the eighteenth century. Jack

Welch, who is quoted at the head of this chapter, certainly knows business. He may or may not have read Marx, but he does understand the motive forces of capitalism: *speed* and *competition*. Speed enables a company to compete, and effective competition is predicated upon the company's ability to move quickly to innovate and produce things faster.

In his writings on the temporal factors in the production process (which were few and scattered) Marx tended to underplay the extent to which speed (the rate of) was implicated in the creation of value. In 'Notebook 1' of his *Grundrisse*, however, he makes the connection explicit:

> Every commodity . . . is equal to the objectification of a given amount of labour time. Their value, the relation in which they are exchanged against other commodities, or other commodities against them, is equal to the quantity of labour time realized in them. (Marx, 1973: 168)

This is the famous 'time is money' connection that had already been identified by Benjamin Franklin as early as 1736 when he stated in his 'Necessary Hints to Those that would be Rich' that: 'Remember, that time is money. He that can earn ten shillings a day by his labour, and goes abroad, or sits idle, one half of that day, though he spends but sixpence during his diversion or idleness, ought not to reckon that the only expense; he has really spent, or rather thrown away, five shillings besides' (cited in Adam, 2004: 42).

What Marx does is to theorize and explain what every business person intuitively knew from at least the beginnings of the Industrial Revolution: time is of the essence in business, and so the faster the production processes, the better. From this it follows that in the general 'circulation of capital' idleness and waiting literally costs money. The faster the circulation of capital, the more profitable it is. David Harvey in his *Limits to Capital* emphasized this point, where he wrote that:

> There is . . . considerable pressure to accelerate the velocity of circulation of capital, because to do so is to increase the

sum of values produced and rate of profit. The barriers to realization are minimized when the 'transition of capital from one phase to the next' occurs 'at the speed of thought'. (Harvey, 1983: 86)

Increases in the 'velocity of circulation' or 'speed of capital' in order to compete has always been found through technological innovation, the invention of faster machines, the 'forcing the pace' of work through 'speed-ups', or through more efficient and productive forms of work organization – the latter tactic having evolved into a whole science and academic discipline called 'organizational management'.

Technology and the systematization of capitalism

As capitalist industrialism develops, and becomes more complex and faster, then the role of technology inevitably moves to centre-stage. Constant innovation in technology allows capitalism to do what Marx argued that it must do – to constantly expand. Profits, or at least part of them, must always be ploughed back into technological solutions that allow the individual business to grow. The alternative is to stagnate and be the victim of competition. As a generalized system, capital accumulation (profit) must be invested into physical space (geographic expansion) in order to seek new markets, new sources of raw material, and new sources of labour, and to create more accumulated capital. This logic develops its own cycle that continues endlessly (Harvey, 1983). Throughout modern history, new technologies have been developed to allow this to occur. Investments in the train network and in the telegraph system, for example, along with macadam-surfaced roads, had the effect of shrinking time and space, making the 'sphere of influence' of the industrial way of life paradoxically larger, more manageable and potentially more profitable.

For much of the eighteenth and nineteenth centuries, this growing into space and the effective use of time through the efficiencies of speed was conducted in the context of a Smithean free market that was loosely regulated, and where the push and pull of market forces was relatively unrestrained – and therefore unpredictable. Uneven economic development between countries, and within countries too, contributed to political tensions. Imperialist expansion exacerbated these tensions yet further, and was itself connected to the capitalist imperative to constantly grow. Technological development and concomitant spatial expansion was one thing, but late-nineteenth-century capitalism had begun to move out of its classical liberal phase of free markets and free trade. Political and economic tensions began to move to the fore. As an official of the US State Department noted in 1900, at the apogee of imperialist expansion: 'Territorial expansion [and the political tensions it creates] is but a by-product of the expansion of commerce' (cited in Hobsbawm, 1996: 45). The last quarter of the nineteenth century, then, was a time when capitalism was beset by a lack of confidence and what Eric Hobsbawm termed 'the breakdown of its old intellectual certainties' that had sustained the classical model and the liberal market that it advocated (1996: 308).

By the turn of the twentieth century, the volatile nature of the world economy and the political and social tensions generated by the boom-and-bust swings led to growing working-class disenchantment in the industrial centres. A burgeoning socialist and communist movement meant that, even at this late stage of its development, capitalism and the liberal democracy of free markets that sustained it were still on trial and by no means an inevitability. More immediately, such swings were, obviously, bad for business and blunted the impacts of technological innovation and efficiency. Industrial capitalism was badly in need of productive processes that would be more *systematic and predictable*.

It was in this context, in 1911, that Frederick Taylor published his book *The Principles of Scientific Management*. It contained a set of ideas that were to lead to a revolution in the 'mode of production'. In its essence, Taylor's was a systematic attempt to infuse the work process, in the factory, in the building site or the office, with a *logic of information*, based on numbers (i.e., the time it took to perform a particular job). The objective was to align the human worker more closely to the rhythms of the machine – machines that were themselves constantly being developed to run faster and more efficiently. In this, it was a proto-computer way of looking at life and work, by seeing them as J. C. R. Licklider would half a century later, in terms of human–computer interaction (HCI) (Licklider, 1960). For Taylor, however, workers had to *adapt* to the machine, not interact with it or control it. He argued that by studying the movement of the worker performing his or her work task, detailed information would be gathered and analysed, and the modification of the work practice – usually the modification of the worker – would automatically and logically suggest itself. Speed, flexibility and efficiency were the driving force behind Taylor's thinking, and, by linking the worker to these machinic tropes, he had hit upon something profound at the core of the capitalist economy.

Henry Ford, the automobile magnate and towering figure in American capitalism during the first half of the twentieth century, took up the ideas of Taylor with enthusiasm. Two years after Taylor's book hit the shelves, Ford was busy applying 'scientific management' techniques to initiate a revolution in manufacturing called the assembly line. The production processes whereby workers stand at specific points along a conveyor belt have become the standard across the world and are today taken for granted by those who work within this logic. However, the gains made in speed, flexibility and efficiency by the Ford Motor Company, who were the first to systematize this technique, were tremendous. Its success gave birth to the term 'Fordism'. The original object of the assembly-line technique was the famous Model T car that symbolized the dawn of the age of true mass production. By 1918, 50 per cent of all cars in the USA were Model Ts. Ford's genius was to see the connections between economies of scale – which could dramatically drive down the price of a finished product – and mass consumption, whereby workers should be able to afford to buy mass-produced objects. This was not a simple matter of supply and demand as the classical liberal economist imagined, but was a process that needed the help of conscious intervention and planning. And so in 1914 Ford began paying his assembly-line workers $5 a day, which at the time was more than double the average wage. Through such a device his workers could for the first time buy the things they produced, thereby creating more demand, spurring increased production, creating the need to hire more workers who would themselves be the source of yet more demand, and so it goes on. In theory, then, the volatile 'business cycle' of boom and bust could be erased through technological innovation and social planning.

All this was a major step forward and inaugurated the beginnings of a greater role for the organizing of capitalist production and consumption on a more systematic basis. It meant that government and its bureaucracies would become more involved, an involvement that would, in the post-Second World War era, lead to the development of a new political articulation in the shape of a social democracy to replace liberal democracy. But Fordism as the dominant means of production in capitalist society would not last. To understand the rise of the information society, we need first to look in more detail at the nature of the Fordist industrial society that preceded it, a society, polity and culture that was oriented around Fordism and a 'total way of life'.

Fordism as a 'total way of life': 1950–1973

The essences of Fordism are mass production, mass consumption and, importantly, the insertion of organization, planning and predictability into the historically volatile business cycle. Ford's pioneering techniques became the basis for a new paradigm in capitalist production – Fordism was even enthusiastically taken up by the Soviet Union in the 1920s and 1930s as it tried to industrialize and modernize as quickly as possible. However, it was during the Second World War that Fordism gradually became dominant across whole economies and across the world as the standard mode of industrial production. In the USA in particular mass-production Fordism made that economy the foremost industrial nation. It was during the decades after the Second World War, however, that Fordism really came into its own. The success of planning and the organization of production and consumption went way beyond the factory assembly line. The philosophy of planning and organization, of linking of mass production and mass consumption, and of the partnership between organized labour, government and big business created more than the so-called 'managed economy' (Olson, 1984). Its effect was felt in every sphere of life in the industrial economies in the decades of boom that followed the end of the Second World War. In the wider process of organizing and planning society along Fordist lines, the new social democratic tide introduced comprehensive welfare programmes, where education, social security and health services would keep workers (as producers and consumers) healthy and secure. Indeed, so deeply infused was the economic and cultural ethos of this 'high Fordism' as a *social system*, that David Harvey, in his *The Condition of Postmodernity*, wrote:

> Post-war Fordism has to be seen, therefore, less as a mere system of mass production and more as a *total way of life*. Mass production meant standardization of product as well as mass consumption; and meant a whole new aesthetic and a commodification of culture. (1989: 135)

Why was Fordism, especially in its post-war 'high Fordism' variant, so successful? Why was it able to produce (that is, at the time) the longest uninterrupted boom in history (Brenner, 1998)? And why did it eventually become crisis-prone? In

France in the mid-1970s the neo-Marxist 'Regulation School', comprised of thinkers such as Robert Boyer, Alain Lipietz and Michel Aglietta, emerged in the attempt to make sense of the crisis of Fordism – which was by then well into its demise in the Anglo-American economies. What they termed 'regulation theory' argued that the process of capital accumulation might be given a degree of stability (avoiding violent swings in boom and depression) through what they called 'modes of regulation'. For Aglietta (1979), the continued 'concentration and centralization' of capital accumulation was made possible by the growing tendency of Fordism to 'fix' capital in space through a reliance on fixed assets such as factories, plant and machinery – as well as a relatively 'fixed' and stable workforce who had grown accustomed to the Fordist notion of 'a job for life'. These were processes and cultural assumptions that were given the backing of governmental policy in all the post-war social democracies.

To understand why this regulated system broke down almost completely, and led to the inauguration of a post-Fordist information society, we need to go back briefly to what I noted on the nature of capital accumulation in space and time. We saw that accumulated capital must expand into fresh territories, create new markets and so on if it is to avoid the problem of 'over-accumulation' where there is too much production and not enough consumption. A precondition for successful accumulation is the relative mobility and flexibility of capital (Harvey, 1989: 187). For much of the post-war period this was not a problem, because in the wake of the war's destruction, the national economies of Western Europe and Japan needed to be rebuilt – and so there was enough flexibility (and space) in the system itself for this to occur. However, as the Fordist system grew, and evolved and matured, with its regulation and planning ethos pervading a 'total way of life', then the need for the mobility of capital became more pronounced. Whole areas of the economy in the social democracies had become off-limits to private investment – however much it was needed. And so

nationalized or heavily subsidized industries in the core sec-
tions of the economy, such as steel, coal, airlines, shipping and
so on, had become common – and had become inefficient and
costly. Lack of investment and growing union power meant
that research and development into new technologies, such as
computer technologies with which to increase speed, flexibility
and efficiency, were low and/or heavily regulated.

In the Marxist analysis, regulation tended to be a problem
over the long term. However, as the 1970s progressed, business leaders, revisionist economists and influential politicians
began to view regulation per se as the core problem. Red tape,
tariff walls, industry subsidies, overly powerful unions and
'socialist' governments were argued to be choking the life out
of rigidifying economies. David Harvey, a Marxist, but not one
of the Regulation School, saw the over-accumulation problem
primarily in terms of there being insufficient space for capital
to expand into, within a crowded global system. He wrote that
the crises of Fordism in the late 1960s and early 1970s:

> can be to some degree interpreted . . . as a running out of
> those options to handle the overaccumulation problem . . . As
> these Fordist production systems came to maturity, they
> became new . . . centres of overaccumulation. Spatial compe-
> tition intensified between geographically distinct Fordist sys-
> tems, with the most efficient regimes (such as the Japanese)
> and the lower labour-cost regimes (such as those found in the
> third world) driving other centres into paroxysms of devalua-
> tion through deindustrialization. Spatial competition inten-
> sified, particularly after 1973, as the capacity to resolve the
> overaccumulation problem through geographical displace-
> ment ran out. (Harvey, 1989: 185)

The world was on the brink of a new revolution, a paradigm
shift regarding how society would be organized. Indeed,
according to Scott Lash and John Urry this phase signalled the
'end of organized capitalism'. This was a new era where the
market would again come to the ascendancy and where social-
interventionist policies would decline (Lash and Urry, 1987). It

is a revolution that continues still, through new technological means, and through new cultural attitudes towards work.

Efficiency, efficiency, efficiency . . .

It was with the demise of Fordism that culture, politics and society began also to experience the eclipse of Marxism, social-ism, and the decline of the rather more tepid social democracy as ways of seeing the world and organizing it. What this meant in practice was the withering and marginalization of any group, body of thought or individual that would stand in the way of the freeing of business from the perceived 'rigidities' of government regulation. The mobility and flexibility of capital were the new watchwords of the newly revitalized right-wing economic theorists and philosophers who were coming to the fore. Modes of thought that had been subsidiary for decades in the universities and the think tanks were now having their day in the sun as a direct outcome of global economic crises. Prominent among these was Friedrich von Hayek whose Adam Smith-derived ideas of individualism and economic freedom were best expressed in his dusted-off 1945 book, *The Road to Serfdom*, that warned that social democracy would inevitably lead to tyranny and crises. Hayek's old ideas of a return to laissez-faire capitalism were being eagerly received by powerful political and economic figures in the Anglo-American countries who attributed the chronic crisis mode of the period to over-regulated societies where 'socialism' had become out of control (Jenkins, 1989).

The rising influence of neoliberalism was aimed at freeing up capital, to make it flexible and mobile and able to promote faster innovation and more rapid change, and then respond to change with yet more innovation. The mantra of 'efficiency, efficiency, efficiency', was to return as the solution to stagna-tion, to loss of productivity and (of course) to the loss of profits that derived from these. Computerization was seen by some visionary engineers and business people as a way to radically improve speed, flexibility and efficiency. With computers automating human tasks and taking fatigue and error out of much of the production process – and injecting potentially limitless and untiring speed into it – productivity levels could, in theory, go off the charts. As Michel Aglietta put it: 'neo-Fordism, like Fordism itself, is based on an organizing principle of the forces of production dictated by the needs of capitalist management . . . *The new complex of productive forces is automatic production control or automation*; the principle of work organization now in embryo is known as the recomposition of tasks' (1979: 122; my italics).

This embryonic 'recomposition of tasks' was a central part of what has been described as the 'remaking of the world' (Harvey, 2005: 1). And, as the political and ideological barriers to this began rapidly to fall, computerization would rush into that vacuum to make it all possible.

The 'closed world' of computing opens up

In his 1956 classic, *The Power Elite*, sociologist C. Wright Mills described the power that had concentrated in the USA within the nexus of the political, military and economic establishments. He observed that:

> As each of these domains becomes enlarged and centralized, the consequences of its activities become greater, and its traffic with the others increases. The decisions of a handful of corporations bear upon the military and political as well as upon economic developments around the world. The decisions of the military rest upon and grievously affect political life as well as the very level of economic activity. The decisions made within the political domain determine economic activities and military programs. (1956: 7)

The prose is somewhat convoluted but the point is clear enough: that there existed, in the USA, a powerful elite who makes the decisions that have tremendous consequences for ordinary people. President Eisenhower, in his outgoing speech in 1961, referred to this relationship as the 'military-industrial complex' that democratic forces should be vigilant against. Emphasizing the role of computerization in this, Eisenhower elaborated:

> In this revolution, research has become central (. . .) Today, the solitary inventor, tinkering in his shop, has been overshadowed by task forces of scientists in laboratories and testing fields. In the same fashion, the free university, historically the fountainhead of free ideas and scientific discovery, has experienced a revolution in the conduct of research. (. . .) For every old blackboard there are now hundreds of new electronic computers. Yet, in holding scientific research and discovery in respect, as we should, we must also be alert to the equal and opposite danger that public policy could itself become the captive of a scientific technological elite. (Eisenhower, 1961)

The 1950s, 1960s and 1970s were the decades when the Cold War between the USA and the USSR was liable to become 'hot' at any time. Both sides were paranoid about the other's nuclear capabilities. It was this mind-set that led the USA to launch the 'technological revolution' in computing that Eisenhower referred to. The determination of the US military-industrial complex to have the most up-to-date research into computers and the knowledge on bomb-creating that this could provide was central to the decision to allocate huge project funding for it. It was realized during the early theoretical work that these new kinds of armaments, as well as the rocket technology needed to make them deliverable, were impossible to develop without the number-crunching capabilities of increasingly powerful computers.

In his book *The Closed World: Computers and the Politics of Discourse in Cold War America*, Paul N. Edwards argues that 'from the early 1940s until the early 1960s, the armed forces of the United States were the single most important driver of computer development' (1996: 43).

However, the intense research effort into uncovering the fundamentals of computing as a scientific discipline was much more than an exercise in gaining the necessary ability to crunch the numbers on the trajectory of a rocket or the explosive power of nuclear fission. Computers were seen as a way to eliminate the human element from the nuclear equation, and the all-too-human propensity for error and the disaster that this may bring in a world balanced on a nuclear precipice. Planners and strategists recognized that appropriate 'command and control' systems in the US military's structures were of central importance. Their faith in the capabilities of computer systems led them to believe that to be able to respond to an outside attack they had to institute command and control systems that are 'pre-programmed because their execution must be virtually automatic' (Edwards, 1996: 131). To emphasize the importance of speed within the automated command and control systems during the 1940s and 1950s, Edwards cites MIT engineer Jay Forrester who played a 'major role' in the military research and development into computing:

> the speed of military operations increased until it became clear that, regardless of the assumed advantages of human judgement decisions, the internal communication speed of the human organization simply was not able to cope with the pace of modern air warfare . . . In the early 1950s experimental demonstrations showed that enough of the decision making process was understood so that machines could process raw data into final weapons guidance instruction and achieve results superior to those being accomplished by the manual systems. (1996: 65)

The lessons of 'superior' *automated* forms of control of complex processes through computing had not been lost on a business community that was already, if sporadically, automating many of its own administrative and production processes in the USA and elsewhere. In a field research essay in the early 1960s, called 'Automation and the Employee', sociologists Faunce, Hardin and Jacobson argued, in a possibly overly optimistic tone, that 'Automation may affect the significance of work in our society by changing job content, redistributing employment opportunities, or decreased working hours. Its effects *will probably be a decrease in the importance of work and a continuation of the trend toward a leisure-oriented society*' (1962: 60; my italics). Workers who participated in the study were not so sanguine. Office workers were worried about the 'disruptions' and the perceived tendency for automation to eliminate jobs, but then again 'they often welcome change and rarely reject mechanization as such' (60). Workers in mass-production factories, such as automobile plants, were rather less ambivalent, with the study finding the unions against almost any form of automation (73).

The essay was part of a journal edition that was devoted to workplace computerization, with viewpoints being expressed in dedicated articles by academics, unions, management and government. Only the essay that forwarded the case of management, by Malcolm Denise, a Vice-President of the Ford Motor Company, was unambiguously keen on it. His fundamental argument, somewhat predictably given his position, was that 'The relationship between automation and unemployment is widely misunderstood' (90). For his part, the Secretary of Labor, a certain Mr Arthur J. Goldberg, stressed the need to 'minimize' through government regulation 'the complex problems that technological change and automation have been causing' (110). These essentially ideological positions were typical for the post-war Fordist economies: business may not have been happy with the situation, but went along with a relative lack of automation because this was a context of high profits that were the short-lived fruit of the 'golden age' boom.

However, by the mid-1970s the system of Fordism had broken down. In the Anglo-American economies, especially, profits were plummeting, unemployment was soaring and levels of productivity and efficiency were going through the floor. This represented an economic crisis, of course, but it was also a political one. The time, as we discussed previously, was quickly becoming ripe for a political-economic solution and the rising neoliberal elite began to provide and implement one. Much effort went into pressing for the automation of as much of industry as possible to drive up efficiency rates. Accordingly, the immense progress in computer science that had been made in the 'closed world' of the military-industrial complex began to filter through into commercial applications. Of course, big corporations such as IBM had been supplying the private sector with computer applications since the 1940s, but with the end of the post-war compact between labour, business and government, the way was being cleared (through defeats inflicted upon organized labour by a newly militant business sector aided and abetted by neoliberal governments) for the unrestricted and widespread introduction of automation. In the 1970s, the government 'Internetworking system' that had been developed to share information and research between scientists began to spill out into the private sector, inaugurating what would become the Internet. Neoliberal pioneers such as the elite policy circles of the Reagan administration in the USA, and the Thatcher government in Britain, fully supported the restructuring of the old Fordist economy and, as much as they were able, created the political and economic conditions to automate and make more flexible the processes of production. Business, in other words, was increasingly calling the shots. The perceived need to focus on cost-cutting, labour-saving and competitiveness, which innumerable management theorists, politicians and neoclassical or neoliberal economists began to stress from the 1980s onwards, meant that investment in the domestic market was increasingly channelled into capital-intensive, high-technology production – flexible automation which cut out, as far as possible, the human factor in the production processes. Significantly, during the early part of the 1980s, more of the investment dollar in the USA went into computer and related high-technology equipment than into traditional labour-intensive machinery (Kolko, 1988: 66).

The radical shift from Fordism to 'flexible accumulation' – a production system based upon the centrality of the flexibility of machines and workers – was fully under way by the mid-1980s (Sabel, 1989; Kumar, 1995). The 1960s dreams of the Ford Motor Company Vice-President were at last becoming a reality, and fully automated production processes, processes that had already been implemented by Japanese companies, notably by Toyota, were being implemented – and not only at Ford. The 'just-in-time' system developed by Toyota in the 1950s became a widespread production technique by the 1980s. It was the very antithesis of the mass-production systems that had dominated in the Western economies for the previous thirty-five years. In Fordist production methods, in auto manufacture and elsewhere, mass production usually meant mass inventories of parts that were stored and waiting to go into the assembly line at some point. This was a cost in terms of both space and the capital tied up in unused stocks. However, automated systems and the timely flow of information throughout the system meant that production could be streamlined and made more flexible and, importantly, able to be accelerated. Instead of the assembly line drawing required parts from large in-house inventories, it simply ordered these from a networked supplier, arriving 'just-in-time' to be used immediately. The flow of information to all parts of the process is of course central here – from supplier to customer to use in production – and results in much more efficiency. Just-in-time has the additional attraction of being extremely flexible. Electronic data is collected to keep track of where the production flow runs smoothly or where it develops bottlenecks, and so 'timely' information on system problems means they can be resolved quickly. Moreover, warehousing and transportation (and the cost associated with these) can be dramatically minimized. For example, General Electric in the USA was able to close twenty-six of its thirty-four warehouses between 1987 and 1997 (Rifkin, 2000: 34). And on a more general level, through such flexibility, businesses were able to respond to fluctuations in demand in an ever more volatile and uncertain market economy that was rapidly sloughing off the relative rigidity, inflexibility and predictability that had been the markers of Fordism.

Of course, systems such as these in auto plants and across the manufacturing sector more generally were never wholly automated – people (workers) had to be part of the process. Flexible systems thus necessitated 'flexible workers' who had to synchronize with the new rhythms and higher speeds. Unions initially resisted the introduction of 'flexibility' into the workplace. However, neoliberalized governments and employers who were more powerful than they had been for decades were able to wear down worker resistance and weaken industrial militancy. A consequence of political defeat, then, was that workers in many instances were compelled to become more flexible in the 'recomposition of tasks' that Aglietta had observed. Just as important was the fact that for new workers entering into economic life from the 1980s onwards, 'flexible systems' and 'flexible working' seemed as natural as the ubiquitous computer systems that were by now integral to the job, be it in the restructured manufacturing sector or in the burgeoning service industries.

Some intellectual responses to the revolution in information

Not quite Utopia: Daniel Bell

It was into this emergent *milieu* of confidence in the transformative powers of computing for the economy, and for social life more generally (observed in the perceived 'trend toward the leisure society', for example), that Daniel Bell published *The Coming of the Post-Industrial Society* in 1973. It was an influential book in policy, in academia and (with some interpretive licence) in business circles too. Indeed, it was Bell who was given credit for coining the term 'information society' that he used as a substitute expression for 'post-industrial society' in his subsequent works. In concrete terms, Bell noted that

this society would be characterized by a shift from manufacturing to a more service-oriented economy. That is to say, the
heavy- and mass-production techniques that had marked
Fordism would be replaced by service industries that are based
more on the application of information and knowledge.
Indeed, when Bell wrote his book, he was reporting structural
changes in economy and society that were already well under
way. In 1973 some 65 per cent of the US workforce was in the
service sector, and nearly 48 per cent of the Western European
workforce was similarly employed (Rifkin, 2000: 84). In 2006
the percentage in the USA had reached 80 per cent (Reuters,
2006). The pattern is broadly similar in the developed
economies. It is clear that in terms of a shift to a services-based
economy, this part of his thesis was unarguable.

More abstractly and more controversially, Bell's thesis argues
that through what he terms 'knowledge technologies' or 'intellectual technologies', the main constitutive axis of this new
society will be *theoretical knowledge* where new sources of innovation 'are increasingly derived from a new relation between
science and technology' (1973: 212). This is a transformation,
he cautions, that will not lead *ipso facto* to a utopian knowledge-
based society where wisdom and happiness would prevail.
Rather, he envisages the rise of a technocratic elite and with it
the 'primacy of theoretical knowledge' that organizes society
for the purpose of social control and the directing of innovation
and change. For Bell, what is central to the successful emergence and development of this knowledge society is that it
needs to be 'managed politically' (1973: 18–19). He ends the
book with the hope that by seeing Utopia as an ideal, and by
keeping it as one, men and women can go about the 'sober construction' of an always-better 'social reality' through democratic
and controlled use of the new knowledge technologies (489).

A problem that has been identified with Bell's theory is that
he conflates information with knowledge (see Webster, 2002:
8–29 for a fuller discussion). In this Bell builds upon and at
the same time tries to distinguish himself from a pioneer in

this realm, Fritz Machlup. In the early 1960s, Machlup was beginning to think about the role of communications, computers and knowledge in the service of the US economy. In respect of knowledge ('knowledge as a product' and the 'value' factor in his equations) (1962: 5), Machlup distinguished between five 'types' of knowledge. These are: practical knowledge, which is knowledge related to work, etc.; intellectual knowledge, which is related to intellectual curiosity in all manner of realms; pastime knowledge, which is the satisfaction of non-intellectual pursuits (entertainment and so on); spiritual knowledge, which is related to the study and profession of religion; and unwanted knowledge, which is 'incidental' and 'aimless' knowledge (1962: 21–2). Importantly, Machlup saw computers as primarily 'machines of knowledge production' and as vectors for their transmission in the new information-based economy (295).

For Bell also, it is the computer-driven 'knowledge technologies' of post-industrialism that were creating the information economy and society. However, Bell rejected Machlup's broader view of knowledge, containing both subjective and objective definitions, for what he terms a 'narrower' definition that is more 'objectively known' and more applicable to the material world (Bell, 1973: 175–6). This is an important distinction when we consider the logic underpinning the information society – especially for the role of computers. When Bell speaks of the 'information' that is constitutive of the information society, he refers to that which is contained in and produced by computerization. It is, in other words, information based on binary logic: on/off, yes/no, stop/go or 0/1. From the perspective of its industrial application, the beauty of computer (binary) logic is that information relates to a means–end instrumentalism. That is to say, it is a process that is narrowly defined in terms of possibilities, is able to be strictly planned out, and success is measured by the simple criteria that it seems to work for a particular task. Such instrumental logic fits easily with productive processes in the capitalist economy, such as the assembly line or the processing of data into quantifiable information ('practical knowledge'). Its chief attraction, for those who plan the production process, is that it is highly efficient and rational because the computerized process does what it is programmed to do – and no more. There is no space for the interpretation of meaning, no grey areas where context or inflection or error can affect what *kind* of information knowledge we are dealing with and the various ways it could be represented as knowledge. There is no uncertainty, in other words. As Theodore Roszak has put it: 'Information [had] come to denote whatever can be coded for transmission through a channel that connects a source with a receiver, regardless of semantic content' (cited in Webster, 2002: 24). In a system where time is money, and where speed of operation is the key factor in competitiveness, a black-and-white instrumentalism is able to achieve a level of predictability and certainty that knowledge based upon trial and error, and constant experimentation, cannot.

Knowledge, we can begin to see, is of a different conceptual order from information. Knowledge emerges through the open and experiential and diverse (and often intuitive) working and interpreting of raw data and information. If codified and computerized into digital form, data, information, and even knowledge become frozen – formalized and oriented towards the purpose the programmer has set – into sequences of instructions that follow a predetermined path. Roszak goes on to argue that 'For the information theorist, it does not matter whether we are transmitting a fact, a judgment, a shallow cliché, a deep teaching, a sublime truth or nasty obscenity' (cited in Webster, 2002: 22). It can thus be argued that, in the 'knowledge society' that Bell tentatively welcomed, 'knowledge' is reduced in its neoliberal context to that which has a measurable and commodifiable outcome.

Writing in the 1970s, French theorist Jean-François Lyotard called this kind of computer-driven knowledge 'performative' – formalized knowledge that has been designed to 'perform', to act in a certain way and produce seemingly effective and efficient results. Knowledge creation and knowledge production under the auspices of computer logic undergoes a particular process of change. As Lyotard puts it, 'technological transformations' in computerization, information storage in databanks, etc., 'can be expected to have a considerable impact on knowledge' (1979: 3–4). He continues: 'the miniaturization and commercialization of machines is already changing the way in which learning is acquired, classified, made available, and exploited' (4). Anticipating the commercialization of the university, Lyotard notes that the old notion that knowledge and pedagogy are inextricably linked has been replaced by a new view of knowledge as a *commodity*, and, as a result, teaching and learning have become part of an alienated and alienating process: 'Knowledge is now produced in order to be sold; it is and will be consumed in order to be valorized in a new process of production: in both cases, the goal is exchange' (1979: 4).

Computerization put to such specific use hollows out what is human in the production of knowledge and reduces it to abstract information. What we *lose* through the formalization of knowledge into means–end information is beautifully described by the photographer Peter Gullers (cited in Rochlin, 1997: 67–8), who writes on the subject of expert knowledge of light in photography:

> When faced with a concrete situation that I have to assess, I observe a number of different factors that affect the quality of light and thus the results of my photography. Is it summer or winter, is it morning or evening? Is the sun breaking through a screen of cloud or am I in semi-shadow under a leafy tree? Are parts of the subject in deep shadow and the rest in bright sunlight . . . In the same way I gather impressions from other situations and other environments. In a new situation, I recall similar situations and environments that I have encountered earlier. They act as comparisons and as association material and my previous perceptions, mistakes and experiences provide the basis for my judgment.

It is not only the memories of the actual practice of photography that play a part. The hours spent in the darkroom developing the film, my curiosity about the results, the arduous work of re-creating the reality and graphic worlds of the picture are also among my memories . . . All of the memories and experiences that are stored away over the years only partly penetrate my consciousness when I make a judgment on the light conditions. The thumb and index finger of my right hand turn the camera's exposure knob to a setting that 'feels right' while my left hand adjusts the filter ring. This process is almost automatic.

What Gullers describes is the creation and inculcation of knowledge through doing and through experience. It is *contextual* knowledge in that it may not work for everyone. But it is also a form of *universal* knowledge in that it contains patterns of 'common sense' that may be applicable to many situations with more or less success. The key point that Lyotard and Roszak make is that this kind of knowledge does not sit easily with codification and pre-programming. It does not fit the efficiency criteria of 'performativity', nor is it easily made into exchangeable or commodifiable forms of knowledge. It is a form of knowledge, in other words, that may be viewed as marginal and not really 'useful' in an efficiency-seeking society.

Pushbutton fantasies and cybernetic capitalism: Mosco, Robins and Webster

As the spread of information technologies deepened and became ever more ubiquitous over the 1980s and 1990s, other scholars, coming from differing intellectual backgrounds, began to apply their own methodological training to the analysis of this growing phenomenon. A relatively early – and subsequently influential – collection of essays edited by Vincent Mosco and Janet Wasko (1988) brought together a range of self-consciously critical perspectives on the effects of information technologies. The book contains the approach that Bell adopted in that it views information technology as more than simply a technology, and argues that its effects reach across culture, politics and, of course, the economy itself. Where these perspectives differ from Bell is in their use of what Mosco calls in the title of the volume a 'political economy of information' that overtly critiques the pre-eminent role of capitalism in the process (18–27).

In his own contribution, Mosco is scathing about the sloganeering and hyperbole that accompanied the coming of the information society. He views it as an ideological process that is used primarily to glorify and justify radical technological change and the social upheaval that was its corollary. For Mosco, it is akin to a form of fantasy – 'pushbutton fantasies' he calls them – that serves to conceal a very different underlying reality. His essay is titled 'Information in the Pay-per Society', which can be read as a witty play on words on the ideology of the 'paperless office' that was supposed to accompany the computerization of office processes in the late 1970s.

For him, the revolution in computers is not simply a technological one, but a revolution in the way the capitalist system organizes production. Mosco thus proceeds from the basic premise that:

> A fundamental source of power in capitalist society is profit from the sale of commodities in the marketplace. In fact, a basic driving force in the development of capitalism has been the incorporation of things and people into the commodity form. (Mosco, 1988: 3)

He goes on to argue that the collection of essays he has brought together show that the information technology revolution is in fact 'the process of incorporating *information* into the commodity form' (3). In other words, the fruit of the research in science and technology that we discussed as germinating within the 'military-industrial complex' of secret laboratories and restricted-access work has been taken over, developed and globalized by the imperatives of the capitalist marketplace. Computerization, based as it is on a binary system of numbers, is well suited (indeed was initially conceived) to *measure* and *monitor* and *instrumentalize*, and thus accelerate, almost any process. This provides the technical ability to conduct production and consumption on a tightly scaled cost-benefit analysis where everything is quantified and everything has its price. Spread this logic across economy and culture and we have the basis of our neoliberal 'user-pays' society where the market (augmented by information technologies) decides what is worthwhile based upon the simple criteria of whether it can be made profitable or not.

In Mosco's analysis the trope of computer-based speed, flexibility and efficiency are once more seen to be the driver of capitalist momentum. Culture and society, in turn, are colonized by this logic as computerization pervades socio-economic life. What this means is that the individual has to be able to pay to take part in what the information society has to offer. To be unable to pay is to become marginalized and gradually more invisible as a member of society. It was from this political economy perspective that Mosco was able to identify, at a relatively early stage, the outlines of what would come to be known as the digital divide. As he observes: 'We have been so caught up in the . . . Pushbutton Fantasies of the computer society that we have lost sight of a growing class of people who cannot afford the prices of admission to the information age' (10). The barring from certain technologies is of course more than a simple lack of access. It is a question of politics and social justice. The existence of a technological divide in a highly technologized society is deeply bound up with processes of social exclusion, of deprived areas and people, of the breakdown of social capital and the fracturing of those forms of community relations that emphasized social inclusion (Warschauer, 2003). This was a theme Manuel Castells had expanded upon when he argued that those who have no place in the information society comprise a 'fourth world':

> composed of people and territories that have lost value for the dominant interests in informational capitalism . . . because they offer little contribution as either producers or

> consumers. (. . .) Thus while valuable people and places have been globally connected, devalued locales become disconnected and people from all countries and cultures are socially excluded by the tens of millions. (Castells, 1999: 10)

And yet the picture is more complex than this critique would suggest, notwithstanding the 'tens of millions' who are cut off from the alleged benefits of 'informational capitalism'. Research by the United Nations Research Institute for Social Development (UNRISD) suggests, for example, that access to all kinds of digital technologies had 'jumped markedly' during the mid- to late-1990s (Hewitt de Alcántara, 2001: 18). Moreover, China today is the fastest growing market for mobile telephony. And even in the rich developed countries where there are substantial levels of unemployment and relative poverty, the falling cost of computer equipment, together with the availability of mobile phones to all but the most destitute, and the sheer ubiquity of networked computers in public libraries, in universities, schools and colleges, mean that *access is available*. But whether or not this offers the kinds of opportunities that 'being connected' may provide is another question. Brian Loader has noted the experience of Britain's UK Online centres, a government digital divide 'solution' that aimed to provide Internet access to all. He writes:

> It is scarcely surprising perhaps that the anecdotal picture which is emerging in the UK is of large numbers of grossly underused Online centres packed with state of the art digital equipment and providing formal training which is regarded as irrelevant to the needs of their intended users. (2002)

Clearly, there is scope for deeper and more fine-grained research into why some regard access to such equipment as 'irrelevant'. Could it be that through simple lack of information, many people are ignorant of such facilities? The evidence of declining standards of education in countries such as the UK, where functional illiteracy is perceived as a major problem, may mean that such individuals are intimidated by high-tech equipment (TUC, 2005). Or it could be that by being on the wrong side of the digital divide, one's outlook and day-to-day life is shaped in such a way that high-speed Internet access may indeed be considered 'irrelevant' when a job has to be got or kept, when rent has to be found, when kids have to be fed, and where the struggles of everyday existence block out almost everything else.

The critical approach by theorists such as Mosco is useful in the context of a social, political, economic and technological revolution that seemed to be both unstoppable and held out as desirable. And so a lesson we might draw from it is that some hidden realities of the information society are not so hard to find if we use our critical faculties and proceed from the relatively simple criteria of asking whether the processes of 'informational capitalism' are just and fair in relation to a logic that inserts the market and technology into more aspects of human relationships whether we want it to or not.

In the same volume, authors Kevin Robins and Frank Webster took a similar perspective to Mosco, initiating in the process a distinctive style of critique that they would develop over the next twenty years in response to the expansion of the information society. They too are concerned to deliver a critique of capitalism – but they push it further than Mosco to describe the information technology revolution as an unremitting nightmare. And again, like Mosco, the analysis 'goes beyond the purely economic' and is applied to the realms of media and culture. First, they take a particular view on the role of information. 'Information', they insist, 'is not a thing, an entity; it is a social relation' which under modern capitalism 'expresses the characteristic and prevailing relations of power' (70). In other words, the technologies of computerization and automation are being used by capitalism to expand and deepen its rule over society. They use Michel Foucault's conception of 'systems of micro-power' to describe how societies are ordered and controlled. Foucault argued that power is based upon knowledge (power-knowledge) and is used to extend the field of power. In appropriating and reproducing knowledge, power thereby reproduces and strengthens itself (see, for example, Foucault, 1980).

Robins and Webster maintain that the forms of domination and control of society that capitalism (and government) extended through the system of Fordism has been immeasurably strengthened in this post-Fordist age through use and development of information technologies. The centralizing tendencies of Fordism, which, as we saw previously, were to emerge as a central weakness in the quest for efficiency, have become radically decentralized, flexible and accelerated through economic restructuring and the computerization of productive systems. At first glance, it may seem that the notions of power-knowledge and 'decentralization' are somewhat at odds. However, they say that the major player in this transformation, the multinational corporation, 'can now use its communication network to coordinate the activities of decentralized units' which means that 'Decentralized activities can be coordinated as if they were centralized' (56). And, of course, the extent of this transformation goes well beyond the economic. As information technologies become the norm in every process and activity, the power of capitalism 'invades the very cracks and pores of social life' (54). In this they again reflect Foucault and his insistence that power is a decentralized, ubiquitous and systemic phenomenon that is highly dynamic.

In this view of the all-pervasiveness of information technologies and the logic of capitalism that it enhances, the ancient boundaries between work and leisure dissolve into a vast and growing cycle of production and consumption. Here, everything is commodified and placed under the criteria of profit, from education and entertainment, to sport, health provision and social relationships more generally in a steadily individualizing society. Information technologies use the social relation of information, they argue, to exploit social relations across time and space. In the late 1980s, when their essay was published, neoliberal globalization was fast becoming a concrete reality, and in projection of what the power of networks would achieve for capitalism, Robins and Webster contended that:

> Increasingly, leisure will become amenable to arrangement by capital, which can now access the consumer via electronic/information consoles capable of penetrating the deepest recesses of the home, *the most private and inaccessible spheres to date*, offering entertainment, purchases, news, education, and much more round the clock – and priced, metered, and monitored by corporate suppliers. In these ways 'free' time becomes increasingly subordinated to the 'labor' of consumption. (1988: 55; my emphasis)

Apart from the somewhat antiquated expressions 'electronic/information consoles', the point is clear and fresh, and what they describe (and much more) is now commonplace. Indeed, we take the ubiquity of information technologies for granted so much that we tend to forget that they are there. We 'move through' communication networks without a thought, emailing, doing our banking, shopping, using mobile phones and Blackberries with little concern that every keystroke, every number we dial, every transaction we make in our daily life is being recorded and that we leave a 'data trail' that can be as clear as footprints in the snow for those (people and automated systems) that take the trouble to look. The authors point to a fundamental dimension of the information society, one that allows, in theory at least, for the power of capitalism, and the power of political systems over individuals, to be augmented even further.

'The real power and political implications of information technologies', Robins and Webster maintain, is their 'intelligence and surveillance capacities' (1988: 57). The fact that information technologies can measure and control processes in society means also that they can *track* and *scrutinize* these too. They build on the work of Jeremy Bentham, an eighteenth-century social philosopher, who drew up plans for a new kind of prison (never built) based on what he called the Panopticon, which was a series of cells built around a circular observation tower. The point of this, in Bentham's words, was to gain the 'unbounded facility of seeing without being seen'. The intended effect would be that prisoners would not know precisely when they were being observed and that this would regulate their behaviour, ensuring that they 'should always feel themselves as if under inspection' (Robins and Webster, 1988: 57). Pervasive and largely unseen (or unnoticed) information technologies, Robins and Webster predict, will have the same panoptical effect in the information society. Invisible computer databases within anonymous buildings in parts of the world that you may never have been near will be able to store information about you. Expressing their darkest fears, they write that they:

> consider the loops and circuits and grids of what has been called the 'wired society' or 'wired city', and we can see that a technological system is being constituted to ensure the centralized, and furtive, inspection, observation, surveillance, and documentation of activities on the circumference of society as a whole. (1988: 59)

In such a closely surveilled *1984*-type society, not only is the individual or group able to be tracked and shaped as a consumer, as a profit centre, but can be *politically* monitored as well, to judge if they may be classified as subversive or dangerous. We see the 'technological system' put to its logical use today in many ways that would have been unimaginable only a generation ago (see Lyon, 2001, for a fuller discussion). Prisoners can now be subjected to what is a direct application of Bentham's idea. Inmates selected for conditional release can now be 'tagged' to enable them to be electronically monitored, to make sure that they stick to a regime of 'home detention' or curfew (Dodgson et al., 2001). We see the same logic of monitoring and tracking on the open Internet through cookies, for example, which are a line of text that passes from a web server to your browser and back again to the server, with the details of your computer logged. In effect, a cookie can track where you browse and for how long, etc., compiling patterns of web use that could be useful to commercial interests – or to the authorities. In the political realm, governments such as those of China and Iran monitor 'suspect' websites to try to find expressions of dissident opinion and try to locate from where they originate. Moreover, these governments use software applications to 'block' sites such as the BBC and CNN, or any site they may feel threatens their political prerogatives.

So far so grim, it would seem. And, to make matters worse, significant elements of Robins and Webster's dark vistas appear to have come true. World production and consumption is now heavily (if not completely) dependent upon automated computer systems and networks. Only a decade after it was popularized, the Internet became the backbone of the global economy, to serve as the network through which all kinds of monitoring and tracking take place. And, no matter how we look at it, the information society seems to have been originated for and developed for the interests of capital first. In many ways *we do* seem to be simply 'nodes' of production and consumption in a vast, interconnected marketplace, where the individual is considered only if he or she can pay – and then becomes a consumer – or falls foul of the law, in which case surveillance may be in order. Finally, these gloomy theorists cannot even end on a bright note of optimism, or point to a chink of light that may offer some hope:

> Our response to the information society is sombre. We are not talking of what information technologies might do; of how cable could further democracy if it was run by the right people; of the possibilities for satellite television or viewdata systems or word processors. We are talking about actually existing technologies – technologies that threaten to constitute a mega-machine, a systematic and integrated mechanism . . . We must confront the reality of existing technologies in the present tense. And we must confront the reality of an 'information age' . . . We can expect no utopia . . . If we want one we will have to invent it ourselves, and the new

technologies do not provide a short cut. (Robins and Webster, 1988: 72)

Has the Internet become the pitiless and exploitative and all-seeing 'mega-machine'? The authors come close to saying that we *need to bypass* information technologies to create our own Utopia, and to create a new kind of politics not based upon digital networks. But how is it possible to uninvent computers, or to make them less pervasive? I would say that it is not. Information technologies, with the Internet and its growing complexity, are here to stay. The note of Luddism that can be read into Robins and Webster's work is no solution. It may be more useful to consider who controls the mega-machine. When the authors wrote their provocative article, economic restructuring and social transformation were just beginning to be left to the abstract forces of the market. Today that process is well developed, and, to paraphrase the futurist Alvin Toffler, in the age of neoliberal globalization, *no one is in control* (Toffler, 1970: 290). As we shall see in chapter 7, however, the ideas of democracy and reason and justice are simply too ingrained in Western society for them to evaporate in the space of a couple of decades. New currents, new political languages, and, crucially, new political spaces and times are emerging that utilize information technologies in ways that the market logic did not intend. It is just possible that deep currents of justice and fairness are powerful and ingenious enough in Western societies to turn information technologies and networks of communication into socially useful platforms that go beyond the instrumental uses of a neoliberal economy.

Ideology wars in the information society

The restructuring of the world economy during the 1970s and 1980s – from a post-war Fordist mode to one dominated by 'flexible accumulation' and driven by information technologies – was by no means a smooth transition. It was in fact distinguished by a profound political and economic upheaval that disrupted the lives of millions upon millions of people, and continues to do so. Above all, restructuring was a war of ideas, ideas over how economies should be run, who should run them, and the technological basis upon which they would run. In such a battle, people can only be pushed so far. To *force* people to be more 'efficient' and 'flexible', to compulsorily require them to synchronize with an increasingly accelerated way of life, and to develop an obsession for computers, is clearly not going to work in ostensibly democratic societies. What was needed, as David Harvey has noted in his analysis of the period, was, following Noam Chomsky, the 'construction of consent'; that is to say, for the engineering of a shift in what kind of ideas dominate society and to make these ideas so deep-seated that they appear as 'common sense' (Harvey, 2005: 39–63). In short, the fundamental battle was (and still is) an *ideological* one.

Neoliberalism became dominant because its ideas were able to capture and motivate powerful people in government, in elite business circles and in the global media. Speed, flexibility and efficiency – and the primacy of market mechanisms vis-à-vis the work process – were the watchwords repeated over and over again, in all these forums, until they became embedded principles. If these terms had a slightly harsh and onerous ring to them, then there were other central tenets such as 'empowerment' and 'freedom', and 'entrepreneurialism' and 'individuality', to act as emolument. These more palatable-sounding ideas were revived from the 'classic' liberalism of the eighteenth century. This was a semi-mythic time when the 'state' and 'state interference' was minimal and men were freer. The state's primary role in this perspective was merely to conduct wars and to levy the absolute minimum of taxes. Moreover, it was supposedly a time when individuals were responsible for themselves and the conduct of their lives and did not require the state to get in the way. As Friedrich von Hayek, that very eminent hero of neoliberal intellectual circles – and someone lauded by early information society theorists such as Fritz Machlup – put it, 'A society that does not recognize that each individual has values of his own which he is entitled to follow can have no respect for the dignity of the individual and cannot really know freedom' (1978: 344).

The ideology of neoliberal individualism filled the space left by the ebb of 1960s counter-culture, but it was inflected with a selfish tone that the 1960s hippies would have blanched at. Margaret Thatcher expressed this more hard-edged Hayekian individualism in an interview in 1987 when she asserted that 'there's no such thing as society. There are [only] individual men and women and there are families . . . and people must look after themselves first.' It was a growing perspective that had been powerfully critiqued in 1979 by Christopher Lasch in his *Culture of Narcissism*, which described the weakening of social bonds due to his impression that many people had 'retreated to purely personal preoccupations' (1979: 4). This process of social individualization was echoed a generation later by Robert Putnam in his *Bowling Alone* which similarly lamented the perceived diminishing fabric of society and the depletion of the 'social capital' that kept communities vibrant and able to form the basis of a democracy (2000). Both these books (and titles with a similar concern, such as Richard Sennett's 1998 *The Corrosion of Character*) were best-sellers, and generated much debate about the nature of post-Fordist society.

However, this is 'theory' compared to the reality that confronts many people every day. They encounter it in their jobs, in the media, in their relationships with other people, in the pressure to consume, to have a bigger house, an even bigger SUV or a private education for their kids. It is a pressure to be flexible and to be oriented towards the self and to consumption and to the immediate gratifications of the present. It is a life that reflects, as Lasch put it, 'the waning of the sense of historical time' (1979: 3). And, in an effect of life seeming to speed up, our sense-making becomes attuned to the here and now, and to the imperatives of multitasking. It is a life, as some writers see it, where the individual has less sense of being part of a larger social history, or much of a feeling for what has gone before or what is to come. It is a situation where, as Donald Barthelme puts it, the individual 'is constantly surprised. He cannot predict his own reaction to events. He is constantly being overtaken by events. A condition of breathlessness and dazzlement surrounds him' (cited in Lasch, 1979: 4).

In the grip of such cognitive helplessness, where the time to reflect and to consider becomes subsumed by a constant present, the individual is exposed to the 'dazzlement' of powerful and pervasive ideology. He or she is susceptible in particular to the ideology of information technologies as offering the way to function in such a life. Without ICTs there would be no neoliberal globalization, and so what Theodore Roszak called the 'cult of information' (1986) became a sub-set of ideology that was able to grow and pervade with the globalization process. New media technologies were promoted not only as a way to make us more productive, but also to engender forms of community, albeit 'virtual' ones (Rheingold, 1993). Neoliberalism claims that information technologies are necessary for the new world that is being created. They are also necessary for *you*. And in the rising culture of individualism, ICTs are engineered towards use by the individual: personal computers, personal digital assistants, mobile phones dedicated only to you, personal email addresses, iPods, peer-to-peer file-sharing where you share with a 'virtual community' in cyberspace, the MySpace website and its clones, or YouTube where you can promote yourself to the virtual world, and of course online gaming where the virtual world is a place where the only flesh and blood around is your own. And, just as in the real-world economy, the free-market ideology will put the failure of a business down to its not being flexible enough, or not responsive enough to market conditions, then so too if you feel the existential pain of digital anomie, what you need are *more* digital connections. The direct corollary of this is that computers or neoliberal society aren't to blame in an individualist society – *you* are. If you feel lonely, buy a laptop. It is a condition of purported freedom, where, according to Michael Heim: 'When online we break free'. We no longer need the physical proximity of people in the information society, Heim goes on to insist, because:

> Telecommunication offers an unrestricted freedom of expression and personal contact, with far less hierarchy and formality than are found in the primary social world. Isolation persists as a major problem of contemporary urban society, and I mean spiritual isolation, the kind that plagues individuals even on crowded city streets. With the telephone and television, the computer network can function as a countermeasure. The computer network appears as a godsend in providing forums for people to gather in surprisingly personal proximity. (1993: 84)

Ideology made flesh

Finally, in any ideological framework it is always useful to elevate people as symbols to positions that the rest of us should aspire to. Accordingly, the coming of the information society saw the rise to prominence of an array of individuals who came to be seen as the embodiment of the 'indomitable force' that Thomas Hughes refers to in the quotation at the beginning of this chapter. Again, the ideology is of the 'dreams' that information technologies can make possible – notwithstanding the fact that these 'dreams' were themselves first suggested to us by neoliberals and by techno-utopians. Journal of choice for this latter group, and barometer of the technological zeitgeist of the 1990s, was *Wired* magazine which was first published in 1991. It was co-founded and part-funded by the MIT Media Lab director, Nicholas Negroponte, who also wrote influential utopian books such as *Being Digital* (1995). Partner in the *Wired* venture was Louis Rossetto who penned an article in a 1998 edition of the magazine in which he reflected upon the early years of the publication, and from where the founders drew their inspiration:

> What we were dreaming about was profound global transformation. We wanted to tell the story of the companies, the ideas and especially the people making the Digital Revolution. Our heroes weren't politicians and generals or priests and pundits, but *those creating and using technology and networks in their professional and private lives* . . . you. (Rossetto, 1998)

Rossetto speaks directly to 'you' as the individual, a 'hero' who is making the 'Digital Revolution' through creative and innovative uses of information technologies. This was the dawning of a new age that needed new role models, people who 'bucked the trend' and were resolutely non-conformist. Primary among these was Bill Gates, the habitually described 'ex-Harvard dropout' who rose from geeky obscurity to be the richest man in the world because, it is heavily implied in the popular perception, he understood and believed in the power of computation to transform the world. Gates himself forcefully promoted the notion of the individualistic entrepreneur in which he, through example, placed himself firmly in the role of leader in leading-edge software. By the mid-1990s, the needs of business and the making of lots of money through the application of software and computers was an area in which Gates had plenty of authority and ideological legitimacy – as well as *chutzpah*. For example, his first book, *The Road Ahead* (1995), proclaimed no less than the solution to capitalism's problems through computerization and automation. He called it 'friction-free capitalism' and saw it as the fullest expression of Adam Smith's concept of the ideal market where 'would-be buyers and would-be sellers' are able to share 'complete information' through which they could make fully informed decisions. The Internet, he proclaimed, would be the seamless electronic middleman that would provide this all-seeing, all-knowing perspective on all possible market conditions (1995: 180–208).

We see a similar trajectory in the stellar career of Steve Jobs, founder, with Steve Wozniak, of Apple Corporation. Another university dropout, Jobs fits the ideological typology of the individualistic hero who pursues his own way, using his own skills and driven by his own entrepreneurial impulses. 'Think different' was the famous Apple advertising slogan during the 1990s. And, along with the burgeoning success of Microsoft, Gates and Jobs were the prominent heroes behind the immense dot-com boom of the late 1990s, where the NASDAQ high-tech stock market ballooned and many multimillionaires were made overnight – and then went broke again when the dot-com bubble burst in 2001.

In retrospect, it seems that the thousands of would-be dot-com heroes were not thinking so differently after all. They were, in classical fashion, merely responding, herd-like, to market signals. 'Complete information' was conspicuous by its absence for many of the buyers of 'red hot' dot-com shares (Cassidy, 2002). Moreover, both Apple and Microsoft, as pre-eminent revolutionaries in the ideological fostering of the information society, have been searching unsuccessfully for 'friction-free capitalism' ever since the heady days of the 1980s and 1990s. Microsoft has had a running battle over a series of anti-trust suits that claimed they were using their powerful position to destroy competition and monopolize the global software market. In 2001 Microsoft was found to have used its market power in a way that Adam Smith, whom Gates looks to for inspiration, would have no doubt disapproved of. Apple, for its part, was found to have infringed the patent of the Creative Corporation for the iPod user interface that Creative said was theirs. In 2006 Apple agreed to pay Creative $100 million for a licence to use the patent (Bangeman, 2006).

Notwithstanding these hurdles, the powerful legitimizing ideology of digital dream-makers continues to pervade the mediascape today. Jaws still collectively drop in amazement and admiration when it is announced that a new generation of digital heroes, the individuals behind the creation of websites and applications such as YouTube and Skype, for example, become overnight billionaires when they sell the digital fruit of their ideas to the highest bidder.

And the old guard still fights the good fight. Bill Gates, for example, despite his corporation being found guilty of monopolization and anti-competitive practices, can still confidently write of the benefits of 'friction-free capitalism'. In a 2006 essay, titled 'The Unified Communications Revolution' (the term 'revolution', it seems, has not gone out of fashion), Gates sets out his vision of the 'coming communication convergence', where communication will become seamless across telephony, mobile phone, desktop, laptop and handheld computers, streaming video, web conferencing, indeed anything that is networkable. This new digital ecology will create 'people-ready business' in the 'new world of work'. And, again, as in the visions contained in *The Road Ahead*, software is key to the delivery of this new phase of the revolution. It is not known if such talk of the 'Unified Communications Revolution' just happened to coincide with the 2007 launch of Windows Vista, the major new Microsoft application, 'the breakthrough computing experience' that would enable all this to come true (Microsoft, 2006).

Gates was specifically addressing the business community in his essay. But he views with some admiration the new generation of people who have grown up during the age of information and who have no real conception of a pre-Internet life or a pre-Internet tempo. These are:

> the young people in your organization – particularly the ones who are fresh out of college. They've lived their entire lives in the digital age, communicating in real-time via text messaging and instant messages. For some of them, even email lacks the immediate gratification they expect when they want to communicate with someone. To this generation, the desktop phone has about as much relevance as an electric typewriter does for those of us a generation or two older. (Microsoft, 2006)

The Microsoft chairman proceeds to confidently sketch a picture of the inhabitants of a new world, a world where the information society is no longer 'coming', as Bell put it, but is *here*, firmly entrenched and creating and sustaining a new way of relating to economy, culture and society. It is a world where information is so central that most of us now take it for granted. But there are questions we still need to ask and reflect upon. For example, how deep does the 'cult of information' go, and what does it mean to have digital logic at the very basis of how we see the world and how we see ourselves?

3

Information Takes Over

Everyone and everything is affected by the disruption.

Poster, 2006: 46

By the 1980s, with the star of neoliberalism and the ICT revolution fully on the ascendant, it was beginning to be generally accepted that business solutions to the crises of the 1970s, i.e., speed, flexibility and efficiency through computerization, was the only way forward. 'There is no alternative' was a famous line attributed to British Prime Minister Margaret Thatcher in the 1980s to assert that the new way was non-negotiable. With this acceptance, a fresh consciousness began to develop in people and a new zeitgeist began to emerge. Where once the free market used to be viewed as a recipe for chaos and boom–bust swings, it was now respectable again. Business was almost cool. Computers were certainly cool – and the faster the processor the cooler it was. Thomas Frank termed the grass-roots support for the New Economy 'market populism' (2001). Computers seemed to open up all sorts of possibilities in all sorts of areas. The 'think different' Apple campaign of the 1990s was in fact reflecting a social trend that was already established.

Business guru Peter Drucker contextualized the new world in this way:

> Every few hundred years in Western history there occurs a sharp transformation . . . Within a few short decades, society rearranges itself – its world-view; its basic values; its social and political structures; its arts; its key institutions. Fifty years later there is a new world. And the people born then cannot even imagine the world in which their grandparents lived and into which their own parents were born. (1993: 1)

It would, indeed, be rather difficult to overestimate the scale and potency of the technological transformation that shook the world in the 1980s and is still shaking it today. If one came out of a coma today that had lasted for ten, or perhaps even five years, one would wake up to new processes, new applications, and new ways of communicating, of working and being entertained that would be largely unrecognizable. Our current obsession with podcasting and blogging and having to obtain the latest gadget from Apple are examples of how rapidly change has been compressed into our lives. It is a point we are reminded of nearly every day if we look at the 'technology' section of any major newspaper. Accelerated transformation is built into the processes of the information revolution. However, to understand what kind of change this is, we need to go deeper. We need to go beyond the glib statements and worn clichés that comprise the general understanding of the spread of information technologies, and consider something that Peter Drucker does not in his *Post-Capitalist Society*, from which the above quote came – and that is to provide a historically based political economy critique.

In the previous chapter I outlined an argument for what I see as the rationale for what Drucker perceived as the 'sharp transformation' that occurs every few centuries. This was the intertwining political, economic and cultural logic of modernity, capitalism and classical liberal democracy that had reached a point of crisis in the 1970s. The effect was a shift from a Fordist to a post-Fordist society and, more broadly, from a society based upon the tenets of modernity, to a postmodern world where our 'basic values' were no longer so clear. In our quest for a greater understanding of the information society, what I wish to do here is to look at the ideas that reflected (and also helped shape) this postmodern world where 'information takes over', as I have termed it, or where, as Ithiel de Sola Pool puts it, 'electronics takes command' (1983).

To do this, first we need to gain some appreciation of what profound technological transformation has meant for the 'world view' and the 'basic values' that Drucker speaks of. This is because without a change in the fundamental ways in which we perceive and judge the world, it would be very difficult for that change to take hold and for it to be accepted in any deep and lasting way. And there seems to be no question that the world view of the individual in the context of widespread computing has been transformed; indeed, the omnipresence of computers constantly *reinforces* a certain perspective concerning their role in society. Kevin Kelly, for example, a founding editor of *Wired* magazine, says that the computer has become a metaphor for how we see the world. Increasing numbers of people in the network society, he writes, believe that the logic of the universe is akin to a computer – and vice versa. And, as the information society becomes the prevalent mode of life, we begin to accept consciously or not that 'thinking is a type of computation, DNA is software [and] evolution is an algorithmic process'. If we persist in this, Kelly continues, 'we will quietly arrive at the notion that all materials and all processes are actually forms of computation [where] our final destination is a view that the atoms of the universe are fundamentally intangible bits' (1998). Speaking from a perspective influenced by the work of Michel Foucault, where power and ideology can be framed by the construction of 'discourses' or modes of communication that are specifically structured through language, Paul N. Edwards extends this metaphor-as-constructor-of-reality thesis when he looks at what is culturally inferred in the Turing Test, 'brain-as-computer'. His list of the most obvious metaphors includes:

> The brain is *hardware*.
> The brain is a *rapid, complex calculating machine*.
> The brain is made up of *digital switches*.
> The mind is *software*.
> The mind is a *program* or set of *programs*.
> The mind *manipulates symbolic representations*.
> The mind is an *information machine*.
> Thinking is *computation*.

Perception is *computation*.
Memory is *looking up stored data*.
The function of the mind and brain is *information processing*.
(Edwards, 1996: 59)

Edwards goes on to point out that the profound claims contained in these sentences have been made in such terms, or something close, by cognitivists and computer scientists such as J. C. R. Licklider and Norbert Wiener since the 1950s (1996: 161). The cumulative effect of this bombardment by metaphor is, as Neil Postman maintains, that the 'energizing of mechanistic metaphors' creates a mindset whereby we believe 'we are at our best when acting like machines, and that in significant ways machines may be trusted to act as our surrogates' (1993: 118).

The philosopher Emmanuel Lévinas claimed along the lines that ideology is both constituted by and concealed in our *weltanschauung* (O'Shaughnessy and Stadler, 2003: 195). Accordingly, perspectives such as those just outlined are congruent with the view that the ideas we use to make sense of the world in some way have to reflect how we experience its reality. In other words, for ideology to function effectively, it must contain elements of what we see as 'truth' or aspects of reality that ring true for us, thus tending to confirm or legitimize this or that claim concerning the necessity or even 'naturalness' of computers. Indeed, in respect of the information society, effective ideology must not only reflect more or less accurately our experience of reality, but must also promote the idea as a way to *improve* our experience of reality, to make our lives better in tangible ways, and point to pathways along which technological development can empower us as both individuals and as members of communities and societies.

We will now consider the exponential and rapid growth of the information society from two differing perspectives. First, we look at the viewpoint of those (usually) powerful individuals (writers, theorists and business consultants) who have shaped a strand of thinking about the information society that has been extremely influential and has had real-world effects in terms of its helping to further promote and extend the 'informationalization' of the world towards specific ends. It is important to understand these perspectives because they have become almost second nature to us, causing us to accept almost unthinkingly that our networked society, though often hectic and stressful, is organized and oriented towards a better life for all of us. Second, we shall consider the views of more critically oriented thinkers, writers, activists and academics who use elements of political economy, social theory and media theory to try to discern patterns of interest. That is to say, they attempt to uncover the operation of power, of politics, and of economics that shape and direct the course of the information society towards goals that are not automatically focused on the needs of people as members of a democratic and pluralist society. Finally, we consider both types of claim in the light of some empirical evidence.

Promoting the dream: Al Gore

To be a booster for the information society and the spread of computers into every possible realm does not necessarily mean having a personal economic stake in the matter. Many people, groups and institutions actually believe it to be the case that computers are, as Theodore Roszak memorably satirized them, 'a solution in search of problems' (1986: 51). And, as we just saw, most of us are now brought up to think in such terms. Since the Industrial Revolution at least, as Arran Gare has reminded us, a mechanistic conception of the world has been at the very core of Western philosophy, influencing the 'quantification of human relationships, culminating with the development of commercial capitalism' (1996: 130). Since the 1950s, the 'machine metaphor' has graduated to the 'computer metaphor'. And so one can honestly, and without any apparent cynicism or ulterior motive, advocate computers to become a way of life for everyone – because 'everyone knows' that the desktop computer is better, more accurate, less noisy and more efficient than, say, the mechanical typewriter.

A personification of this mindset is Al Gore, a late 1990s 'conviction' politician and latterly an influential environmentalist. In his role as Vice President of the United States, Gore launched the National Information Infrastructure (NII) in 1993. This was a government–private industry initiative to give all Americans access to the new information technologies that were becoming progressively important through the mainstreaming of the Internet. Accentuating the 'people centeredness' of the NII, Gore set forth shining new vistas when he wrote in the Executive Summary of the document:

> All Americans have a stake in the construction of an advanced National Information Infrastructure (NII), a seamless web of communications networks, computers, databases, and consumer electronics that will put vast amounts of information at users' fingertips. Development of the NII can help unleash an information revolution that will change forever the way people live, work, and interact with each other. (Gore, 1993)

And more:

> People could live almost anywhere they wanted, without foregoing opportunities for useful and fulfilling employment, by 'telecommuting' to their offices through an electronic highway;
> The best schools, teachers, and courses would be available to all students, without regard to geography, distance, resources, or disability;
> Services that improve America's health care system and respond to other important social needs could be available on-line, without waiting in line, when and where you needed them. (Gore, 1993)

The NII was a document of its time. In its wholesome enthusiasm it reflected a phase in the short history of post-Fordism and the possibilities allegedly inherent in this wonderful new thing called the Internet. Moreover, it may have been a US invention, but the information society was not to be a case of American exceptionalism – the Internet and its advantages were to change the world. Indeed, Gore went on something of a roadshow at this time, and took what was called the Global Information Infrastructure (GII) to Kyoto, Japan, the following year. Addressing an International Telecommunication Union (ITU) meeting, Gore was careful once again to establish at the outset of his speech that the information society would be about people, about you and me, and the things we care about:

> The effort to build the GII provides us with an opportunity to reach beyond ideology to forge a common goal of providing an infrastructure that will benefit all the citizens of our nations. We will use this infrastructure to help our respective economies and to promote health, education, environmental protection and democracy. (Gore, 1994)

Gore is an important, though I believe still underrated, figure in the development of the Internet. He was no pioneer technician like Vinton Cerf, or software visionary like Tim Berners-Lee, but at a crucial stage of its development he, along with the then cult hero Bill Gates, was the unthreatening public face of the information revolution. The not inconsiderable 'buzz' that the NII caused inserted the idea of the information society into the public consciousness as an incontrovertibly 'good thing'. Prizes were awarded by Gore, and by President Clinton himself, to people in fields such as medicine, education and community relations who were judged to have made the most innovative use of the Internet. This was exemplified in the 'NII Awards' that were created in 1995, again with a people-centred mission 'to help the global community realize the potential of a networked society by identifying examples of excellence and helping others learn from those examples' (DO-IT, 1995).

Importantly, what this connection did, according to Campbell-Kelly and Aspray in their 1996 book, *Computer: A History of the Information Machine,* was to 'politicize' the 'networking idea', by bringing what was in essence a technical process into the highest realms of public discourse. Gore lent legitimacy to a process that would not be possible through the efforts of business alone. The clearly honest and genuine imprimatur of the second most powerful man in the country would go far. Its most important effect was that it ensured widespread media exposure, inspiring individuals, institutions, and of course businesses, to inquire what all the fuss was about. Accordingly, Gore, the US government and US big business were able to create and then ride the tidal wave of Internet mania that reached a new high-water mark with the launch of Windows 95. And as Campbell-Kelly and Aspray note: 'In the early 1990s the Internet was big news . . . In the fall of 1990 there were just 313,000 computers on the Internet; by 1996, there were close to 10 million' (1996: 283).

The connections broker: Esther Dyson

Gore may have been the skilled raconteur who could dominate the mediascape and dazzle the masses with visions of exciting new worlds. However, there were other, less widely known, but still powerful people, who pressed and cajoled and inspired and spread the memes of info-ideology to other powerful people who could act upon them.

One such figure is Esther Dyson. In 1993, Paulina Borsook, writing in *Wired* magazine, identified her as 'the most powerful woman in computing' (Borsook, 1993). Dyson was not the CEO of some large IT company, or legendary hardware engineer or software programmer, but a venture capitalist who specialized in investing in Internet start-up companies. Her talent was to identify trends in IT, to speculate about the course of Internet development and scout out companies with innovative applications who could make things happen. Borsook characterizes Dyson as 'Silicon Valley's answer to a Hollywood agent . . . Esther's power is in connecting people with ideas . . . a connections-broker *par excellence* whose introductions can make or save companies' (1993: website). Dyson also had a profile outside the hothouse of Silicon Valley's power networks. In 1997 she wrote a much-discussed book called *Release 2.0: A Design for Living in the Digital Age.* The paperback edition a year later was titled *Release 2.1.* Written in a short paragraph-per-subject, staccato style, it ranges over what were some of the salient issues of the Internet at that time (and they still are): from communities, work and governance to security, privacy and content control. Throughout, Dyson is relentlessly upbeat about the Internet – what it then was, and what it promised to be. Running right through the book is a neoliberal 'libertarian' streak where it is *individuals* within communities who will be the main beneficiaries. Quoting eminent Americans such as Thomas Jefferson, Dyson reasons that the Internet will not change the basic characteristics of 'freedom' and 'individuality', because 'it is a medium for us to extend our intellectual and emotional selves' (8). She drives home the libertarian view in no uncertain terms a few pages later when she proclaims, in language close to Gore's, that:

> The Net offers us a chance to take charge of our own lives and redefine our role as citizens of local communities and of a global society. It also hands us the responsibility to govern ourselves, to think for ourselves, to educate our children to do business honestly, and to work with fellow citizens to design rules we want to live by. (Dyson, 1998: 14)

It is important to recognize that in her role as 'change agent' for Silicon Valley's establishment and start-up players, Dyson was a part of the coming together of a powerful critical mass in the 1990s. Prior to it being coherently and aggressively advertised by the IT multinationals, it brought the Internet to the mass public of the USA and the world. I do not claim that Dyson was some nefarious Svengali who operated clandestinely, but she was part of a synergy that is still in operation today, where powerful cross-promotions between governments and business are oriented towards the public, in the genuine belief (by some) that saturation Internet is truly the way towards a better society. We see an interesting insight

into this fairly closed network of information society promotion that straddles the realms of ideas, of business and of
governance, when it is noted that Dyson was part of the
Advisory Committee for Gore's NII, and Ira Magaziner, a
Clinton White House aide and adviser on the information
society, could say of her that 'Her value is as a thinker. She
is one of the premier philosophers of the digital age'
(Salon.com, 2000).

A similar change agent from the very same time is George
Gilder. In echoes of the perceptions of Dyson, Gilder was
tagged in Wikipedia in 2007 as a 'techno-utopian intellectual'.
Gilder is also an important figure because he straddles several
important realms that are necessary for the promotion of the
information society idea to the largest possible constituency.
Gilder spoke to an essentially different (but no less important)
audience from Dyson. The Silicon Valley/California Ivy
League university/and cool start-up nexus that Dyson helped
supply the glue for was seen as a distinct culture that had its
own appeal. Many on the right wing of politics and society saw
this as infected by a post-1960s counter-culture ethos that had
(by the 1980s) begun to merge with a market fundamentalism
through the ideas of freedom and libertarianism that were
made possible by ICTs (Frank, 2001: 33–4). The archetypal
bearded-and-ponytailed IT geeks who were developing the cool
hardware and software, and the university dropouts who were
becoming millionaire entrepreneurs through marketing this
stuff, were seen as suspect by social conservatives. Richard
Barbrook and Andy Cameron saw this milieu in which Dyson
mixed as expressive of what they termed the 'Californian ideology' which was a 'bizarre fusion of the cultural bohemianism
of San Francisco with the high-tech industries of Silicon
Valley', a radically new world where, flying in the face of 200
years of economic and social history, 'everybody can be both
hip and rich' (cited in Flew, 2003: 34).

Gilder's own social conservatism was also politically militant and his advocacy spoke directly to those in business who

were considering the pros and cons of the Internet revolution, and whether or not to invest in its future. Gilder was a speechwriter for various Republican Party officials and candidates during the 1960s, including Richard Nixon, and was an early advocate of the supply-side economics that would be the centrepiece of 1970s neoliberalism. He worked as an economics writer and published in various economic reports and in the *Wall Street Journal*. His politics were overt, as were his economics, and so his audience constituted an important part of the US political and business scene. He was also an advocate of the information revolution. In his 1992 book, *Life After Television*, Gilder tried to show that television had had its day. Its good points were now being outweighed by the bad, to the extent that television was now warping the minds and constraining the liberties of Americans. Television had become 'dumb', monolithic and monological, determining 'which books and magazines we read, which cultural figures ascended to celebrity and wealth, and which politicians prospered or collapsed' (23). Television, Gilder maintained, had become 'a tool of tyrants [and] its overthrow will be a major force for freedom and individuality, culture and morality. That overthrow is now at hand' (35).

The contrast with Dyson is stark. Whereas she sees the positive in new information technologies, the *enhancing* of existing freedoms, of individuality and communities through new ideas and new information technologies, Gilder sees only demons to be slain, old technologies to be consciously junked, and old values and ways of life to be *re-established* through control over the new information technologies. Before the term 'Internet' had become popularized, Gilder saw the 'rise of the [networked] *telecomputer*' as the way 'to enlarge freedom, revitalize culture, and to prosper' (126).

As the 1990s rolled on, and as the Internet began to flourish and networks proliferate, Gilder's role within a critical constituency (the NASDAQ high-tech stock market) became increasingly important. This was a time when the tide of neoliberalism was at its highest, with the idea that investing in the stock market was no longer the redoubt of the monied elites in the world's capitals, but was now a mass-based expression of Frank's 'market populism' (Frank, 2001). In the wake of changes in tax laws, and the freeing-up of economic life more generally, and in a context of fast money and fast profits, millions of 'individuals' were now investing and looking for advice about where to put their money. In this overheated period, in the years prior to the NASDAQ implosion of 2000, Gilder was able to wed his knowledge of economics and the market with his zealotry regarding the possibilities of information technologies. He did this through his enormously influential *Gilder Report*. At its peak before the meltdown, the *Report* was selling 75,000 yearly subscriptions at $295.00 each. As Frank relates it, readers of the *Report* were told they could 'grow rich on the coming technology revolution' if they followed its stock-picking tips (2001: 355). Many who ploughed money into the vast enlargement of the information revolution did so through reliance on his seeming insight, and what came to be called the 'Gilder effect'. This helped mobilize Wall Street and in turn the investment capital of millions of ordinary people, not only in the promotion of the dream of personal profit, but in the realization of a high-tech Nirvana where, as Gilder himself put it, information technologies will 'transform business, education and art . . . [and] can renew our entire culture' (1992: 16).

Perhaps the most potent description of Gilder's influencing and shaping role in promoting the information society in the realms of politics and economics comes from Thomas Frank. He deserves quoting at some length as his 2001 book, *One Market Under God* (Gilder himself is strongly religious and a long-time promoter of so-called 'intelligent design' through the Discovery Institute), captures well the mood Gilder helped create in the rush to be 'part of the future':

the future as George saw it *did* happen, again and again. Not because of Gilder's psychic powers, but because the stock market had transformed him from the man who talked the microchip into the object of one of the long prosperity's most peculiar manias. 'Listen to the technology,' Gilder liked to say. 'Listen to Gilder,' chanted the rest of the world, logging on to his website on the day a new issue was scheduled to appear and desperately buying shares in whatever company the great man had touted. By the year 2000, financial journalists were discussing the 'Gilder effect,' the massive and immediate movement in a company's share price that the ideologue was capable of setting in motion with even the most indirect pronouncements. Novell, a maker of network software, saw its market capitalization leap by $2 billion in one day in December 1999 after Gilder wrote favourably of it in his newsletter. When Gilder steered his followers towards Xcelera.com in February 2000, its price climbed 47 percent in one day; when he touted NorthEast Optic Network a month later, its price nearly doubled. And Qualcomm, which he had boosted for years, became one of the great bubble stocks of the late nineties, appreciating some *2,618 percent* over the course of 1999 as investors rushed to be a part of the future. And when Gilder pooh-poohed a technology, its makers discovered themselves on the wrong side of history in no uncertain terms, shunned by investors and their share price plummeting. Having conjured the 'New Economy' up out of the backlash mud, having transformed the lexicon of social class into the language of free-markets, Gilder himself was now transformed into the archetypal character of the new era: the stock picker infallible, the bubble-blower as *philosophe*. (Frank, 2001: 355–6; italics in original)

The intellectual legitimacy that an idea needs to gain sufficient purchase in society was *ascribed* to Dyson and Gilder by those who may have been themselves hypnotized by the zeitgeist. However, intellectual legitimacy regarding the inevitability and desirability of the information revolution has also *emerged* from the academy itself by leading thinkers – bona fide information society *philosophes* – who could boost the idea and the dream still more powerfully.

Combining bits with atoms: Nicholas Negroponte

A first-ranking source of intellectual legitimacy in the promotion of the purported benefits of the information society is Nicholas Negroponte. Central to Negroponte's influence is that his work straddles the intellectual domains of the university, the practical applications of the laboratory, and the business- and market-centred functions of putting 'dreams' into application and making them a social reality.

Negroponte was involved with thinking about the possibilities inherent in ICTs long before either Dyson or Gilder were. His CV is near perfect. Educated in architecture at MIT in the mid-1960s, he subsequently worked in professorial roles in other Ivy League universities such as Yale. His main interest at this time centred on the possibilities that computer-aided design (CAD) could bring to his academic discipline. Soon, however, he began to think almost exclusively about the nature of computing in society more broadly and the potential of human–computer interaction (HCI). In HCI, Negroponte was working in the same realm as the visionary J. C. R. Licklider whose theorizing of the 'man–computer symbiosis' was beginning to have real-world effects through the intellectual and practical dynamism that individuals such as Negroponte were bringing to the idea. By the 1980s, just as the information technology revolution was getting under way, Negroponte had undertaken a significant intellectual move: he had become a techno-utopian. He now saw the future of computer technology in wholly positive terms, and he theorized these futures and expounded his visions in his monthly column in the pages of *Wired* magazine, the journal he backed when it was founded in 1993.

A decade previously, while at MIT, he established, along with Jerome B. Wiesner, the MIT Media Lab. It was a position he held until he stepped down in 2000. The Media Lab, from its inception, has been viewed by many as a new kind of institution for the new times. The Lab sought ways, in Negroponte's phraseology, to combine 'bits with atoms' (1995). Others have termed it variously as 'a high-tech playground for investigating the human–computer interface' (Wikipedia); or, as Nancy Madlin described it, 'a kind of genius institution, a place of wild and woolly intellectual endeavour holding nothing back. If the place were a person, it would be a mad scientist, someone who breaks the rules and is unafraid to experiment with radical ideas' (1999: 35). Negroponte made a point of promoting such an image. From the beginning, he and Wiesner sought to attract the best and brightest from universities around the world who would apply their creativity and brainpower to the development of new ideas and new directions in the pursuit, as the Lab's website puts it, of the 'study, invention, and creative use of digital technologies to enhance the ways that people think, express, and communicate ideas' (MIT Media Lab, 2007). Reflecting its open and diverse remit, the Media Lab's Faculty research staff are drawn not only from the traditional disciplines of computer and software engineering, but also include people with backgrounds and expertise in disciplines such as business, economics, psychology, physiology, neurobiology, linguistics and digital art.

What makes all this possible is not funding by grants from the government, or subventions from MIT's central university funds, but sponsorship from corporate capital. The range of sponsors of MIT Media Lab is startling and is testimony to Negroponte's skill in selling his vision of merging 'bits with atoms' to all kinds of parties – some of whom would not ostensibly be associated with such endeavours. For example, alongside the long list of donors you would expect to find involved with the Media Lab, such as Intel, Hewlett Packard and Nokia Corporation, there is also sponsorship by the makers of Lego toys, the tobacconists Phillip Morris and the corporate behemoth behind all kinds of stuff that we use every day, Johnson and Johnson (MIT Media Lab, 2007a). Since the early 1980s Negroponte's work has gone a long way to promote the idea of not only a utopian world bathed in the beneficent flows of information, but also a *profitable* one where the Campbell Soup Company can flourish alongside Cisco Systems. It is the 'human–computer interface' idea that underpins Negroponte's ecumenical appeal. His quest to merge 'bits with atoms' opens up the possibility of the ubiquitous computing we discussed earlier *really* becoming ubiquitous to the extent that information technologies inhabit every realm of life – indeed human life itself. It was a vision that began to take on concrete reality with the opening of the MIT Center for Bits and Atoms (CBA) in 2001. The CBA's brief is to look 'beyond the end of the Digital Revolution to ask how a functional description of a system can be embodied in, and abstracted from, a physical form' (CBA, 2007). In other words, it seeks to find ways to join 'bits' of computer information with the 'atoms' that make up the physical world, including humans.

Negroponte had outlined this thinking in his best-seller *Being Digital* which was published in 1995. In it, he explicitly built on the early work of J. C. R. Licklider and the theory of HCI whose time, he believed, had finally come (Negroponte, 1995: 95). In *Being Digital*, Negroponte begins with the assumption that bit and atom are not so very different. Indeed, he uses the contraction 'DNA' to describe what constitutes a digital bit comprised of ones and zeros: 'A bit has no color, size, or weight, and it can travel at the speed of light. It is the smallest atomic element in the DNA of information' (1995: 14). Of course he does not equate these exactly, but through developments in nanocomputing (at the scale of a billionth of a metre), and quantum computing where information processing obviates silicon-based processing altogether, the commingling of the human body with the logic of information draws ever closer. In the website of the CBA, the prospect is held out tantalizingly (for computer nerds and investors alike) where it states that:

> if [binary] logic can be introduced into the process of physical assembly then perfect macroscopic structures could be built out of imperfect microscopic parts. Biological proteins are in

fact produced in exactly this way, by programs run by cellular molecular machinery; CBA researchers have shown how nanocluster antennae can be attached to these proteins in order to provide for radiofrequency control over cellular signaling pathways. This promises to create a 'digital' technology for molecular manufacturing, with implications for atoms as profound as they have been for bits. (CBA website, 2007)

Relatively modest but nonetheless radical implementations of this principle are already under way. In *Being Digital* Negroponte speculated on what he called 'wearable media'. In alliterative mode he muses that 'Computing corduroy, memory muslin, and solar silk, might be the literal fabric of tomorrow's digital dress. Instead of carrying your laptop, you wear it' (1995: 209–10). A decade and more later, MIT Media Lab is still working on bringing these and other innovative ideas into reality, bringing information technologies into the very core of people's lives – and it is this ubiquity that has sponsors from every sector of corporate capital supporting it (see the list of research projects at MIT Media Lab Research).

The power of these (and many other individuals) in 'selling' the dream of the information society is very strong indeed. It derives from being 'part of the system' they wish to promote. Inclusivity gives access to the machinery of dissemination such as the mass media of television, newspapers, magazines, books – and of course the Internet itself. Those on the inside track of this process, if not personally acquainted, mix in the same circles, share the same assumptions about the world and see what they are doing in the main as useful, unproblematic and 'good' for society. Their interaction follows a positive feedback loop where the idea of the information society is carried by information technologies themselves, validating the message, and strengthening it as it spreads. From the Vice President of the USA telling about the wonders of the NII, to the documentary on television that informs us how a mobile phone has transformed the life of a Bangladeshi farmer, the direction and the preponderance of the message is clear. It is also, for many people, something 'natural'; a progression through life with faster and faster computers and ever more dense networks through which information about every conceivable subject will flow. The effort to keep up with this increasingly accelerated life is thought of (when thought about at all) as a 'challenge' or 'opportunity' or, possibly more apathetically, as the 'price of progress'.

However, against this hegemony others resist. They are scattered and they are isolated, and they have much greater difficulty in getting their ideas on the information society across. Moreover, unlike Gates and Gore and Jobs and Bezos, they are largely unknown outside academic and policy circles. But what they do provide is a critique and a reflective insight into the information society – a perspective that is wholly lacking in the world of the boosters. It is to these theorists that we now turn.

Revealing the nightmare?

Let us begin, appropriately at this point, with a warning about technology. It comes from French philosopher and theologian Jacques Ellul. In his 1990 book, *The Technological Bluff*, he reasoned from the broad bases of philosophy and theology that 'there is no [such thing as] absolute technical progress' (40). Modern technology, he maintained throughout his long career, always has a cost somewhere else in society, an unanticipated outcome that would nullify the gains made by the technology itself. We will consider this equation in relation to speed and social acceleration in some detail in chapter 6. However, in the preface to his 1980 book, the *Technological System*, Ellul made a point that is eerily prescient of the forces that would underpin neoliberalism and the information society. He wrote that 'Modern technology has become a total phenomenon for civilization, the defining force of a new social order in which *efficiency is no longer an option but a necessity* imposed on all human activity' (italics mine).

For Ellul, the drive for 'efficiency' through computerization would not only give the totalizing logic of ICTs infinitely more power and scope, but the unanticipated consequences would also be inevitably greater as well. Instead of spreading freedom and diversity, as the boosters would aver, systems of technique, for Ellul, serve to imprison the individual and culture in a form of 'information alienation' and present a 'broken vision of the world' (1990: 329–30).

Ellul's work is useful as a way to frame the following theorists, as it links with our concern with the effects of *systems of technology*, of networked technologies that are oriented towards the nebulously beneficial effects of speed, flexibility and efficiency.

The sociology of information: Manuel Castells

In terms of a more focused academic perspective on the nature of the information society, we have to begin with the work of Manuel Castells. Quite possibly he is the most quoted and cited theorist there is on the subject. A Spanish-born sociologist, he worked in France in the University of Paris and the École des Hautes Études en Sciences Sociales, before moving to Berkeley in the USA in 1979. He came from a politically active background and his earlier work on urban sociology was Marxist-inspired. In the 1980s, he began to move away from an explicit Marxism in urbanism towards a more broadly focused analysis of the emerging information society.

The transition was apparent in his 1989 book, *The Informational City*, where he began to theorize more on the abstract effects of ICTs on society. It was here that he began to forward the idea that capitalism and its productive forces were being transformed in new, wide-ranging and complex ways across the world, a 'technological revolution of historic proportions', as he termed it (1989: 1). A key element of his analysis of the 'informational mode of development' is the conclusion that it represents a new mode of capitalist development that is constituted by what he called a virtual 'space of flows', where the central mode of production has shifted from labour (and machines) to information (13–14). These 'flows' of information in virtual space were collapsing the traditional boundaries of modernity and were enabling not only the transformation of cities and urban society, but also bringing city and country, local and global into a networked, *globalized* whole.

It was in the first of his three-volumed series, beginning in 1996, *The Rise of the Network Society*, that Castells began to expand and develop these key ideas. Castells saw the information technology revolution as profound, and as an all-encompassing phenomenon – as did all the writers we have encountered so far in this chapter. Castells, however, like Ellul, attempts to reflect upon the phenomenon through a philosophical system that seeks to *understand* it instead of *exploiting* it in an unreflective way. It is in his consideration of the 'space of flows' where he gets to the crux of what information technologies make possible – and what information technologies transform. 'Flows' of computerized information are of course amenable to acceleration, to the speeding up not only of technological systems but also the people and societies of which these flows are an intrinsic part. Networked flows of information, then, become 'the expression of the processes dominating our economic, political, and symbolic life' (1996: 412). Referring to the generalized effects of these networked flows, Castells goes on to write that:

> Networks are open structures, able to expand without limits, integrating new nodes as long as they are able to communicate within the network, namely as long as they share the same communication codes (. . .) Networks are appropriate instruments for a capitalist economy based on innovation, globalization, and decentralized concentration; for work, workers, and firms based on flexibility, and adaptability; for a culture of endless deconstruction and reconstruction; for a polity geared towards the instant processing of new values and public moods; and for a social organization aimed at the suppression of space and the annihilation of time. (1996: 470–1)

There are several things going on in these few sentences that speak to an admirable Castellsian vision that is at once panoramic and multidimensional. Most prominent is that network structures are first and foremost *capitalist structures*; the 'open structures' and 'appropriate instruments' for the globalizing of a neoliberal form of capitalism that has become utterly hegemonic. Moreover, there is no sense of there being any alternative in the matter for the mass of humanity. Notwithstanding the advertiser's rhetoric regarding choice – or 'Where do you want to go to today?' in the words of a Microsoft slogan – it is the users of these technologies (the vast mass of ordinary workers in capitalist industries who did not ask for them) who are those most affected by the mania for 'flexibility' and 'adaptability'. It is they who must get used to what Marx called the 'constant revolutionizing of the means of production' and be prepared for their working practices to change with each innovation, and have their skills rapidly diminished as the demand for new skills increases. And it is they who must synchronize their lives with the accelerating effects of the 'annihilation of time' where networked flows drive people faster, blurring the traditional realms of public life and private life, of work time and leisure time into a constant flow of temporal 'nows' where a frantic 'multitasking' ability becomes the most important skill that a person can have.

Writing in the mid-1990s, Castells also touches upon a dimension of the information society that is having increasing repercussions today, and is something we will consider in some more detail in the final chapter of this book. That the hegemonic nature of networked and neoliberalized capitalism has left no register of culture and society untouched is a thesis that Castells takes into the realm of politics. Neoliberalism is after all a political ideology, but what does it mean when the 'polity [is] geared towards the instant processing of new values and public moods'? 'Instant' is the temporal term that provides the clue to Castells's thinking here. Many, if not all, political parties, who seek to be taken seriously by big business, have had to

remake themselves since the beginning of the information revolution in the 1970s. In this process of 'repoliticization of informational capitalism' (1996: 88–9), right-wing and traditionally
pro-business parties, such as the British Conservatives, became
even more pro-business and market-oriented; and the left-wing
parties, typified by Britain's Labour Party, have moved in the
same ideological direction, becoming 'New Labour' and the
new friend of corporate capital. This abrogation of the historical goals of representing the wishes of ordinary people has rapidly changed the nature of politics and how people themselves
now perceive the political system. Millions of voters across the
Western democracies and beyond have, since the 1970s, abandoned the idea that political parties any longer speak to their
day-to-day concerns, so deeply has traditional politics been
implicated with the aims of big business and the 'free' market.
Apathy in the form of a declining voter turnout at elections, or
cynicism in the shape of large-scale opinion polls, showing the
low esteem in which politicians are now held (Whitaker, 2005),
has been the political effect of neoliberalism and its pursuit of
'flexibility' and 'adaptability'.

And here too we anticipate our discussion of what I term 'bad
speed'. As the polity synchronizes with the fast speed of the
economy – more executive-centred government, less democratic deliberation (there is increasingly no time for it) – it must
also try to retain at least some sense of legitimacy with people,
through 'reading' the mood of the voter, or, as Castells puts it, be
'geared towards the instant processing of new values and public
moods'. This process of 'reading' is a highly mediated form that
is usually conducted through specialist media agencies and the
'focus group' research they do, a traditional 'market research'
tool that has migrated to the political realm. The effect is policy
construction through highly alienated means, conducted within
small windows of perspective that give the polity no real indication of the aspirations and needs of people. Political institutions and the people they are supposed to represent, then, in
this reading of Castells, have suffered a long-term estrangement

since the beginnings of the information age, and this is expressed in an apathetic and thread-slender relationship that threatens complete disconnection.

In much of his analysis – as one might expect from someone who approaches the subject of the information society within a political economy framework – Castells reaches some fairly sombre conclusions. However, the apathy towards institutional politics, symptomatic of the 'repoliticization' process, is also expressed in more vibrant forms in other, sometimes anti-institutional and subversive realms, and it is here that Castells dispels any overall negativity and sees hope for the future and promise for the longer-term project of the information society as an emerging social good. He makes this quite clear at the beginning of the book, in the *Prologue* in fact. Surveying the fall-out for institutional politics that came from information technologies in the service of neoliberal economics, Castells observes that: 'Political systems are engulfed in a structural crisis of legitimacy, periodically wrecked by scandals, essentially dependent on media coverage and personalized leadership, and increasingly isolated from the citizenry' (1996: 6). In response to such 'uncontrolled, confusing change', people try to reorganize themselves around 'primary identities' such as faith, nation, ethnicity and language. This kind of atavism has been present in human affairs throughout history. However, the particular turbulence created by the market-led spread of information technologies has brought this tendency to the surface and globalized it. The search for meaning through identity is enhanced by this process. As the information society subsumes more of our life, this leads, in the first instance, to a bifurcation between our 'being' in the 'real world' and our life on the Net. As Castells puts it:

> People increasingly organize their meaning not around what they do but on the basis of what they are, or believe they are. Meanwhile, on the other hand, global networks of instrumental exchanges selectively switch on and off individuals, groups, regions, and even countries, according to their

relevance in fulfilling the goals processed in the network . . .
It follows a fundamental split between abstract, universal
instrumentalism, and historically rooted, particularist identities. Our societies are increasingly structures around a bipo-
lar opposition between the Net and the Self. (1996: 3)

This 'structural schizophrenia' has negative outcomes, to be
sure, in the shape of intolerant fundamentalist religions, or
neo-fascist organizations, but in the final analysis Castells
believes in what he calls the 'liberating power of identity', a
power that does not necessarily lead to 'its individualization or
its capture by fundamentalism' (1996: 4). His political economy of the network society, Castells maintains, leads him to
'swim against the streams . . . of intellectual nihilism' and he
believes that 'observing, analysing, and theorizing is a way of
helping to build a different, better world' (ibid.).

New political formations are central to this longer-term project, and Castells begins to concentrate more on the political
aspects of the information society in volume 2 of his trilogy.
Here he acknowledges the essential fact that the institutions of
liberal democracy are in crisis. It is a crisis that involves the
blurring of the boundaries of the nation-state by neoliberal
globalization. Politics (in its institutional forms) has become,
largely, 'informational politics', meaning that if they want to
reach out to 'the people', mainstream political parties now
must effectively conduct their work of policy formation, tactics
and strategies of political struggle and the ideological dimensions of these through a shared media space, i.e., through the
Internet, and through the mass-media channels of the global,
digital media. Cyberspace had become 'the privileged space of
politics' (1997: 312). This space also became the space where
elements of the evolving networked civil society began to form,
organizing and sharing information and projects that were
antithetical to institutional political agendas. Several years
later, in his 2001 *The Internet Galaxy*, Castells could write that
'civil society has been able to use the Internet to broaden its
space of freedom, to articulate the defence of human rights,

and to propose alternative views in the political debate' (164). In a dialectical movement, then, the fragmentary logic of neoliberal globalization upon traditional forms of nation, place and space also set in place the network structures of informational 'flows' that people are able to use in ways that were unintended by the capitalist system, and that act as the basis for a new language of politics. We see this process in the growing influence and attraction of networked political communities that come together in the shape of the World Social Forum, for example, a truly global phenomenon that articulates a broadly anti-neoliberal perspective, seeking to fill the democratic void that has opened since the 1970s and the shift by institution politics to a pro-market stance regardless of the social costs (see WSF, 2007).

Computer-driven capitalism: Dan Schiller

Castells's canvas is vast, and its main value is that it is broad enough to allow others to focus on specific aspects of the general tendencies he describes. Dan Schiller, in his *Digital Capitalism* (2000), does this in respect of how he sees the 'neoliberal networking drive' as the force that changed the substance of the capitalist mode of production. *Digital Capitalism* was probably the first sustained critique, from the perspective of political economy, on how the Internet was transforming capitalism. The *ideology* of digital capitalism, as Schiller tells us, is the utopian vision that information technologies, as Bill Gates and others had predicted, would produce a 'friction-free capitalism'. And, once relieved of those elements that cause friction, such as miscommunication and non-communication, the age-old system of production that had evolved in the eighteenth century would finally, as Schiller says, excoriating Gates's idea, 'somehow morph into a kinder, gentler place' (2000: xv).

The very first sentences of Schiller's book reveal his take on the logic that underpins the networked economy, and the reality behind the cyberdreams of many of its boosters. He writes: 'The architects of digital capitalism have pursued one major objective: to develop an economywide network that can support an ever-growing range of intracorporate and intercorporate business processes. This objective encompasses everything from production scheduling and product engineering to accounting, advertising, banking and training' (2000: 1). He argues that those who actually built and developed the Internet, and made the connections – the 'intranets' within corporations and 'extranets' between corporations – were not concerned (even vaguely) with 'networking communities' as Dyson or Gilder would have it, but with ordering and rationalizing business systems across the whole economy and beyond. And all this is in the singular pursuit of profit. The likely effects 'for much of the population' are, as Schiller puts it, 'unpropitious' (xvii).

The deregulation of the telecommunications industry in particular created the optimal environment for 'neoliberal networking' to proceed at breakneck pace during the 1980s and 1990s. A positive feedback process was set in motion, where, as more corporate investments were poured into ICTs, the ICT industries themselves became able to plough more of their profits into research and development to produce more innovative and faster products that would keep corporate capitalism coming back for more. As Schiller notes: 'Computers, telecommunications equipment, and software accounted for nearly 12 percent of overall U.S. capital stock in the mid-1990s' (2000: 16). Or, put another way, by 1997 'information technology hardware expenditures alone totalled $282 billion – 17 percent more than U.S. purchases of new motor vehicles and parts, 49 percent more than outlays for new homes, and 168 percent more than commercial and industrial construction' (17). The overall effect of the digitalization of US capitalism was, in the space of a decade, to make it the largest industry in the United States (ibid.).

Much of this frantic activity was driven by competition. The pressure to computerize was intense and it was felt in almost every boardroom that if they did not streamline to make their processes of manufacturing, administration, distribution and so on more efficient, then their very survival would be at stake. Intranets (the in-house networking of a discrete business entity) worked in conjunction with 'extranets' that allowed corporations to link up their 'firewalled' networks with collaborators. Hence we see a classic symptom of capitalist development where 'competitors' must also cooperate and collaborate to ensure the wider functionality of the system.

Network functionality was aimed at developing new processes and procedures that would, as noted before, consign Fordism and its alleged inefficiencies to the dustbin of history. Schiller provides a useful illustration of the process from the Ford Corporation itself, which in 1998 had installed a networking system that epitomized the quest for post-Fordist 'flexible accumulation'. The new system:

> connected 12,000 workstations at offices and factories worldwide to thousands of proprietary web sites with information regarding markets, competitors, and part-suppliers' efficiency. As a product-development system, Ford selectively opened its intranets to let engineers, designers, and suppliers work from the same data, and updated that data hourly. Ford hoped to link its 15,000 dealers to its intranet and to move to building cars on demand, thereby saving billions of dollars in inventory costs. (Schiller, 2000: 21)

Driven in part by the perceived need to 'computerize or die' that stemmed from the competition in the neoliberalizing marketplace, and driven also in no small part by the influence of Dyson, Gilder and others, there seemed to be no limit to what computerization could not be applied to in the quest for 'friction-free capitalism'. The year 1995 saw the launch, for example, of Amazon.com. Online shopping was thus born. Hotel bookings could now be purchased easily online, as could tickets to sports, movies, theatre, and so on. It was the potential profits from this generalized 'networking drive' that helped to inflate the NASDAQ bubble from the mid-1990s.

Networking and using the Internet as a common platform allowed the interoperability and complementarity of once fairly discrete parts of many industries. Inflating the bubble still further was what came to be known as 'digital convergence', where more and more industries were using compatible systems – the bits and bytes of digital information that was becoming the central focus of what businesses now did, from automobile construction and steel-making to insurance and tourism. Schiller gives an example of the effects of digital convergence in the media industry in the USA, where competition, once again, was pushing corporations into either 'friendly mergers' or hostile takeovers:

> The Web platform . . . comprises a venue that is perfectly matched to the diversified entertainment conglomerates that have been assembled during the last fifteen years. In a cascade of huge mergers and acquisitions, multibillion-dollar media properties – film studios, broadcast networks, program packagers, cable systems, satellite channels – changed hands like marbles. Such vertically integrated megamedia as Time-Warner, Disney, and News Corporation were created to fulfil the goal of cross-promotion and cross-media program development. (2000: 99)

During the 1980s and 1990s, global capitalism, and not just its US variant, was at once succumbing to the logic of neoliberal information, and at the same time driving itself into unknown realms and uncertain futures. However, one thing was clear in the minds of the Internet builders – it was not going to be a free-space in the sense that Al Gore (1994) had envisaged it, where 'Preserving the free flow of information requires open access'. The virtual spaces of the networks of the information superhighway were created to be the profit centres of the twenty-first century. Schiller shows how the privatization of public telecommunications industries in Britain, continental Europe and elsewhere around the world allowed the transference of the broadcast spectrum from the democratic control of parliaments to the shareholder control of corporate boardrooms. The privatization boom of the period saw formerly national telecommunications carriers, with their satellite systems and extensive cable networks, embark on 'unprecedented system-building' across borders, transmuting into globalized and privatized entities that constitute the backbone of the Internet and the information society. For Schiller, this constituted a 'political victory' for neoliberalism and an ideological triumph for the tenets of the globalization project itself (43). It was a point emphasized by Noam Chomsky in 1999 as the first Internet fever was approaching its zenith. For Chomsky, digital capitalism was not about the fostering of democracy; it was about the usurpation of public goods (the spectrum) and the insertion of a commercialized communication system into every aspect of life. In an interview for the *Boston Phoenix*, Chomsky encapsulated the essence of Schiller's argument and the thrust of 'digital capitalism':

> Handing over the digital spectrum, or for that matter the Internet, to private power [is] a huge blow against democracy. In the case of the Internet, it's a particularly dramatic . . . because [it] was paid for by the public. How undemocratic can you get? Here is a major instrument, developed by the public – first part of the Pentagon, and then universities and the National Science Foundation – handed over . . . to private corporations who want to turn it into an instrument of control. They want to turn it into a home shopping center . . . where it will help them convert you into the kind of person they want. Namely, someone who is passive, apathetic, sees their life only as a matter of having more commodities that they don't want. Why give them a powerful weapon to turn you into that kind of a person? Especially after you paid for the weapon? Well, that's what's happening right in front of our eyes. (Chomsky, 1999: website)

The incorporation and commodification of the Internet is a theme Schiller interrogates once more in his 2007 book, *How to Think About Information*. Essentially, Schiller argues that the logic of commodification of ideas and processes in the service of profits continues, and that only the scale has dramatically increased, with no socially compelling or humanistic impulse behind it. Moreover, it is a process, he contends, notwithstanding all the hype surrounding 'social networking', Web 2.0 and 3.0 technologies, that 'at a basic level . . . has been thoroughly, even necessarily, uncreative' (2007: 161). He makes the case that 'accelerated commodification reorients institutional infrastructure' and social power relations become distorted in favour of the 'increasingly omnipresent capital logic' (121). This is a political problem, he asserts, because 'Unless . . . power is broadly shared, democracy itself is threatened' (57). Schiller remains profoundly sceptical of the idea that the information technology revolution, as currently constituted, is in any way leading to the kind of society that Dyson or Gilder promote, writing that: 'the dominant approach treats with contempt the idea that networks should be shaped, overseen, and used with regards for any substantial public interest. The contempt has been concealed, however, beneath a veneer of theory that, by equating the public interest to marketplace efficiency, purports to vitiate the former' (111).

Overall, the political economy-based message has been consistently critical since the 1980s. It argues that information technologies were conceived and implemented not for the common good or for ideas of freedom and liberty – but in the interests of a market-based economy whose logic and imperative are antithetical to the public interest.

So how do the information 'dreams' stack up against the 'nightmares'? We can begin with an overarching neoliberal claim for globalization and the information technology revolution: that it would create a prosperous society, where the 'trickle-down effect' would raise everyone's standard of living and where unemployment, the scourge of earlier economic systems, would be all but abolished. Indeed, against this most basic benchmark all else could be measured, because if a society (global or national) cannot provide jobs for all its members, then how can 'progress' of any kind be said to have taken place? In 2006, the International Labor Organization (ILO) released a study that showed that despite overall GDP growth, the global unemployment rate in 2005 had *reached new highs*. The report states that 'In total, nearly 191.8 million people were unemployed around the world in 2005, an increase of 2.2 million since 1994 and 34.4 million since 1995' – and this in the context of a global labour force participation rate that was lower in 2005 than it was a decade earlier. Moreover, the world total of 'working poor', those who subsist on $2 a day, had risen in that decade from 1,354.3 million to 1,374.6 million (ILO Report, 2006: 5–11). It is in figures such as these that we see the social effects of neoliberal globalization and the information society it creates. GDP *growth* is the pre-eminent imperative and so the orientation is geared towards this end.

This palpable unfairness is even more apparent when we look at the yawning gaps between the earnings of ordinary workers in a free-market system, compared with the CEOs who create the context of our networked lives. In 1980, that long-ago time when free-market post-Fordism and the information technology revolution were in their infancy, the typical chief executive earned, on average, forty-two times the salary of the average worker. The ratio rose to 525:1 during the Internet boom peak of 2000, and by 2005 had dipped slightly to 411:1 (AFL-CIO, 2005).

From these general trends it may be argued that the foundation stones for a better society have not yet been laid. A decade and more of the Internet – and a generation of the unfettered implementation of 'networked solutions' and ubiquitous computing – has not led to a planet of 'friction-free capitalism'. Capitalism is in turmoil, perhaps as never before, and the constantly changing and constantly churning information society that reflects it can hardly be called a 'better' world. However, the 'individualism' that the new economic system was said to promote has in a way actually come about. We are individualistic as never before, but for most of us the transformation has not been voluntary or conscious. It has been brought about by an anomie that has inserted itself into the lives of millions, in high-speed, high-stress living, driven by the 'flexibility' that computers construct for us. What this creates is a process of 'isolation of individuals within social groups' (Beck and Beck-Gernsheim, 2002: 33). More, that ours is a stress-filled society seems to be evidenced in the immense growth of the pharmaceuticals industry and the proliferation of stress-related products that earn it billions of dollars (Angell, 2004).

So far, in this book, the neoliberal mantra of 'efficiency' through competition is usually framed in ironic quotation marks. This is because, on a generalized level, the networking of society has in fact been incredibly inefficient. Capitalism has always been prodigiously wasteful: we see it in the millions of cars that go unsold each year, the profligacy in terms of fossil-fuels in the 'food miles' that bring mangoes or strawberries to our supermarkets in winter, the waste involved in the resources devoted to non-essential goods, the mountains of rubbish that clutter our throwaway society, and so on. The information society has not changed this; indeed, it has massively added to it. The building of the networks themselves is a revealing example of how inefficient neoliberal globalization has been. Schiller made the point in *Digital Capitalism* when, citing a *Wall Street Journal* article on the 'staggering' waste in ICT projects within companies, he noted that 'fully 42 per cent of corporate information technology initiatives are abandoned prior to completion' (2000: 15). However, many *are* completed, but are never used. In the computer industry, such waste of resources is called dark fibre. This is the cabling and the fibre optic wires that are in place, but not in use; they are called 'dark' because fibre optics send information by way of light pulses and so, when they are not in use, they are 'dark'. The cooperative part of the capitalist dialectic often takes second place to the competitive part, so it is by no means uncommon for business rivals to ignore the fact that they are both investing colossal amounts in the same technologies in the full knowledge that only one of them will prevail. Writing about the late-1990s dot-com boom, Robert Brenner shows that such profligacy is an indelible feature of capitalism, a feature not erased with the coming of the information society:

> Thanks to the unregulated product and financial markets, everyone was [expanding]. In 2000 no fewer than six US companies were building new, mutually competitive, nation-wide fibre-optic networks. Hundreds more were laying down local lines and several were also competing on sub-oceanic links. All told, 39 million miles of fibre-optic line now criss-cross the US, enough to circle the globe 1566 times. The unavoidable by-product has been a mountainous glut: the utilization rate of telecom networks hovers today at a disastrously low 2.5–3 per cent, that of undersea cable at just 13 per cent. There could hardly be clearer evidence that the market – and especially the market for finance – does not know best. The consequence was an amassing of sunk capital that could not but weigh on the rate of return for the foreseeable future, in the same way as did the railway stock built up during the booms of the 19th century. (2003: 54)

Jacques Ellul's warnings of the 'myth' of technological progress are salient today as never before. And so it is difficult, for all our current technological sophistication, to say without significant qualification that this represents progress for humanity. To be sure, the vast number-crunching capability of computers has unlocked the human genome and much good can come of this. But a large proportion of medical science is market-driven, and, where progress is made for 'modern' diseases such as cancer and heart disease, this is largely because huge profits can be made from treatments. Study into older diseases, such as malaria and tuberculosis, stays relatively under-funded because it is the poor, overwhelmingly, who die from them – and in much bigger numbers than from first-world lifestyle illnesses.

Ellul's writings on the possible 'unintended consequences' of 'systems of technique' are equally relevant when we look critically at a quarter-century of information technology development. We see examples in books about the loneliness of postmodern life by writers such as Robert Putnam, whose *Bowling Alone* (2000) chronicles the collapse of the American form of community, and Richard Sennett's *The Corrosion of Character* (1998) – whose subtitle is *The Personal Consequences of Work in the New Capitalism* – which surveys the global work scene and how neoliberal 'flexibility' has devastated millions of lives. These, and many others like them, may be read as a litany of the unintended consequences of life in the networked society where information has been created as an abstract, instrumentally oriented means of production that is developed, not for the well-being of people within democratic polities, but for a globalized digital capitalism that people must adapt to and synchronize with.

4

A Shrinking Planet

six thousand beans fit into one
Gaston Bachelard, *The Poetics of Space* (1994: 149)

This is the year the world got smaller
Alcatel advertisement (1987)

If there is an indisputable fact concerning the information society, it must be that it has given us a very much smaller world. Thinking in abstract terms, the world today brings people together in virtual proximity to a degree that is unprecedented. Being in the information society is to be within (and be a constitutive part of) a network of networks that span the globe, putting one in the same space and time of information flows as billions of others. The geometric space- and Newtonian time-perspectives that had shaped our modernist world have become transformed utterly in the present post-Fordist postmodernity. In reference to the above line from the communications company Alcatel, we can safely say that in many ways *every* year the world gets smaller.

A smaller world is undoubtedly a greatly accelerated social world too. For example, no longer does it matter so much that you may live, say, in Australia and your mother in the UK. An important aspect of neoliberal globalization has been the dramatic reduction in transportation costs since the 1970s. This means that almost anyone with a job can afford to travel a long way after only a bit of saving. This is reflected in the fact that in 2006 the world's combined airlines carried on average more than 6.3 million passengers every day. This translates as a record 3.3 billion seats on 28.2 million flights during that year,

[handwritten margin note: Castells says.]

an increase of 3.4 per cent and 1.8 per cent respectively on 2005 (Aviation News, 2007). Getting on a plane is becoming just as common as getting on a bus or train, and so family and friends are never more than a few hours away. This is remarkable because, as recently as the 1960s, people came from or went to Australia predominantly by sea, a mammoth, consciousness-shifting journey that could take six weeks. Today, one doesn't even need to bother getting a taxi to the airport to wait around for a flight. You can be in virtual touch through using voice-over Internet protocols (VoIP). Downloadable software from a business such as Skype means you can speak to and see anyone, anywhere, who is similarly connected – immediately and for next to no cost.

Our shrinking world means that, for billions of us, almost the whole world is literally at our fingertips through computer keyboard or mobile phone pad. We are stretched over time and space through networks, and, through everyday use of these networks, the miniaturized time and space of our worlds become part of who and what we are: information nodes that form part of a global communications network where everything seems to be available, and available almost immediately. Our old-fashioned and modernist conceptions of geometric space and clock-based time are fast becoming irrelevant.

In the new economy, businesses, as we have already seen, are transforming themselves, or dying, and new ones are constantly being born. When looking for a new job nowadays, growing numbers of people simply log on to sites such as Jobsearch.co.uk and are able to build an exact profile of the job they want in seconds – and can also see the jobs that are available in the UK and across the world. No longer do they need to sit down with a cup of tea and a pen, poring over column after column of every kind of job before coming to something remotely related to their interests and skills. That job may be applied for through a telephone interview where, with a mobile in your pocket, you can be on a Greek holiday from your home in New Zealand and still be in line for a new job in San

Francisco. Such prospective employers will, if they are willing to conduct a global search for candidates through the Internet, doubtless consider themselves a 'globalized' entity. Moreover, such companies are unconcerned now by the fact that their next hire may come from half a world away. The dramatic shrinking of the planet means that they would view the world as their potential marketplace, and the whole world is similarly the potential source of their raw materials, their human capital as well as their finance capital.

This notional corporation may be headquartered in San Francisco, but its field of operations will cross (or will be prepared to cross) all national boundaries. The goal of 'weightlessness' that we discussed previously in relation to corporations means that the outsourcing of 'cost-effective' processes will be simply automatic, a reflex response for managers in the globalized economy. If this corporation makes computer chips or T-shirts, then having them produced in a *maquiladora* in Mexico, or a Special Economic Zone (SEZ) factory in Shenzen, China, is just a normalized part of business, with the only ones giving it a second thought being those San Francisco workers whose jobs have suddenly evaporated through outsourcing. Outsourcing, indeed, may be seen as a kind metaphor for the shrinking of the world. What this conveys is 'ability' and 'mobility' – the *ability* of capitalism, for all the reasons we have previously discussed, to scour a very much more manageable-sized planet for the optimization of business opportunities, and the use of the new *mobility* of workers and of capital to follow this logic in the search – the never-ending search – for profit.

For many in business, and for many ordinary workers keen to get on in life, this fundamental aspect of the information society is (or seems to be) yet another 'good thing'. The 'tyranny of distance' that not so very long ago kept most of us locked into a localized life with localized opportunities, engendering a localized perspective, has been blown away by the gales of neoliberal change that now regularly sweep the planet. The world is no longer our oyster – whatever that terrible cliché was supposed to mean – but potentially it is now literally ours to possess and to dominate, to range over and manipulate at will. Is this 'progress'? What can possibly be wrong with seeing my mother every day on the computer, and chatting with her via VoIP? What can be wrong with her seeing her grandchildren grow up in real time, and not having to depend on occasional letters and photographs that cannot speak, or laugh, or cry?

In theory, all this is good, maybe. However, to make sound judgements about a shrinking world we need to go beyond the unthinking generalization of our own experience. We need to understand what it means to have the world at the ends of our fingers, and so we need to know *what kinds of theory* underpin the reality of our being what Mark Poster terms 'nomads who daily wander at will . . . without necessarily moving our bodies at all' (1990: 15). To do this we shall look here at two theorists, both influential in important ways, and from both ends of the political/ideological spectrum, who see the contraction of space and the acceleration of time as the key elements of our post-industrial world. The persuasiveness and critical insight of these respective theories are assessed from within the framework of my own arguments on the centrality of neoliberalist globalization and social acceleration through information technologies.

'. . . profoundly democratic and liberating': Frances Cairncross

Frances Cairncross wrote an influential book titled *The Death of Distance*, in 1997, just as we were nearing the cusp of the first Internet boom. The author was also an award-winning journalist for the business weekly *The Economist*, and a senior academic at Oxford University. The CV is not without interest as it shows once more the value in being able to traverse those powerful institutional realms of *media* and *ideas* that make the successful promulgation of a concept so very much easier.

The book was influential in the Dyson-Gilder *milieu* and was read and admired by the powerful change agents of the time. For example, the blurb on the front cover of the book comes from Rupert Murdoch, CEO of News Corp, who lauds it as 'essential reading' for those who wish to understand the future of the information society. The publishing success of the book meant that it was extensively rewritten and reprinted in 2001. The existence of these two editions is fortunate as it allows us to compare and contrast them over a critical period in the development of the information society (1997–2001) and to consider also how Cairncross's list of 'future trends' – that constituted much of the book's importance – was able to stand the test of subsequent events.

In its written style and its focus, *The Death of Distance* is clearly addressed to a business readership. Penned by a business journalist, the title itself connotes 'globalization' from the perspective of corporate capitalism. The extent of Rupert Murdoch's interest, for example, is obvious. The 'death of distance' for media tycoons such as Murdoch signals that through technological innovation (new media technologies) the functional ability to manipulate space (and time) will offer tremendous new business opportunities. For canny business executives and corporate planners, the idea of the world getting 'smaller' does not mean that markets shrink. In fact they see the opposite to be the case. The technological ability to more effectively manipulate and control space and time means that more markets are reachable and new media technologies, such as the Internet and satellite TV, create new markets. Indeed, the vista of a shrinking planet is the book's main attraction, I believe, and the ideas and the salient 'trends' contained within it are somewhat secondary. What really interests business people is the concept of a world that is small enough to *control* and *manipulate* through technology.

As is customary within the business-oriented genre, the book takes as given that technology and technological innovations are positive. Indeed, Cairncross urges the reader to cast aside any fears about the constant change that untrammelled technological systems bring and to surrender willingly to the logic of earth-shrinking communications systems. She writes: 'For many people, this prospective new world is frightening. Change is always unsettling, and we are now seeing the fastest technological change the world has ever known' (1997: 4). Change is described and change is forecast along specific paths that we have since come to recognize. We see this in her 'predictions' of the convergence of the telephone and the PC through a mobile phone, or the coming difficulties over intellectual property (IP) rights. However, what I want to focus on more is Cairncross's occasional *focus on people*, and what the 'death of distance' will do for them, and how it will change them, as opposed to what it will do for globalizing corporations.

In what reads like her mission statement, Cairncross argues strongly that we need to grasp the opportunities afforded by ICT systems, systems organized and guided by the dynamics of market competition, so as to be able to reap the fabulous benefits that await us. She writes:

> at the heart of the communications revolution lies something that will, in the main, benefit humanity: global diffusion of knowledge. Information once available only to the few will be available to the many, instantly and inexpensively. [N]ew ideas will spread faster, leaping borders. Poor countries will have immediate access to information that was once restricted to the industrial world and travelled only slowly, if at all, beyond it. Entire electorates will learn things that once only a few bureaucrats knew . . . In these ways, the communications revolution is profoundly democratic and liberating, levelling the imbalance between large and small, rich and poor. The death of distance, overall, should be welcomed and enjoyed. (1997: 4)

An information society, we can see, is also a knowledge society. In this she echoes the work of Daniel Bell in the 1970s and Peter Drucker in the 1990s; and like them she conflates information with knowledge.

Let us look, first of all, at the 'global diffusion of knowledge' that Cairncross predicts and compare it with recent developments. There is no doubt that there has been a massive global diffusion of *information* – but is that the same as knowledge? Cairncross thinks it is, and that this explosion of knowledge will benefit our reading and writing skills, making for a more literate humanity. The positive effect of the 'global diffusion of knowledge' is outlined in number 28 of her list of coming trends, which is: 'Improved Writing and Reading Skills. Electronic mail will induce young people to express themselves effectively and to admire clear and lively written prose. Dull or muddled communicators will fall by the wayside' (1997: xvi).

Now, the non-equivalence of information and knowledge is something that we have already looked at, when I argued, through the work of Lyotard, that knowledge created under the regime of the ICT revolution has become 'performative' and 'commodified'. How would an increasing glut of information/knowledge improve literacy? Cairncross does admit that a 'deluge of information' might be a problem, but she sees this only from the perspective of business, not the individual, and so prescribes 'filters to sift, process and edit it' (1997: xii). This is a lot of sifting and editing when we consider the 60 billion emails that we send to and from each other every day (Reuters, 2006a). And this is just a fairly small part of the 161 billion gigabytes that was being produced in total by that year. To get this in some perspective, this equates to filling 161 billion iPods with data, or, even more breathtakingly, it amounts to '12 stacks of books that each reach from the Earth to the sun . . . or 3 million times the information in all the books ever written' (Bergstein, 2007). We are drowning in information, the production of which has no objective limits. We are subject to a thickening 'data smog' which, as David Shenk put it, 'simply gets in the way' (Shenk, 1997: 31). The tendency is for the blizzard of information to crowd out quiet moments of reflection and obstruct the spaces for contemplation and learning. It instrumentalizes conversation, transforms literature and reorganizes entertainment. Importantly, it thwarts a natural scepticism, rendering us less sophisticated as consumers and as citizens, and as naturally inquisitive beings (Hassan, 2003).

What 'data smog' also 'gets in the way' of, I argue, is a solid concept of precisely where knowledge comes from. Literacy is a form of knowledge that comes from learning – an essential part of which is achieved through contemplation. We learn to read and write through the time-consuming process of *learning* to read and write – processes that are antithetical to increased speed and acceleration across society. I just gave some theoretical consequences of the torrents of information being generated each day, but there is also growing empirical evidence to support this. For example, businesses themselves are becoming concerned that people are less able to write in 'clear and lively written prose'. In 2004 the *New York Times* published an article on a survey of 120 US corporations, which found that a third of employees write poorly. More alarming for corporate America is the fact that it is forced to spend 'as much as $3.1 billion annually on remedial training'. Expressing a concern on this particular mode of communication, the article cites a professor of English who heads an online business school and who notes, with rather poor sarcasm, that 'E-mail is a party to which English teachers have not been invited.' It goes on to conclude that this poor standard of literacy is bad for productivity and efficiency because 'Millions of inscrutable e-mail messages are clogging corporate computers by setting off requests for clarification, and many of the requests, in turn, are also chaotically written, resulting in whole cycles of confusion' (Dillon, 2004). Tellingly, perhaps, this particular 'trend' was dropped from Cairncross's rewritten 2001 edition. This omission may point to a tacit acceptance that there are not nearly enough sifting and editing processes available to individuals with which to counter the intellectually clouding effect of information production systems. Indeed, it points to the more intuitively recognized fact that we are increasingly asked to deal with more information, across all realms of culture and society – and are coping badly (de Zengotita, 2005).

Cairncross maintains, as we just saw, that such free-market-based information systems are 'profoundly democratic and liberating'. Knowledge once shared only between the elites could now be available to us all – presumably to enable and empower people to act and seek redress through energized democratic processes. One can see the logic in this argument, and there are many observers, from Howard Rheingold's *Virtual Community* and *Smart Mobs* (1993; 2002) to William Mitchell's *City of Bits* (1996), who were early boosters of the idea that the digital domain was potentially the new agora of ancient Athens. Concrete evidence of this argument is difficult to find, however. Not so for the contrary opinion that the information society has a dark political side. For example, in 2007, after being invisible from the global political radar for many years, the country of Burma (or Myanmar) suddenly filled our screens. Led by Buddhist monks, demonstrations against the price of petrol began to spread rapidly and increase in frequency. Armed with mobile phones and Internet access, protesters were able to get vision out through the Internet to dissident Burmese groups in cities such as London and New Delhi. The demonstrators themselves were suddenly opening an essentially closed country and its repressive regime to global scrutiny. Local Burmese bloggers were able to augment the footage with reportage from the demonstrations, commenting on the supposed vacillations of the government who seemingly were caught unawares by being suddenly thrust into the glare of global media – from sources inside the country itself. ICTs had become a kind of Trojan horse for the regime, and initially it did not know how to respond. Recovering its balance, the regime moved quickly to use its near-monopoly of the network and its servers to shut down Internet access completely. The information flow instantly slowed to a trickle, and access to the '.mm Burma' domain name suffix was closed off (Johnson, 2007). The momentum of the protest movement was immediately lost and the government regained the initiative with a wave of arrests throughout the country. This represents a stark example of how what might be termed the *innately anti-democratic* function of the Internet is closer to the truth because governments have the ultimate control over whether or not the people have access to it. When the situation is serious, in other words, it is a relatively easy thing to shut down potentially dangerous 'network communities'.

Indeed, Cairncross herself seems to think that the 'profoundly democratic' effect of ICTs may not, in fact, be so profound after all. We see this shift in the general political dimension of the 'death of distance' in point number 30 of her 'trend spotting' list called 'Global Peace'. The second edition, published in 2001, with 'over 70% new material', decided to keep this particular trend in her list (some, such as 'The Rebalance of Political Power', did not make it into the new edition). However, the rewriting of her 'Global Peace' for the 2001 edition incorporated a subtle and illuminating change of language. Compare the entries and judge for yourself:

> (1997) Global Peace. As countries become even more economically interdependent and as global trade and foreign investment grow, people will communicate more freely and learn more about the ideas and aspirations of human beings in other parts of the globe. The effect will be to increase understanding, foster tolerance and ultimately promote worldwide peace. (xvi)

And:

> (2001) Global Peace. Democracy will continue to spread: people who live in dictatorial regimes will be more aware of their governments' failures. Democracies have always been more reluctant to fight than dictatorships. In addition, countries will grow yet more economically interdependent. People will communicate more freely with human beings in other parts of the globe. As a result, while *wars will still be fought*, the effect *may be* to foster world peace. (xvii; my italics)

Note how the confident tone from the refulgent days of the first Internet boom has turned into weaker hedging of the bets concerning war and peace. Of course the information technology revolution continued over the period between these publications, and global trade and capitalist interdependence has grown massively too. However, as Cairncross's caution reveals, there is little sign of the 'near-frictionless markets' she predicted in the 1990s (1997: xii). Instead, there has been friction aplenty and this shows in a disturbing global political scene. Many countries, and a diversity of social movements within countries, now see globalization as simply the attempted imposition of Anglo-American economic and cultural hegemony, and they try to resist it (see Klein, 2002, for example).

As for people being able to 'communicate more freely' with others in this shrinking world, in one sense this is true enough. Blogs and listservs and email, and the myriad means of expressing oneself to the whole world through YouTube or MySpace, do exist and millions take advantage of these. However, when we consider the political realm, the 'death of distance' as inaugurating new forms of freedom of expression presents a different reality. The case of Burma is instructive and salutary. Moreover, people in, say, China or Iran certainly know of the political aspirations of their fellow global citizens, but if they try to discuss these aspirations 'freely' and in the context of their own country, they quickly come up against the antithesis of such freedom in the shape of repressive state apparatuses that limit online free expression as much as possible, while trying to keep their economy high-tech and ICT-oriented to the maximum degree (Tait, 2007).

What the evidence points to is that, far from freedom being *enabled* by ICTs and the 'death of distance' as Cairncross suggests (and subsequently modifies), political freedom and democratic practice is a never-changing terrain of struggle under capitalism. Freedom to use communications systems does not make a democracy; democracy is about power relations, and the democratic use of social power. Neither can ICTs bring freedom in any deterministic sense. Freedom needs to be fought for, and in a networked, but still class-based and ideologically structured global system, struggle continues in cyberspace as well as on the street. No matter how small the world has become, defeat and victory are part of the ongoing fight for freedom by peoples everywhere. What is certain is that the fostering of 'world peace' will only come through more equality and more democracy – and not through simply being able to communicate on YouTube or MySpace. These can help, but they are easily closed-off vectors for democratic communication – and when they are closed off, then the struggle for democracy suddenly becomes old-fashioned and sometimes painfully slow.

The shrinking of space and the acceleration of time: David Harvey

The social geographer and Marxist theorist David Harvey brought a powerful vision to the issues of time and space in his 1989 book, *The Condition of Postmodernity*. In it he was concerned with theorizing what he called the 'transition from Fordism to flexible accumulation', which for him constituted the political, economic and cultural underpinnings of a much broader shift from a society (or societies) dominated by the ideas of modernity and progress, to become characterized instead by modernity's historical antithesis, postmodernity.

Earlier, we discussed the transition to flexible accumulation and saw how this process restructured the world around the principles of so-called 'free markets', combined with the abrogation by governments of their role in the managing of the economy, and how this enabled 'globalization' through the revolution in information and communication technologies. As Harvey sees it, this process greatly accelerated time–space compression, and has had two principal effects: one in our heads, and the other on the concrete reality of the capitalist world.

Both have been transformed fundamentally. Let us take these in their turn. In the first instance, Harvey argues, the transformation to a globalizing regime of flexible accumulation has changed how we relate to the world and how we make sense of the world. In reference to the term 'time–space compression', Harvey wrote: 'I mean to signal by that term processes that so revolutionize the objective qualities of space and time that we are forced to alter, sometimes in quite radical ways, how we represent the world to ourselves' (1989: 240). This intense process, a process enabled by information technologies and the rise of neoliberalism, disrupted our previous view of the world that was based much more upon the sureties of modernity.

Notwithstanding the ideology of neoliberalism that promoted the information society as a bright and efficient and welcoming new world, the collapse of the 'whole way of life' that had seemed so normal and permanent has had a 'disorienting and disruptive impact' (1989: 284) that shook the very foundations of established practices, established values and established ways of being conscious of the world and our place in it. A similar idea was forwarded by Anthony Giddens with his theory of 'time–space distantiation' that argued that social practices are stretched across time and space, and that remote action and the effects of remote action become more prevalent at the level of the institution down to the level of the individual (Giddens, 1990).

The idea of the world being a single, capitalist marketplace, driven by a single instrumental logic, is something we will take up in more detail shortly. However, cultural theorist Fredric Jameson, like Harvey (Giddens hedges his bets), also saw the processes of time–space compression as invoking a dystopian sense of what computerization and the information society might bring. In his *Postmodernism, or, The Cultural Logic of Late Capitalism*, Jameson writes that our 'faulty representations of some immense communicational and computer network are themselves but a distorted figuration of something deeper, namely, the whole world system of a present-day multinational capitalism' (Jameson, 1991: 37). The seeming overriding dominance of capital, into all areas of society, across the whole planet – and based upon a generalized speed-up of life – threw into salience questions not only of the possible negative effects of global capitalism as a 'whole way of life', but also the validity of the 'truths' that held modernity together as a narrative story.

The status of 'truth' in our postmodernity has been hotly debated since the mid- to late 1970s, the very period (not coincidentally) when the shift to neoliberal globalization began. Jean-François Lyotard argued famously in his 1979 book, *The Postmodern Condition*, that, with the collapse of the metanarratives of modernity, 'truth' or 'reality' was contestable between a proliferation of many different versions that were constructed through what he termed 'language games'. The 'truth' of science and technology as being legitimized through their orientation towards 'efficiency' and performativity, Lyotard argues, is but one version of truth and reality in the postmodern condition. However, Lyotard also saw that science and technology had become indissolubly linked to the project of capitalism, indeed had become *subordinated* to capital, and so ceased to be 'science and technology' in the objective sense, but were linked more to the idea of performativity and efficiency. In a context where science and technology in the service of the economy appear as a 'truth' amidst a sea of proliferating versions of who we are and what we should be, the ideas projected by globalizing capitalism and the high value it places on the science and technology of computers seem all the more assuring. In other words, in the absence of any solid and recognizable truths that act as a unifying anchor for all kinds of people from a myriad of cultural and social traditions (an impossible task), the ideology or 'language game' of capitalism/science and technology becomes powerfully enhanced. We may not like what we hear regarding the information society, but the world is framed in such a highly ideologized way that there appear to be no options, no alternatives, despite the seeming diversity of ways of interpreting the postmodern era that we are living through.

Moreover, the aspect of *where power resides* in this transition from modernity to postmodernity is occluded in many of the disputes on truth (Lyotard's thesis included). However, Terry Eagleton, in his criticism of Lyotard's position and his advocacy of multiple truths, makes the useful point that if one takes this position to its rational and logical end point we find that: 'there can be no difference between truth, authority and rhetorical seductiveness; he who has the smoothest tongue or the raciest story has the power' (cited in Harvey, 1989: 117).

This argument in effect posits a new postmodern consciousness. The cultural, political and economic anchorlessness that emerges through the compression of time and space effectively makes the majority of people more amenable to the 'smooth tongue' of the capitalist and the advocates for a wired world. And this process, this new consciousness, enables the second principal effect of time–space compression – which is the imposition of a capitalist concrete reality across every corner of the globe.

In purely economic terms, the 'death of distance' seemed to be good for capitalism. Indeed, it is official policy in institutions such as the International Telecommunications Union (ITU), the world's oldest international organization that was set up in 1865 to coordinate and standardize communications between countries. Its Secretary General, Yoshio Utsumi, addressed the World Summit on the Information Society (WSIS) in 2005, and declared that:

> Today, information is a source of power and a route to riches. God gave us the power to see and hear. Our parents and teachers taught us to read and write and to use information to make sense of the world around us. Now, the power of information and communication technology is removing the boundaries of time and space, which have long kept us apart. (Utsumi, 2005)

In this mirroring of Frances Cairncross, Utsumi envisions a single world marketplace operating within the same circuits of production, distribution and consumption through the rational functioning of information technologies that are used to bring people and markets together. Capital, raw materials and labour could be integrated through global networks. This offers the opportunity for businesses to access these inputs cheaply, wherever they may be found, and to use them to access markets that were formerly too far away, or to create new markets altogether in the new industries that the information technology revolution was creating. Quite suddenly, from the late 1970s onwards, through the rise of neoliberal ideology in particular, the world seemed to be much more manipulable and controllable from the perspective of business, and it was able, finally, to be ordered on a rational and profitable basis.

The flow of capital as information through spreading and deepening digital networks, and the flow of goods and services through dramatic improvements in distribution and transportation, quickly made business (in potential at least) a planet-wide operation. Moreover, the word 'potential' is connoted with 'freedom' in neoliberal discourse: the freedom to expand, invest, restructure – to do whatever was deemed necessary by business leaders to increase the 'bottom line'. Not only was the global spread of capital now politically possible through the rise of neoliberalism – it was also *technologically possible* through the proliferation and growing effectiveness of ICTs.

This 'potential' or 'freedom' meant that local or national businesses (even quite small ones) could step up a level and restructure themselves as multinational or global companies. For instance, a local shoe company may have manufactured quite profitably at the local level, using local suppliers and local labour for the past 100 years. But from the 1980s onwards, the growing compression of time and space meant that it was increasingly cheaper (and economically more logical) to outsource all of these operations. This local shoe manufacturer was now able to shut down its local production facilities and become a multinational. It could do this by contracting the production to, say, China; by sourcing the procurement of raw materials (leather, plastic, rubber, etc.) to an agent in Hong Kong; by creating distribution links with overseas partners for the exploitation of new markets; and by employing the services of a global shipping agent in Singapore. All this could be financed by turning to a multinational bank that will lend on the basis of a global monetary system that is currently predicated on cheap money and low interest rates. Importantly, all this interactivity is made possible (and profitable) through growing information networks that are geared towards bringing cheaper shoes, not only to the original local market, but also to a globalizing marketplace. We can see the dramatic effects of this logic (of suddenly being able to become a multinational within a shrinking world) when we consider the estimate that the number of multinational corporations rose from 7,000 in 1969 to 37,000 in 1994 (*The Economist*, 1994).

Through neoliberal globalization, time and space were being compressed to enhance business efficiency, and business used the new information technologies to augment this transformation. Nonetheless, there have been difficulties with this process since its inception in the late 1970s, and we have already touched upon some of them. Unemployment in many countries has reached serious levels, especially in the early 1980s and then again in the early 1990s; in the 2000s it has reached historic highs as a global phenomenon; the reduced role of the government in economic management has left many people exposed to economic volatility; and the perceived dwindling of social solidarity with its replacement by an 'acquisitive individualism' has been argued to have produced a less caring society (Sennett, 1998; Putnam, 2000).

However, there are other ways of looking at this transformation. For some, the 'neoliberalization of culture', as Harvey (2005: 47) puts it, appears to be nowhere near as bad as the doomsayers of the 1980s had predicted. Until the 'credit crunch' of 2008, at first glance many of us seemed to be better off – at least in material terms. In the advanced economies of the West, people now regularly, and in their millions, take overseas holidays. Car sales steadily increase, as do purchases of computers and mobile phones and MP3 players, and many other kinds of new media equipment. There are more homeowners than ever before, more jobs in more diverse industries than ever before. More people finish secondary education and go on to take higher degrees than ever before. Clothing and air transport are cheaper than ever before – and, by the approaching end of the first decade of the new century, globalized capitalism appears to have been riding what a Deutsche Bank analyst termed the 'longest ever [economic] recovery' (Deutsche Bank, 2007).

From this it would seem that through its unprecedented 'control' over time and space the neoliberal logic is now able to deliver the kind of world that it has always promised: a world of increasing material wealth, of dense interconnectivity, a life full of gadgets and innovation and growth, with capitalism nestling in every corner of the planet and busily developing, extracting, building, producing, creating and placing us (or increasing numbers of us) on an upward spiral of well-being. However, the fact that time–space compression has been so radical and palpable over the last twenty or so years, under the regime of neoliberalism, suggests something else, something more alarming about the nature of the capitalist drive for unlimited growth and unlimited consumption – we live on a planet of finite resources. The abstract pros and cons that have just been outlined may be (and are) debated ad infinitum. But the environmental limits to our common home are something we all at least intuitively understand and accept. The earth is finite in terms of the space available, and it is finite in terms of its carrying capacity for humans. Harvey considers what he sees as a fundamental contradiction in the neoliberal project as it relates to time–space compression and rapid technological change. As he observes in his book *A Brief History of Neoliberalism*:

The neoliberal theory of technological change relies upon the coercive powers of competition to drive the search for new products, new production methods, and new organizational forms. This drive becomes so deeply embedded in entrepreneurial common sense, however, that it becomes a fetish belief: there is a technological fix for every problem. [This can] produce powerful independent trends of technological change that can become destabilizing, if not counterproductive. (2005: 68–9)

Then he gets to the crux of the matter:

There is an inner contradiction . . . between technological dynamism, instability, dissolution of social solidarities, environmental degradation, deindustrialization, and rapid shifts in space–time relations, speculative bubbles, and the general tendency towards crisis formation within capitalism. (69)

We have noted some of the salient and negative social, cultural and political issues concerning the rise of neoliberalism and the information society in the previous chapters. However, what Harvey called the 'coercive powers of competition' and the technological 'fetish' regarding ICTs has contributed massively to a problem that has been simmering away almost since the beginning of the industrialization process itself, but has worsened markedly over the last twenty-five years – and that is environmental degradation and the depletion of the world's natural resources (Flannery, 2006). We currently live in a global economic system dominated by neoliberal, free-market rule, where technology and the market are posited as the solution to all of our difficulties. But our problems as a global society have never been greater or more pressing than in the realm of our global ecology, and it is here we find the 'inner contradiction' Harvey speaks of. Capitalism is predicated on constant spatial expansion and constant material consumption. This intrinsic process has been turbocharged by neoliberalism and ICTs. Since the end of the Cold War the so-called socialist and communist societies of China and Russia, as well as the state-dominated society of India – major economies with huge populations – have all enthusiastically joined the circuits of the neoliberal free market, in practice if not in theory. This has led to the *neoliberal model* of growth, with expansion and consumption becoming general, and conceived as the natural way forward for the whole of humanity. Under this model, the six billion (and counting) inhabitants of the earth are encouraged to believe that they can *all* achieve, and should strive for, and view as their right, the growing levels of consumption that are taken as standard in the advanced Western countries.

However, seen from the critical perspective of political economy that Harvey articulates in his space–time compression thesis, it becomes clear that the planet cannot sustain such a drain on its natural resources. The neoliberal model is a danger to the ecosystem, and it is an issue which people are waking up to with some difficulty, notwithstanding the salience of global warming in the mainstream media (Monbiot, 2006). It seems that in the context of the shrinking of space, we as individuals and as collectivities have a cognitive problem with the nature of the environmental threat. Even the linking of the information society with ecological crisis is a rare intellectual move. This may have something to do with the potential enormity of the predicament that has come to us from the hitherto obscure realms of climatology. As John Lanchester writes on the issue of global warming: 'Part of the problem is one of scale. Global warming is a subject so much more important than almost anything else that it is difficult to frame or discuss' (2007: 24).

It follows that current Western levels of consumption and production will be as nothing compared with a future of growing demands and aspirations of the 2 billion proto-consumers of China and India. These societies are already becoming heavily networked and people from Shenzen and Beijing to Bangalore and Mumbai take the Western standard of living in the form of a car, a house full of gadgets, and a well-paid job in a free-market economy, as an entitlement, something that belongs to them as much as it does to the citizens of New York or London or Berlin. And, indeed, who can say that a first-world lifestyle can be 'ours' but not 'theirs'?

Take the example of China. Previously overwhelmingly poor and dominated by the agricultural sector, this country of 1.3 billion people is now experiencing a massive transfer of population from the countryside to the cities in search of work and wealth. It is a movement of humanity the likes of which is historically unprecedented, and is driven principally by the logic that underpins time–space compression. Its erstwhile 'closed' economy is becoming fully integrated into the world economy, and hundreds of millions of Chinese are now more or less easily able to connect to a global network of economic-information flows that would have been not only politically impossible a generation ago, but technologically impossible too.

The dynamics of neoliberalism and the ICT revolution in China are contributing to an immense economic-environmental contradiction. On the one hand, these processes act as magnets that draw people to the large urbanizing coastal areas that supply many of the manufactured goods that flood the Western economies – from textiles and toys to cars and computers. Large-scale production has meant that China is now the largest single supplier of high-tech goods to the USA (Branstetter and Lardy, 2006: 36). On the other hand, the booming Chinese economy acts as a vast 'sink' for the world's extractable resources. The demands for non-renewable resources such as coal, oil, gas, uranium and other minerals are so large that commentators regularly ascribe this as the principal reason for the ongoing world economic boom. Indeed, it has been estimated that in 2007 a new coal-fired power plant was being opened *every week* (Shukman, 2006). The domestic Chinese economy itself, of course, is a part of this boom, and, since 1984 when Deng Xiaoping told the Chinese people that 'to get rich is glorious', the focus for millions of citizens in this ostensibly communist country has been to own and to consume on a par with people in the advanced Western countries. Accordingly, domestic demand for items like automobiles is now enormous. With no tax levied on fuel, and more and more people attaining the relative affluence needed to buy them, China is on a car-buying binge. In 1994 there were 1 million private cars in the country. By 2004 this had ballooned to 16 million – and, by 2020, China is set to overtake the USA in private car ownership, with a projected 170 million cars on the roads at that time, requiring yearly some 100 million tonnes of oil to power them (China Development Brief, 2006).

Car consumption is only one aspect of the process, and within the overall picture China is only one country, albeit a highly illustrative one. Breakneck development in countries such as these, and growth-at-any-price policies in all parts of the world, has ensured that the pressure on the planetary ecosystem is not sustainable. In parentheses it is interesting (and alarming) to note that, as Harvey reminds us, 'The era of neoliberalization also happens to be the era of the fastest mass extinction of species in the Earth's recent history' (2005: 173). But to the example of cars can be added the growth in demand for buses, trains, aircraft and air conditioners, and the development of the widespread infrastructure that the mass movement of people on a global scale demands.

Many cities are now densely crowded and choking in clouds of particulate matter that spew from cars and smokestack industries; major rivers are either fouled by industrial waste, or they are diverted into massive dam-building projects to provide energy for yet more development. Cities across the world, both old and new ones, now sprawl with unprecedented rapidity, drawing more energy from the finite supply that the earth has.

The growth of industry and urbanization is most marked in the developing regions of Asia, Latin America and Africa – the 'South' in the global divide of the neoliberal development process. The urban sociologist Mike Davis has considered the rise of 'megacities' as a particularly neoliberal phenomenon whereby a rapidly globalizing economy has concentrated immense agglomerations of people, ramshackle infrastructure, polluting industries and human misery into spaces with numbers approaching 20 million souls (2006). All in all, the South contains a billion people who live not in a Western affluence, but in slums. Davis's book *Planet of Slums* shows that their existence is directly due to the model of capitalism that has given us globalization and the information society. He writes that 'In 1950 there were 86 cities in the world with a population of more than one million . . . by 2015 there will be at least 550' (11). Moreover, and to put the era of neoliberalism into frightening context, Davis notes that 'neoliberal capitalism since 1970 has multiplied Dickens's notorious slum of Tom-all-Alone's in *Bleak House* by exponential powers. Residents of slums, while only 6% of the city population of the developed countries, constitute a staggering 78.2% of urbanites in the least-developed countries'; and 'China . . . added more city-dwellers in the 1980s than did all of Europe (including Russia) in the entire 19th century!' (11). The information society, at the most fundamental level, is a society – as these figures suggest – where more people than ever before in history have lives of precarious instability, between absolute poverty and the sliver of luminescence on the horizon that indicates some kind of hope.

In what way do these 1 billion slum-dwellers constitute a direct effect of Harvey's time–space compression and the information society? First, many of them would formerly have been rural dwellers, farmers or workers and traders in villages that dotted the countryside in China, or Mexico, or Nigeria, or the Philippines. In the globalizing process, Castells writes of the 'complexity of the interaction between technology, society, and space' (1996: 377). And it is through this increasingly complex interaction that globalizing capital *creates* the megacities, as the shift to industrialization in once-rural economies forces the transfer of millions of people to places where work may be found in the *now easily exploitable* pools of cheap labour in the South that underpin the relative wealth of the North. The process is truly global. As Deane Neubauer puts it:

> Throughout the world, the rural poor flock to cities as the only practical solution to endemic rural poverty. National governments support intra-country migration for the urban economic development it supports. Mexico City, Sao Paulo, Taipei, Seoul, and Yokohama are older industrial and commercial cities that have exploded into global production centers built largely on migratory growth. Other cities – Lagos, Cairo, Mumbai (Bombay), Lima, Buenos Aires, Bangkok, Shanghai, Shenzhen-Pearl River Delta, Manila, and Jakarta – owe even more to their magnetic pull of labor from the agricultural sector into contemporary globalized industries in transportation, communication, manufacture, finance, and the like. (2004: 22)

Second, the fact that 1 billion slum-dwellers would have relatively little access to networked computers, and would not enjoy the 'connected' life of the denizens of New York or Tokyo, does not mean that they are not *directly connected* to the *logic* of the information society. They are a *consequence of its logic*, in that the time–space compression the information society creates assigns megacities to function as 'nodes' of production and exploitation in a global economy. They constitute what Marx identified in the nineteenth century as the 'reserve army of labour'. In Marx's time this 'reserve army' was locally or regionally based. But by the end of the twentieth century, it had, according to the economist Andrew Glyn, 'gone global' (Glyn, 2006). Moreover, the importance of global communication systems, even in the slum megacities themselves, is shown in the burgeoning rise of mobile phone ownership (or rental), even amongst the poorest, as well as access to the Internet, because both are seen as a means with which to escape the poverty trap (Slater and Kwami, 2005). We can perhaps see that the former 'first-world/third-world' divides, or the 'North–South' geographic appellation that it was sometimes given, no longer accurately depict what happens under globalization. These were supposedly distinct worlds where the first world (the North) exploited and colonized the third world (the South). The information society and the particular form of globalization it has engendered have meant that the 'death of distance' has brought the whole world into a closeness where each is affected both positively and negatively by the other. The balance of this effect, as my discussion of Cairncross and Harvey has indicated, seems to be in the negative.

These thinkers give us two very different causes and effects of the shrinking of the planet. Cairncross accentuates the positive in ways that are laudable and reveal a genuine hope and belief that the world may become a better, more literate and more peaceful place through the possibilities that the information society brings. Harvey, for his part, relies upon a more sceptical political-economy tradition that sees capitalism and its 'forces of production' such as computerization and the Internet as being inherently undemocratic, having the interests of production, profit and 'efficiency' above those of ordinary people. Crucially, the latter perspective looks at the role of ideology, the role of dominant ideas that rightly or wrongly help to determine and shape the paths that economy and society take. We have already seen in the previous chapter how the ideas of neoliberalism fail to match up against the empirical reality of some of its effects. The environmental crisis is another such empirical reality, one which amounts to a terrible dilemma for humanity: how can we advocate the kind of limitless material world the information society encourages and seems to make possible, against the limits of what our planet can physically sustain?

This rather depressing thought leads us to a consideration of all that 'material stuff' that fills our contemporary lives. We produce and consume commodities, and societies have done so on an increasing scale since the beginning of the Industrial Revolution. But, thanks to the processes of globalization and the information society, we have never produced and consumed to such a gigantic extent. To get some idea of how this process works and what it means for our world we need to think some more about the nature of the commodity and our relationship with it.

5

Commodification and Culture in the Information Society

A commodity appears at first sight an extremely obvious, trivial thing. But its analysis brings out that it is a very strange thing.

Marx, *Capital* (1982: 163)

To commodify or not to commodify?

The capacity for information technologies to act as a double-edged sword in terms of their positive or negative effects upon economy, culture and society has been a primary narrative of this book – the dreams and the nightmares that the information age has engendered. We have touched briefly upon the subject in the works of Dan Schiller (2000; 2007) and Kevin Robins and Frank Webster (1988; 1999) who see the logic of information as bringing the logic of the commodity into every part of life. We have also discussed those theorists and boosters such as Esther Dyson (1998) and Nicholas Negroponte (1995) who see commodification, implicitly, as unproblematic because they also see the insertion of the market in more and more realms of life as a positive thing, producing, in the main, positive outcomes for people.

In this chapter we will look in some more detail at the processes of *commodification* in the information society. The purpose is to encourage a more reflective look at commodification – what it is and what it does – so as to allow the consideration of these questions in the context provided by a political-economy analysis of information technologies.

What is commodification?

There is of course a vast literature on this subject, the core of which need not detain us here. It has an intellectual history that goes back to the dawn of the Industrial Revolution and was theorized most influentially by Marx in volume 1 of *Capital*. To gain what may be a more profound insight into the nature of capitalism (and, by extension, the information society), Marx's work would be the indispensable starting point. However, it will suffice here to offer a brief definition of the process of commodification and then illustrate how it operates in the information society by way of some contemporary examples.

All human societies, from the earliest civilizations, produced their own material conditions of existence. We saw how, during the Enlightenment, philosophers of 'political economy' saw this as emerging in 'stages' of progression: from hunter-gatherer societies, through to feudal agriculture and on to capitalist industrialism. It is during the latter phase that the commodity became the central material condition of modern society. For Marx, and for generations of Marxist-inspired theorists, the commodity represented not an abstract thing, but the physical embodiment of a *social relation*. The insertion of a particular logic of production and consumption into the lives of people was constituted around the 'cash nexus' – or the marketization of increasing realms of social interaction. This was a process that grew in tandem with the spread of capitalism itself.

It would of course be absurd and futile to argue that the commodity is inherently negative, as many orthodox Marxists might argue. Without commodification there would have been no industrialization, or modernity, or anything in the way of the life (good and bad) that we take so much for granted. The real issue, as it so often is, is the *extent* of the process and whether it may have run too far and into social realms that make it destructive of those realms.

A useful way to think about commodification and the growth of the capitalist way of life is to see it also as a process of *colonization*. An example might be the simple act of social communication. Informal networks of communication, such as people speaking face-to-face, is colonized or commodified when those same people begin to text or email each other. Why? The process becomes commodified because they *pay* for it through a third party. It is a logic that is both powerful and flexible. For example, instead of colonizing realms already in existence (such as where people simply talk to each other) commodification can also create entirely new social realms; new markets for products and services to which people (consumers) gravitate towards to 'claim' a part of it for themselves, through paying for it. In both senses the effect is to connect the individual with an instrumental logic that has buying and selling as its core rationale. A further effect is the tendency towards the marginalization of other forms of social interaction – we email instead of talk, for example; or we browse the Internet alone where we used to be with people. Like the intrinsic limits to our natural environment that we discussed in the previous chapter, it would seem logical to argue that there are limits to the extent to which our culture may be commodified before it mutates into something qualitatively different; into what might be called a 'culture of commodification'. This would constitute a transformation of what it is to be human in the world, and would take our sense of self and of the social into uncharted waters.

In what follows, I want to develop the premise that neoliberal globalization and the revolution in information and communication technologies has indeed created a digitally enabled 'culture of commodification'. Stemming from this premise, the question of what this would indicate about the nature of the information society is posed. The chapter will conclude with a look at some counter-trends to the commodification dynamic within the context of the information society itself, and consider whether these suggest genuine alternatives to the 'culture of commodification'.

The commodification of culture

The premise begins with the claim that today we live in a world that is commercialized and commodified to an extent that would have been greeted with horror by many only a generation ago. Work I have done elsewhere gives a theoretical underpinning for this process (Hassan, 2003). However, here I think that concrete illustrative examples can go a long way in the pursuit of understanding how commodification and the market have seeped into almost every pore of the cultural and social body.

The growing commodification of culture and society began to dawn on me (and doubtless many others) when, around the late 1970s, my favourite football team, Glasgow Celtic, began to put the name of a sponsor on their shirts. For the club this was an instrumental business decision, brought on by the increasing pressures to secure non-traditional revenue streams in the new market environment. For many of the supporters, however, the appearance of an unerringly tasteless brand logo across the chests of their idols was a desecration of the traditions and the historic culture of the game. In football, the shirt, with its specific colours, is a symbol of more than the formal identification of the team, and is more important than any player who happens to wear it. It represented, in many instances, the personal biography of the supporter, a symbol of growing up and watching 'their' team, of collecting pictures of the stars in scrap books or in swap cards. More generally, the shirt could be said to represent the cultural memory of many thousands of supporters, with its colours and design; especially its colours, these being essentially unchanged for decades or even generations. Translate this attachment to the 100 or so professional clubs in the UK and you have a large and potent tradition of cultural identification with myriad meanings, memories and understandings for millions of people. However, the introduction of the name of a beer company or car manufacturer, or whatever, scrawled across the chest of the shirt was greeted with dismay by many. Just how, exactly, was the logo of a local double-glazing firm or broadband service provider supposed to reflect the values and the culture of the club that were intrinsic to the shirt? Well, in fact it didn't; and it wasn't intended to. The shirt became an item of exchange, a 'thing' wherein the meanings and identifications of generations of supporters disappeared into the commodity form of the shirt-symbol.

The depressing story of shirt sponsorship says something, I think, about the power of the commodity form in our postmodern culture. Until the arrival of sponsorship in that pivotal decade of the 1970s, very few people (apart from the footballers themselves) actually wore the shirt. It was primarily an abstract symbol, not a material artefact. Kids sometimes bought those few that could be ordered in the fans' magazines, so as to emulate their heroes while playing on the street corners or school fields. There was no 'market' in shirt sales, and no one had yet found the need to create one. Today, however, at any professional game in the UK, many thousands will be wearing the replica 'branded' shirts: father and son, mother and daughter. They are worn not only at games, but have become acceptable garb at almost any other occasion, and have become a powerful cultural statement in themselves. To capitalize on this propensity, and to encourage it enormously, the marketing division of clubs (or more likely outsourced design companies) will now remodel these very expensive shirts every year or so with hardly any devotion to the traditional colour system. Different colours (any colour) can be used, with the clubs and the designers confident that the supporters will buy them (Bhat, 2007). In a notorious episode, the chairman of Newcastle United, an English club with a long history of loyal and fanatical support, was caught on tape by an undercover reporter bragging about the gullibility of the club's supporters who continue to buy shirts year after year (Conn, 2006). This exposé did nothing to dent shirt sales in Newcastle.

So central have shirt sales become, indeed, they can even drive the choice of players who will be in the team, something that would have been unimaginable prior to the commodification of football culture. For example, the transfer, in 2003, of the Manchester United player David Beckham to Real Madrid in Spain was fundamentally a business arrangement where the consideration of potential shirt sales with Beckham's name on the back was a major factor. Indeed, the sports marketing firm Apex predicted that the £25 million transfer fee paid for Beckham would be recouped through shirt sales alone during the term of his four-year contract (Hale, 2003).

Of course the processes of the commodification of culture and society go well beyond this personal (though illustrative) obsession. We see it evidenced, for example, in the waves of privatization of industries by neoliberal governments. Across the world since the 1980s, 'public utilities' such as electricity, water, gas, railways, airlines, steel-making and so on have been sold to multinational corporations. In the post-war culture of the leading Fordist economies it was accepted as natural that there were sectors of the economy where the government had a legitimate role. No longer. Government assets are now seen *ipso facto* as 'inefficient' and as loss-making black holes for public money that require the application of 'market mechanisms' – no matter what the social consequences (see Stiglitz (2002) for an analysis of the consequences of neoliberal privatization).

The writ of the market and of the commodity runs deeply into the education system too. Institutions such as universities and schools have traditionally been seen as part of the public sphere, where rational argument and critique were core elements of what a 'liberal education' could offer the individual and society more generally (Noble, 1999). Indeed, the broad intellectual culture of Western democracies could be argued to have emerged from the university system, as its best graduates, trained in the critical tradition, went on into the professions to enrich the culture through the application of their knowledge of philosophy, history, politics, literature and so on. Notions of the market or competition within and between universities were largely alien to those in the system and within government too. Today, however, the university functions in a global education marketplace, and must consider itself first and foremost a business. And, as with all global businesses, the university could not be 'competitive' or 'efficient', in either its business, administrative or pedagogical roles, without the requisite high levels of digital automation and computer skills, for students and teachers alike. Here we see the effect of the neoliberal globalization/ICT revolution nexus again.

What this has meant, as Slaughter and Leslie have argued, is a form of 'academic capitalism' where universities now have to compete and 'engage in market and market like behavior' in order to attract resources (1997: 114). Acting as businesses, the rationale for teaching and learning becomes skewed, because for both students and teachers: 'competition . . . becomes the basis for the logic of discovery' (Delanty, 2001: 108). The 'production of knowledge' through market competition and ubiquitous ICTs thus becomes inevitably oriented towards technical-rational forms, reflected in the burgeoning of vocational courses at universities. This has usually been at the expense of the more critically oriented liberal arts subjects that are seen as 'not relevant' to today's world because such knowledge is unable to connect with the 'needs of industry' (Hassan, 2003). The forms of culture in society that emerged from the university system – through a more vibrant blend of technical-rational and critical pedagogy – are now being commodified and/or marginalized by an education system that is increasingly tied to the needs of industry and the 'production' of the kinds of graduates who not only see this new world as normal and/or inevitable, but go on to replicate and reinforce this commodified cultural world view when they enter the workplace and pursue their careers.

The arrival of the information society, then, if we accept the theorization set out above, represents far more than the mere expansion of capitalism and the growing pervasiveness of computers in our lives. If we see our world as spatially finite (which it is) and if we accept that capitalism is inherently expansionistic (which would be difficult to deny), then the commodification impulse must accompany it into every space that it colonizes or creates. For example, in what has been a dual movement since the 1970s, the orbit of commodification has expanded *outwards* to those physical territories (such as Russia, India and China) that had been relatively untouched, and *inwards* into more subjective realms of culture more generally. Many politicians, economists and information society opinion formers view this as fairly unproblematic; and many other 'ordinary people' accept this 'reality' in an unreflective manner, or as evidence of 'progress'. Some others, however, see this as an ambiguous disaster. The philosopher Slavoj Žižek, for example, notes that today 'the logic of [commodification] follows its own path, its own mad dance, irrespective of the real needs of people . . . [and] pushes into every pore of our social lives, into the most intimate of spheres, and installs an ever present dynamic' (2001).

Cultures of commodification in the information society

It has been my contention that the combined effects of neoliberal globalization and the ICT revolution have massively augmented the commodification process. I have also tried to show that this has created new forms of culture, what might be termed 'cultures of commodification'. So what might these look like? Let us look at computer game culture. We saw in chapter 1 that this is a massive area in terms of the numbers who participate, and highly lucrative for the corporations who supply the hardware and software. It was noted too that it could be a very addictive head space wherein the boundaries between actual and virtual reality can become fatally blurred. Notwithstanding these markers of game culture as an industry and as a realm that can be less than utopian, the image of game

culture as cool, subversive, and somehow resistant to commodification is still dominant in mainstream media and in
strands of academic discourse. For example, theorist Sue
Morris argues that gaming 'communities' generate a:

> sense of self-governance [that] combined with the creative
> input of players, has led to a high level of involvement and
> investment by players in an online community that is vocal,
> influential, highly social and considers itself self-regulating
> and, to a certain degree, self-determining. (2004: 118)

A self-regulating culture it may be, but regulated around what
kind of logic? The majority of its practitioners are attracted to it
because it has many connotations with the lifestyle made
famous in Douglas Copeland's anti-Baby Boomer tract
Generation X: Tales for an Accelerated Culture (1991). Copeland
inspires many in this cohort through the manifesto-like chapters in his book. Titles such as 'I Am Not a Target Market', or
'Purchased Experiences Don't Count', purportedly define the
anti-business Generation X zeitgeist. Gaming is widely seen as
a hip, non-mainstream activity where individuals can express
themselves in true Generation X fashion and compete with
each other using cutting-edge computer applications and
highly trained hand–eye coordination skills, in a context where
a Marinetti-like glorification of speed pervades. Not for them,
so the rhetoric goes, the slavery of conformity or complicity
with the consumerism and commodification that had blighted
the world view of the baby boomers.

Notwithstanding its youth and its radical connotations –
mixed-up, it should be added, with the fascination with some
of the more lawless aspects of hacker culture – the real name
of game culture is business. And it is an immense business.
Accountancy firm PricewaterhouseCoopers predicts that the
industry (game consoles and software sales) will grow from
$21.2 billion in 2003 to $35.8 billion in 2007. It is claimed that
such growth would make gaming a bigger industry than
Hollywood movies (PWC, 2005). The market, moreover, has

enormous room for further expansion as the network society itself spreads and deepens. For example, the number of users in China went from zero in 2000 to 14 million in 2005; and industry leaders Microsoft, Nintendo and Sony are deliberately seeking to expand the market out from its young male demographic (Joseph, 2005). And, as in any capitalist industry, the tendency towards exploitation and commodification emerges. It is an age-old pattern and follows an inexorable economic logic that is clearly expressed in the gaming industry. The logic is: as hardware and software become more complex and powerful, the producers incur increasing development costs. The innovators of many of the popular games, however, are from small independent software producers comprising fewer than ten people working on game development. These companies have two choices: devote their entire workforce to a single project; or seek buyers for the business and be subsumed into a multinational. The first option comprises a considerable risk in a fickle industry, and the second is one that tends to iron out any kinks of creativity and originality in game design, and goes with what will predictably sell in the marketplace (Joseph, 2005).

Users are not immune to the effects of the dictates of business either. The laws of globalizing capital flow through the networks of online game users along with the bits and bytes of information that drive the games themselves. Online gaming is the burgeoning centre of the games industry. Users are linked through the Internet and compete with each other. They play games where killing virtual opponents, finding secret keys, more powerful weapons and so on make up much of the challenge. More powerful games allow players from anywhere around the world to join forces against others in these virtual global battles. Players coming from 'virtually' any point on the face of the earth can band together to form alliances in cyberspace. However, we live in a world of uneven development and the structure of these virtual armies reflects and sustains the concrete reality of global class stratification and exploitation.

Tony Thompson, writing in the London *Observer* in 2005, describes an entrenched development in game culture whereby wealthy users in developed countries can pay users in less developed countries to do much of the routine work for their characters (avatars). Thompson writes that:

> The most valuable commodity in [online games] is time, and this has spawned the rise of the virtual sweatshops. Every player starts with little 'virtual money' and few skills. Moving up to the next level involves carrying out dull, repetitive tasks such as killing thousands of virtual monsters. But thanks to companies such as Gamersloot.net, players now have an alternative. They simply pay someone else to do the dull work, and buy a ready-made character at a more advanced level. (2005: website)

And so gamers in the USA or the UK, for example, can pay gamers in Romania (the example in the article) the equivalent of 50 cents an hour to perform the tedious work of killing virtual monsters for up to ten hours a day. The term for this exploitation is 'gold farming' where wealthy users can employ 'a whole factory of gamers to play through games to acquire in-game goods' (Armstrong, 2007).

Freed from the tedium of slaying enemies all the time, wealthy gamers can involve themselves in the higher levels of the game, where the virtual rewards are greater. The very businesslike nature of online gaming culture is further revealed when we learn that avatars can be bought and sold on eBay for four-figure sums (Winokur, 2003). As we saw in chapter 1, with the case of the Chinese gamer who was convicted of killing a person who allegedly stole his sword-avatar, the real-world stresses that accompany this virtual space have other – predictably human – effects. The feeling of social solidarity in the sense that Morris describes is, of course, as absent from the virtual game world as it is from the actual world of bosses and workers in the information society. Virtual sweatshops simply illustrate the commodity production logic transferred to virtual space.

Game culture is useful to reflect upon because it is seen by many as *something different* from the instrumental reality of day-to-day jobs in the network society, and as a more positive and assertive form of non-capitalist culture. However, what I have tried to show is that it is a culture that is stamped with the same logic as any other realm within the information society. Indeed, Generation X and the cohorts beyond are consumers who enthusiastically buy into this logic (Heath and Potter, 2004). The virtual world of gaming, for its part, is a component of the parallel world of business that impinges on our lives. Through its growing preponderance, it seals off access to other worlds and other ways of thinking about our own lives. The screen becomes the closed world of the quick-thinking gamer, and, as a mode of cultural production, this virtual culture is as commodified and reliant on big business as football now is.

Decommodification

In a fast-paced world it is impossible to 'see in slow motion' (Gleick, 2000: 57–65). An effect of this is that many people simply do not have the time to think reflectively about the information society and tend to just get on with life as best they can. Others do think about it critically, but see it (sensibly) as an irreversible reality. They try to work within its logic but at the same time endeavour to exert some sort of influence on the directions of the information society and the forms that it takes. Much of the most salient activity here takes place precisely around issues of commodification and the perception that information technologies have taken the process too far.

We see this tendency in the wide and varied movements whose passion and work goes to the very core of the ownership of the code (the operating systems of computers) that so profoundly shape our digital lives. For these individuals and groups, the rise and domination of software manufacturers such as Microsoft were seen as evidence of a constriction of the creative talents of people who could do more interesting things with code. Corporations such as Microsoft, it was alleged, grew fat and complacent through their zealous guarding of the proprietary rights of the 'source code' that was at the heart of their fantastically successful Windows-based products. If this code was free for users to experiment with and distribute to others, it was argued, then the collective talents of thousands of amateur and professional programmers could take software to places that a few in-house Microsoft coders could never do on their own. Some people realized early on that Microsoft was not going to legally open its source code to anyone, and so they decided that they would create their own.

A seminal figure in the movement to make programming code open and free is the programmer and activist Richard Stallman. In 1983 he launched the GNU movement, and, two years later, the Free Software Foundation. The object of these was, as Stallman put it, to develop a 'sufficient body of free software so that I will be able to get along without any software that is not free' (Stallman, 1985). In other words, it was specifically designed to allow users to be released from the compulsion to use Windows- or Mac-based products. This movement developed into what has been termed the 'copyleft' system that was designed to directly counter the perceived 'copyright' restrictions of proprietary software. This is fundamentally a process of decommodification. How does copyleft work? It is, in effect, a 'free software licence' where a programmer is able to access and modify 'open-source' software, provided that the modifications made to that program are themselves freely available to others. The philosophy is that if many thousands of programmers are working on the same open-source software and are constantly modifying and improving it, ironing out bugs and developing new functionalities, then the product will be much more useful than the proprietary software that can only be legally modified by a select group.

One of the most successful examples of this movement is the Linux operating system. Developed in the early 1990s by

Linus Torvalds, Linux began as an open-source system he wrote as a student at the University of Helsinki. The program became what is known as the 'Linux kernel'. This 'kernel' has grown and spread to become a powerful and respected operating system that is used in all kinds of machines – from desktops to supercomputers – and for all kinds of applications, all for free (Lyons, 2005). The beauty is that the operating system is being continually refined and improved by professionals (and amateurs) in their own time, programmers who may themselves work for IBM, or Microsoft, or Hewlett Packard. To the chagrin of the titans of proprietary software, open sources such as Linux are now leaching money away from the market for operating systems. One can even put a dollar price on the extent of this decommodification. The market research firm IDC reckoned the market share of Linux, including servers, PCs and packaged software, was expected to register a 26 per cent compound annual growth rate to reach $35.7 billion in 2008 (Abramson, 2005). Linux even has its own rivals in the movement against proprietary software, and operating systems such as Ubuntu (meaning 'humanity toward others') have been developed on the GNU/Linux kernel primarily as software for desktops. In 2007, Dell Computers began to sell all their desktops and laptops with Ubuntu preloaded (Dell, 2007).

This kind of resistance to the commodification of ideas is conducted in the world of technology, within the relatively closed world of programmers and systems analysts who strive for more freedom in how people develop and use computers. However, in culture and in civil society more broadly, there are battles being waged against ICT-driven commodification and its relationship to law. Lawrence Lessig has been an influential figure here. A Stanford University academic and lawyer, Lessig set up, in 2000, the Center for the Internet and Society (CIS) to coordinate and act as a hub for the differing projects he is involved in, many of which intersect with the work of the open-source movement. The Center's website describes its works as providing 'law students and the general public with educational resources and analyses of policy issues arising at the intersection of law, technology and the public interest' (CIS, 2007). More detail of the philosophy that guides the Center is set out in his books. For example, in *Code and Other Laws of Cyberspace* (2000), Lessig pointed out that the spread of proprietary code was in essence the spread of law – hence his slogan: 'code is law'. What this means, as Lessig sees it, is that as privatized and commodified cyberspace colonizes ever more of culture and society, then so do the laws which protect the code, and these laws now shape the nature of cyberspace to reflect the imperatives of multinational corporations. So-called 'fair use' laws that governed 'old media' copyright, where limited use of copyrighted materials could take place without permission, were diminished by the code proprietor's super-strict interpretation of their rights under copyright laws. He acted as lawyer in several high-profile cases to argue for the extension of fair use to cyberspace, such as A&M Records v. Napster (2000), where he acted as 'defendants' expert' for the file-sharing website.

In his *The Future of Ideas* (2002) Lessig develops this idea further. He argues that the duration of copyright protection, and its distribution and enforcement throughout the expanding domain of cyberspace, will blunt creativity and innovation in not only the arts, but across culture and society as well. The Internet will become so choked by the enforced 'rights' of those who produce and distribute material, that an innovation-protected 'commons' must be developed as a counterbalance so that ideas can flow as freely as possible. His 2004 book, *Free Culture*, was accessible on the Internet without charge and its fundamental argument, following on from his previous books, can be detected in its subtitle: *How Big Media Uses Technology and the Law to Lock Down Culture and Control Creativity*. In it he reissues his warning of the commodification of culture when he states that: 'there has never been a time in history when more of our "culture" was as "owned" as it is now. And yet there has never been a time when the concentration of power to control the uses of culture has been as unquestioningly accepted as it is now' (2004: 28). With these two sentences, Lessig goes to the heart of the effects of the commodification process to show that: (1) the process itself knows no spatial or cultural bounds; and (2) the more deeply and widely it spreads, the more 'natural' it appears.

Lessig is no anti-technology Luddite. He uses information technologies to exert their maximum potential in terms of both making his work public and enjoining others to become involved in debate and activism. This enables him to create and share knowledge that would promote the cause of 'free culture', open-source software, and the creative commons more generally. Lessig's website, for example, makes use of wiki technologies to do this. Wikis are software applications, first developed by Ward Cunningham in the mid-1990s, with the objective to make easy the editing and linking of web-sites. Importantly, wikis allow users to simply develop collaborative websites where *everyone* can contribute in something approaching real-time.

This little preamble brings us to the mother of all wikis, the online dictionary Wikipedia – which is a prominent example of the existence of a vast community of computer users who do not take commodification for granted or as a 'natural' condition. Indeed they work actively to create another reality.

Wikipedia is a not-for-profit online encyclopaedia that was created in the USA by Jimmy Wales in 2001. By allowing anyone to write up an encyclopaedia definition on any subject, whether they are formally qualified to do so or not, Wikipedia has proven to be a radical development on the Internet, and something directly counterposed to the Internet's impulse to spread and commodify across culture and society. It was an idea that can be traced back to Richard Stallman's essay 'The Free Universal Encyclopedia and Learning Resource' (Stallman, 1999). On the surface, this project to develop a free online encyclopaedia seemed to be somewhat obscure.

However, it immediately caught the imagination of millions of people across the world and mirror sites in many other languages quickly appeared. Marshall Poe compares Wikipedia to a beehive and wrote, slightly tongue-in-cheek, in the *Atlantic Monthly* that:

> A quarter century ago it was inconceivable that a legion of unpaid, unorganized amateurs scattered about the globe could create anything of value, let alone what may one day be the most comprehensive repository of knowledge in human history. Back then we knew that people do not work for free; or if they do work for free, they do a poor job; and if they work for free in large numbers, the result is a muddle. (2006: website)

Today, however, Wikipedia is consistently one of the most visited sites on the Internet – and, as any student or teacher now knows, people do take it seriously, both as creators and consumers of the knowledge it offers. There are relatively few muddles, and Wikipedia's moderators can quickly rectify any 'vandalism'. In contrast to paper-based referencing systems, Wikipedia constantly evolves and is able to rapidly respond to new knowledge and new insights on any conceivable topic. For example, during late 2007, Wikipedia contained 2,076,194 articles in English that had been subject to 176,451,331 edits, which averages 16.39 edits per page since July 2002. It may indeed seem somewhat chaotic if the knowledge you seek might change from one minute to the next. However, in 2005, the much-respected journal *Nature* conducted a survey that found that Wikipedia was able to almost match the *Encyclopaedia Britannica* in terms of its factual reliability (Terdiman, 2005). The finding was significant as it indicated that people can use the Internet to collaborate effectively, and in ways that are not geared automatically towards profit or 'efficiency'. Indeed, Poe suggests that any muddles tend to take place in the commercialized space of the wider Internet and that Wikipedia, by contrast, is relatively rational and self-ordering – like bees in a hive. He goes on to state that:

The private-property regime that governs the Internet allows it to grow freely, but it makes organization and improvement very difficult. In contrast, Wikipedia's communal regime permits growth *plus* organization and improvement. The result of this difference is there for all to see: much of the Internet is a chaotic mess and therefore useless, whereas Wikipedia is well ordered and hence very useful. (2006: website)

From software uses, and development to the changing status of law and technology, we have seen two spheres of resistance against commodification and the insertion of the cash nexus. As part of the information society, however, there is the wider sphere of day-to-day communication between people. Here too there seem to be burgeoning forms of online communication, ways of using the network, that are not simply about business, or buying or selling, or getting information for whatever reason. The objective seems to be more about people meeting people and expressing oneself inside what might be termed a 'community of interest'. This online phenomenon has been termed 'social networking'.

Social networking is the connection of (potentially) large groups of people through Web 2.0 software where users can upload and download information quickly and easily. An early advocate of social networking as a 'social good' was Howard Rheingold, who wrote a much-discussed book called *The Virtual Community* in 1993. In it he argued that social networking (or what he termed 'many-to-many' communication) would benefit society tremendously. Rheingold believed that through ICTs the simple act of communication would be enhanced to the point of transformation where 'virtual communities might [become] real communities . . . something entirely new in the realm of social contracts' (1993: 362). With the advent of Web 2.0 technologies in the early 2000s, it seemed that Rheingold's forecast was becoming a reality. Today 'virtual communities' now permeate the network. They fill the lives of millions with new ways to communicate with each other, to share ideas and images and texts in ways that had until recently been technologically impossible on a mass scale.

The names of websites that enable social networking are rapidly becoming part of the information society lexicon: Bebo, MySpace, Friendster and hi5 are but the most current in a rapidly changing cyberspace. However, Facebook may well typify these. Created by software programmer Mark Zuckerberg in 2004, Facebook has spread across the world as an immensely popular site. In 2007 it had 16 million registered users and was growing at a rate of 3 per cent per month (Fastcompany.com, 2007). In fact, Facebook grew so fast and was seemingly so compulsive that businesses began to express concern that employees were wasting too much time on it during work hours (BBC, 2007). The attraction of such sites appears to be that they fulfil a deep human need to communicate and be social. On Facebook, users can search for people who they may have lost contact with; they can receive requests from strangers to be their 'friend'. Although a privately owned company, Facebook ostensibly adheres to the 'creative commons' ethos by opening the site to programmers who can write novel or useful applications to make the site even more attractive. There have been additions such as 'zombies', allowing users to turn their friends into virtual zombies, or more useful tools like Superwall that enables users to show images of their favourite movies, books, etc., on their profile pages (Stone, 2007).

Social networking sites that are more 'specialized' also proliferate. One such is Second Life which allows users to assume a second identity, and to inhabit the virtual world, a '3D digital online world imagined and created by its residents' as its banner proclaims (SecondLife.com, 2008). It too has millions of registered users and a quick check on my computer reveals that it has 45,017 users currently 'inhabiting' this space. Other sites encourage more individual creativity as an online social act by allowing users to upload photos, such as Flickr, where another check tells me that over 4,000 photos were uploaded during the last minute; or users can experiment with movies or video diaries, on sites such as YouTube, where you are able to 'broadcast yourself'.

Taken together, what does all this ostensibly non-commercial activity mean? Does it signify the creation of vast decommod-ified (or uncommodified) spaces where creativity, sociality and culture can develop without the deadening and predictable imperatives of the cash nexus? Let us look at the examples in a bit more detail.

I think we can bracket the works of Richard Stallman, Linus Torvalds and Lawrence Lessig together in the 'creative com-mons' movement. They share the objective to limit the domi-nation of proprietary ownership of ubiquitous software applications; they want to develop a 'commons' where pro-grammers and users can enjoy the benefits of free intellectual and technical association. These and many others who share their concerns fight a tremendously important battle and have created some useful alternatives. But does it pose a real chal-lenge to the logic of commodification that permeates the infor-mation society? I think not. Open-source or creative commons initiatives such as Linux or Ubuntu may look like impressive achievements, but in reality they are programs that merely mirror what a Microsoft or Apple application will do. These may be 'free', but they still follow the logic of 'efficiency' and emulate the instrumental rationality (doing things faster) of the network system as a whole. The fact that major corpora-tions use Linux, for example, shows not only that it is a system that fits easily with theirs, but also that they are prepared to have a 'free ride' on the open-source code to promote their larger commercial aims. So, for example, by using the Ubuntu operating system, Dell Computers merely makes its product more competitive by not having to pay licence fees to Microsoft.

Similarly, the 'free culture' project that Lessig promotes is a very laudable and important aim. But the incorporation of open-source software into mass-produced computer products and their applications serves also to strengthen the grip of corporations on the *uses* of computation. McLuhan told us that 'the medium is the message'. The message contained within the medium of open-source or creative commons, I suspect, is essentially the same as that of the proprietary software – do things faster, more 'efficiently' and with minimal human input. The bottom line is that for all the good intentions behind open-source software, none of it is actually oriented towards thinking about how we might use computers *differently* – to change their inherently instrumental mode, and to make them more responsive to social needs instead of economic ones.

Wikipedia, for its part, is fundamentally an encyclopaedia. It will be decommodificationary only to the extent that it eats into the profits of rivals such as *Britannica*. Without a doubt it is useful to millions across the world, and it is probably galling to just as many who feel uncomfortable at the seeming 'fluidity' of what constitutes truth, knowledge and the historical record on its evanescent pages. What is important about Wikipedia, however, is that it shows what is possible through online collaboration, and in a context where the cash nexus, for once, does not dictate events. Poe's analogy of the beehive illustrates a small example of what people are capable of in their uses of information technologies. It is wholly positive, in my view, because it allows a glimpse of alternative uses of computer networks – people working together for no other purpose than the common good, and for the enrichment of knowledge and of culture.

We looked finally at social networking as possible examples of culture and society using the network in ways that people themselves decide, to connect with others, to collaborate, to innovate and to share. How successful has this been in creating a decommodified space where the market does not dominate? Well, the prospects don't look good here either. The first thing to say about sites such as Facebook is how *commercial* they are. Click the refresh button on Facebook and see a different ad every time. Indeed, ads are inserted into the user's profile. Visit any of the popular sites and you will get a similarly commercial experience. This is not surprising. They are created and maintained by business people. As Charles Arthur mischievously put it: 'did you think that hosting websites with millions of users was something they did for fun? Not at all – there are hefty hosting bills to pay, but more importantly, big profits potentially to be made' (Arthur, 2007). Microsoft seems to agree with this, prompting it to buy a 1.6 per cent share in Facebook for $240 million (MSNBC, 2007). Facebook also makes money from selling the details (their names and pictures, etc.) of its millions of users to corporations such as Google and Yahoo! to enable them to do their own marketing (Arthur, 2007). That these sites are potential money-spinners is no secret. News Corporation owns MySpace, and Flickr is a Yahoo! subsidiary. In fact, these and other major social networking sites are embedded deep into the corporate structures of digital capitalism – functioning primarily as a marketing tool. As 'communities of interest' social networking sites assemble groups of people who are of similar ages and share similar tastes – and this makes them very attractive to advertisers who want to target their audience as closely as possible.

It seems pretty clear that the much-hyped websites that have evolved since 2004 are not going to make any impact as far as stopping the commodificationary logic of networked capitalism is concerned. But what of 'social networking' per se? Is there any hope here? Castells views networks, and by extension the information society, as a new 'morphology' within capitalism, one that pervades the 'entire social structure' as he puts it (1996: 469). What he suggests is that networks set the parameters for new forms of social, cultural and economic interaction. It is an idea followed up by Andreas Wittel. In his article 'Toward a Network Sociality', Wittel ponders the nature of social networking as a new form of interaction, just a few years before it became a phenomenon that swept the Internet. The structures of 'network sociality', as Wittel suggests – and as we have seen in our discussion of Facebook – are immanently commercial. They are fundamentally business platforms. And in an information society, where social practices are increasingly 'network practices', the unavoidable effect of social networking in such a context is 'a commodification of social relationships' (2001: 53). Much social networking, he maintains, is oriented towards business and personal advancement through making the right connections. While much that goes on in, say, Facebook interaction between people is purpose-free (albeit within a virtual advertising space) and is not necessarily about making the right connections – there is always the potential for another side to emerge. What social networking contains is what Wittel calls an 'inherent ambivalence' (53). MySpace Music, for example, is fairly obviously about bands getting themselves known to as many people as possible, but this instrumental impulse is masked to an extent with the emphasis upon making 'friends' and making endless connections to other sites where new 'friends' might be found. Moreover, the ephemerality of social networking is striking. And so, to the extent that they are communities, social networking sites display a distinct lack of social coherence, stability, embeddedness and belonging – the very opposite of traditional forms of community (Wittel, 2001: 51).

Before there can be any definitive statements regarding the ostensibly anti-commodificationary nature of open source and social networking there needs to be much more ethnography conducted. However, emerging theory seems to indicate that in the network society as a whole, the preponderance of the logic of commodification far outweighs anything else, and the global-wide 'culture of commodification' is a primary effect of our networked society.

The ephemerality of social networking that Wittel notes, along with its incoherence and flux as the basis upon which forms of enduring culture might be built, point to what I see as the detrimental effects of network society speed. Connections are increasingly loose and tenuous, and, in the blizzard of network possibilities, something else always comes along to attract us or distract us. Social acceleration has been a key concern that I have tried to express in broad terms in each of the chapters thus far. It is time, however, to look at the nature of speed in the network society more closely. In so doing I want to give a deeper understanding of the importance of speed in the information society, and to try to give an answer to my conference interlocutor whom we met in chapter 1 – for whom social acceleration through ICTs was unambiguously positive.

6

Faster and Faster

High-speed technology plays a pivotal role in the velocity of human affairs.

'Globalization', *The Stanford Encyclopaedia of Philosophy*

Faster things for faster living. Get with the program! Right now!

Mark Kingwell, *Harper's Magazine* (May 1998)

The speed of information, as the above quote from the *Stanford Encyclopaedia of Philosophy* indicates, has a direct and profound influence on human society. Constant acceleration is a core rationale for computing, and it follows that as computers become more common, even faster and more deeply networked, the accelerative logic flows into society. We have already looked at this in general terms, a phenomenon stemming from the 'need for speed' within capitalism. We have also considered the idea that 'late capitalism' – merging with the revolution in information technologies – has produced a neoliberalized form of globalization where acceleration through computers forms the 'pivotal role'. I want to develop this relatively neglected but highly important aspect of the information society with a couple of framing questions. If information technologies have no intrinsic 'speed limit', how fast can human society go in order to keep up with constant acceleration? Who decides when acceleration is 'good' for society and when it is 'bad'? Or do we simply place our trust in the combination of technology and the free market?

In laboratories across the world, computer scientists and engineers are embarked upon an unceasing quest to make

computer processors go as fast as possible. Discussion surrounding computer chips is primarily discussion about processing speeds. This stems from the commercial rivalry of
high-technology firms and has given rise to what is known as
Moore's Law, after Gordon E. Moore, a co-founder of the
microprocessor-maker Intel, who observed in the mid-1960s
that the number of transistors on an integrated circuit
(microchip) tended to double every two years. The Law seems
to have been borne out as the computational speed of
microchips has grown immensely over the last few decades. So
much so, that the silicon chip that the transistors are embedded in has become so small, and is required to compute so
many instructions, that its physical limit is being reached. The
problem is that they begin to get too hot and become unstable.
Silicon may have limits in its speed of processing capacity, but
the need for faster computers per se has no intrinsic limits,
and so engineers are now experimenting with non-silicon-
based materials (such as chemical computing) and forms of
quantum computing that function on a completely different
basis from binary code. Technological developments such as
these promise to push the computers of the future towards
what Ray Kurzweil, in his *The Law of Accelerating Returns*, sees
as 'infinite' increases in processing speed (2001).

To examine the concept of speed more closely I build on my
previous work in this area, drawing together related perspectives in social theory, sociology and cognitive psychology
(Hassan, 2003, 2004, 2008). We can begin by considering the
material expression of my theory, which is exemplified in the
computer that I write these words on: an iMac desktop. This
aesthetically pleasing and entirely functional workplace
machine is new. However, a year or so from now a technician
will knock on my door and proceed to replace it with a brand
new (and faster) one. As part of doubtlessly complex leasing
arrangements that I was not party to, computers are upgraded
regularly at my place of work. The idea is that the latest
machines with even more processing power are able to

perform more networking applications that will improve my 'productivity'. This is a blanket logic that does not take into account what I actually do – which is to teach, read and write, and I am sure that those who make such decisions could not tell me how precisely my 'productivity' will rise with a new computer.

My case is not special. This is typical of work in universities and in many businesses. But it does beg a more general question: *why is it* that 'speed is everything', as Jack Welch puts it? Why is it that in the information society, to slow down, or even to stay at the same pace, is, as Welch suggests, a form of economic suicide? The same can be said at the level of the private individual: if you don't constantly look for ways of working faster, of communicating more easily, of thinking and acting faster, of mastering the art of 'multitasking', then you too will fall by the wayside and be left behind by a momentum that seems to be going not in the direction of progress – but nowhere in particular.

The information society as an accelerated life

In chapter 2 we briefly looked at what I termed the 'need for speed' that lurks at the heart of the capitalist economy. Since the beginning of the Industrial Revolution, this need has been in many ways regulated by the *meter of the clock*. And the time of the clock, as Lewis Mumford noted in his 1934 book, *Technics and Civilization*, was the most important technology of the Industrial Revolution (1934/1967: 14). Note that Mumford categorizes the clock as a *technological artefact*. It follows from this that the clock, and its representation of time as seconds, minutes, hours and so on, is a *social construction* that has little to do with what time is and what time does in the deeper philosophical sense (Adam, 2004). Nevertheless, this clock-time rhythm was represented in the economic, technological and political contexts in a form that made the speed of modernity a more-or-less *manageable* speed – that is, until the collapse of Fordism in the 1970s. With the demise of Fordism and the shift to neoliberal globalization and the information society, Jeremy Rifkin argues that what we experienced was a transition from economies of scale to 'economies of speed' (2000: 22). Hypercompetition has led to speed becoming the central consideration. And, as competition between capitalists heightened, then so did the 'need for speed' become more acute. In an environment of intense competition, the business that can move fastest, in terms of inventing a product and getting it to market, becomes the leader whom others will seek to emulate. We see an example of this with the Apple iPod MP3 player. From the time of its late-2001 launch it was the only product of its kind in the marketplace and so Apple sold millions of them, making the iPod the biggest source of corporate revenue for what was then an ailing company. Then, in early 2004, *Forbes.com* magazine reported that 'The would-be iPod killers are [now] starting to line up like ambitious fighters eager for a shot at the champ' (Hesseldahl, 2004). However, relative to the standard they had become used to, industry analysts saw such a competition-free time frame (around two years) as being extraordinarily long. When Sony's Network Walkman was finally released in mid-2004, a common market refrain was 'what took you so long?' (Chmielewski, 2004).

It is not enough today for corporations to simply speed up production or install new computer systems every two years or so to make the production process go faster. To become 'efficient' it is necessary to become as 'weightless' as possible (Rifkin, 2000: 30–55). Holding physical assets such as plant and machinery (not to mention lots of expensive workers with expectation of a pension) is slow, uncompetitive and constitutes a 'drag' on the requisite nimbleness of the corporation. Beginning in the 1980s, it thus became 'sound business sense' to get someone else to do it. The objective was to be 'lean and mean' in the parlance of the time where, in the fashion of WalMart, large corporations were able to squeeze contractors and suppliers to get the best price and quickest delivery.

WalMart became the template for those 'old' industries that sought to transform themselves in the context of globalization and the revolution in ICTs. Indeed, Sam Walton, the founder of the WalMart retailing empire, observed that: 'everyone thinks WalMart's success is because of economies of scale. The real reason is that we replaced inventory with information'. Sam Walton's belief in the power of information is illuminated by the fact that WalMart's computing power in the 1990s was second only to the Pentagon's (*Time*, 1992).

Just as the productive mode of Fordism evolved into what David Harvey termed a 'total way of life', where mass production for mass consumption enabled a culture and society to emerge that were to a large extent plannable and predictable, then so does our present phase of post-Fordism reflect (and is in turn shaped by) a specific kind of culture and society. Whereas Fordism was schematic and dominated by the clock, post-Fordism is much more chaotic and is temporally dominated by the time of the ever-accelerating pace of the digital network. Temporally speaking, then, the conjunction of neoliberal globalization and the information society has produced what James Gleick termed in his 2000 book, *Faster*, 'the acceleration of just about everything'. In it he describes a culture, a society, a world, where a ramped-up pace of life permeates everything and everyone; a frantic world where we are increasingly pressed for time. Gleick shows that we have become so consciously or unconsciously desperate to think up ways of trying to 'gain' time, that we revert to ultimately pointless coping strategies such as pushing the 'door close' button in the lift because we feel it is taking too long, or we repeatedly push the 'walk' button at a road crossing in the hope that it will stop the traffic sooner (Gleick, 2000: 15–30). Gleick also rehashes the old intuitive feeling about time and money as being the source of the major economic and social transformations in society when he writes that: 'The modern economy lives and dies by precision in time's measurement and efficiency in its employment. If money is the visible currency of trade, time is its doppelganger, a coin over which companies and consumers battle, consciously or unconsciously, with ever-greater urgency' (2000: 11).

Gleick's book is a useful popular-level treatment of the effects of the speeding-up of everyday life. However, it tends to skate over the surface of the issues, with no real indication of what the underlying dynamics of this process might be – although he does nod in the direction of information technologies as being a prime suspect. For a more detailed analysis, and an explicit thesis of the causes and consequences of the accelerating speed of life, we can look to the German theorist Hartmut Rosa and his ideas on what he terms 'social acceleration' (2003). First of all, Rosa states that in direct reference to Gleick's sweeping treatment of speed, it is obvious that 'the acceleration of just about everything' is in fact wrong if taken literally. He notes that the quest for speed sometimes has consequences which are precisely the opposite of what was intended. Obvious examples are the constant building of freeways which simply encourages more people to drive, thereby quickly resulting in more traffic jams; we see it in slow-moving airports at peak periods; we see it on the Internet where heavy traffic on a site will cause it to 'go down'; or where that social obsession, the mobile phone, will often be rendered useless because the user is out of range, and so it continues.

Rosa goes on, however, to identify at least two important areas where acceleration may be empirically measured. The first is 'technological acceleration' which is the 'intentional, goal-directed processes of transport, communication and production' (2003: 6). This is a core element that can influence other realms and Rosa cites research that suggests that over the last few decades 'the speed of communication is said to have increased by 10^7, the speed of personal transport by 10^2 and the speed of data-processing by 10^6 (ibid.). Second, is what he terms the 'acceleration of social change'. He differentiates this from the first category, which describes acceleration processes within society, to the 'acceleration *of* society itself' (7)

(emphasis in original). This is a move away from the technological to the general-social. It is a process that has been identified as emblematic of modernity since the time of Marx, and
sees acceleration as a constant in social dynamics such as in
fashions, lifestyles, modes of social relations and so on. Rosa
concedes that it is very difficult to measure precisely this kind
of change, and it 'remains an unresolved challenge' in the
social sciences. However, he suggests utilization of the work of
German social philosopher Hermann Lubbe whose 'measure
is as simple as it is constructive' (7). Rosa writes that Lubbe's
insight is to see the past as defined 'as that which no longer
holds/is no longer valid while the future denotes that which
does not hold/is not yet valid' (7). The present thus becomes the
time span through which past and future coincide. Thinking
about the present is key, for it is only 'within these time-spans
of relative stability can we draw on past experiences to orient
our actions . . . with regard to the future' (7). 'Relative stability'
is the operative term here, and Rosa argues, through Lubbe,
that potentially social acceleration may be measured 'by an
increase in the decay-rates of the reliability of experiences
and expectations and by the contraction of the time-spans
definable as "present"' (ibid.). In the attempt to verify this
empirically, Rosa looks at what he sees as the basic structures
within the realm of production and reproduction that help
organize and stabilize social life – the family and work. These
spheres of life, according to Rosa, have 'accelerated from an
inter-generational pace in early modern society to a genera-
tional pace in "classical modernity", to an intra-generational
pace in [our] late modernity' (8). He goes on to explain that:

> the ideal-typical family structure in agrarian society tended to
> remain stable over the centuries, with generational turnover
> leaving the basic structure intact. In classical modernity, this
> structure was built to last for just a generation: it was organ-
> ized around a couple and tended to disperse with the death of
> the couple. In late modernity, there is a growing tendency for
> family life-cycles to last less than an individual life-span:

increasing rates of divorce and remarriage are the most obvious evidence for this. Similarly, in the world of work, in premodern societies the father's occupation was inherited by the son – again, potentially over many generations. In classical modernity, occupational structures tended to change with generations: sons (and daughters) were free to choose their own profession, but they generally chose only once, i.e., for a lifetime. In late modernity, occupations no longer extend over the whole of a work-life; jobs change at a higher rate than generations. (ibid.)

Combined, these technological, economic and social transformations feed into what Rosa terms the 'acceleration of the pace of life', where time compression comes to the fore in the sense that David Harvey means in his 'time–space compression' thesis that we discussed in the previous chapter. Here, on the macro-social level, we see the emergence of the weightless corporation, and hyper-fast ICTs networks propelling business as fast as possible. For those individuals who are connected into this level, 'acceleration of the pace of life' is expressed in the form of the multitasking that is a pervasive fact of life, in the need to pack more activities into the working day and into our so-called 'leisure time' – temporal categories that are increasingly becoming indistinct (Schor, 1993).

Applying Rosa's thesis to my own analysis, then, would suggest that the historically unprecedented 'need for speed' that is at the core of neoliberal globalization and the information technology revolution drives the technological capacity for *speed-enhancing solutions*. A fundamental consequence of this is the inherently unstable and social solidarity-shattering imperatives of a globalized economy that draws billions of people into its accelerating orbit (Hassan, 2003). The social acceleration that stems from this process permeates every realm of life and forms the basis of new occupational, economic and communicative processes that generate new and evanescent patterns of social connectivity and new ways (faster ways) of being in the world.

Rosa is primarily concerned with the negative consequences of 'social acceleration' upon ethics and politics – and we shall discuss some of what I have elsewhere termed the 'pathologies of speed' (2003: 8) later in this chapter. However, I think it is necessary to remember that computer-driven speed need not always be a negative factor in social life. Indeed, it can have positive effects for humans across a range of activities, and any theory of speed in the information society must take these positives into account. For example, faster and more powerful computers have produced positive innovation in music (Battino and Richards, 2005), in art (Greene, 2004) and in cinema (Manovich and Kratky, 2005). Moreover, in cultural production more generally, the Internet has thousands of sites on every conceivable subject, many of which are thoughtful, innovative, sometimes brilliant, and help to contribute to the richness of life in late modernity. And so, to continue, let us briefly consider an example where high-speed technology produces positive outcomes within the information society, one that is beyond culture and beyond the economy – health.

Good speed

The massive number-crunching potential of computers that drove the scientists and engineers of the 1940s and 1950s to develop the computing power needed to enable the development of the atomic and nuclear bomb had also, though somewhat later, many unintended consequences in the form of benefits across the whole range of the medical sciences. In this respect, we can say that the positive potential of computers that occupied the dreams of many an information society booster have in fact been realized in some instances. For example, using powerful computerized tools, surgeons are now able to perform 'virtual operations' where they can operate on a patient who may physically be thousands of miles away, thereby overcoming the sometimes impossible task of bringing patient and surgeon together in the same room. This, surely, is an unambiguously positive effect of Harvey's 'time–space compression'. More, the increasingly fast processing power of computers has opened up whole new fields of bio-medical inquiry (such as bioinformatics) that were formerly only theoretically possible. The Human Genome Project (HGP), for instance, would have been unimaginable outside the context of the information society (HGP, 2007). This heavily computer-dependent project commenced in 1990 and was completed around thirteen years later. The initial goals of the HGP were to:

- identify all the approximately 20,000–25,000 genes in human DNA;
- determine the sequences of the 3 billion chemical base pairs that make up human DNA;
- store this information in databases;
- improve tools for data analysis.

As a 'public–private' partnership, the HGP could be seen as a case where the market and government and ICTs are able to converge in a positive way. And so, of course, given what we discussed earlier regarding the long-standing political support for the creation of an information society, the Clinton administration was hyper-enthusiastic at the completion of the 'first draft' of the human genome in 2000. Interestingly, the official White House Press Release makes much of how the computer-powered HGP had *accelerated* the processes of scientific discovery. The White House statement noted that: 'Before the advent of the Human Genome Project, a joint project of . . . international partners in the United Kingdom, France, Germany, Japan, China, [found that] connecting a gene with a disease was a slow, arduous, painstaking, and frequently imprecise process. Today, genes are discovered and described within days' (White House, 2000).

Today, 'breakthroughs' in all manner of disease, and exciting future possibilities of disease detection, prevention and cure emerge almost every week as scientists across the world deepen their knowledge of the genetic and molecular level functioning of the human body. The worldwide competitive motivation in the development of high-speed computing makes this possible. For example, the bioinformatics pioneer Charles DeLisi has described how computing power is central to his research work on AIDS. He observes that 'The research [on AIDS] goes from basic chemistry to clinical testing, with several points [in between] where you can't do things without high-intensity computing' (Davies, 2007). It is clear, then, that without the aid of 'high-intensity computing' our knowledge of the human genome and the practical applications that this now offers would be comparatively rudimentary. Moreover, our knowledge of possible ways to defeat the blight of AIDS would be a good deal less, and whole new medical disciplines such as bioinformatics would simply not exist at all.

Speed that is not primarily concerned with economic efficiency stands a good chance of being beneficial to humans and to society more generally. The examples in the health sciences show what is possible when science is largely 'disinterested' in terms of the politics and economics of the inquiry. Unfortunately, however, the preponderance of much research and development into information systems is skewed by political and economic considerations to the point where the overriding motivation is to develop a computer application or device that is: (1) marketable; (2) connectable; and (3) *faster* than its competitors. The result of such instrumental logic is to have unintended consequences in society and for people on an individual level.

Bad speed

In an essay written just before the general uptake of the Internet around the mid-1990s, Paul Virilio argued that through the connection between 'speed and information' humans were beginning to experience what he termed a 'fundamental loss of orientation' in the world (1995). In other words, in our postmodern society we are required to deal with increasing amounts of information at an increasing rate of speed, and in ways that have negative consequences for the individual and society. We are compelled to adapt to this increasing tempo because the new information society is characterized by a 'dictatorship of speed' that presents a problem not only for democracy, but also for the ways that individuals perceive what reality is. Virilio sees this process as a form of 'shock' or 'mental concussion' (1995). In a 1995 essay – written, remember, prior to the Internet taking over, and before the saturation of mobile phones, of broadband connections and so on – Virilio marked the beginnings of a consistent theme in the literature that saw 'speed and information' as having *psychological* effects. These are the 'pathologies' that are now becoming evident at the level of the individual and across society more generally. They are also the expressions of what I understand to be deep-level unintended consequences stemming from ICT-driven speed within the context of neoliberal globalization.

Stephen Bertman's 1998 book, *Hyperculture: The Human Cost of Speed*, is an example of this trend. He observes that 'Supported by a network of instantaneous communications, our culture has been transformed into a "synchronous society", a nationally and globally integrated culture in which the prime and unchallenged directive is to keep up with change' (1). Bertman conjures up the mental picture of the caged mouse on the spinning wheel, where no matter how fast it runs, it is only ever just keeping up. Humans in the information society, he argues, are just like that mouse: running faster, expending more and more energy, devoting more and more time to 'keeping up', but never really getting anywhere. Moreover, as Bertman goes on to suggest, with the introduction of each new information technology, and with each new advance in computing power and data-processing speed, the human condition, psychologically speaking, degenerates from 'an acute state to a chronic condition' (8).

It was noted previously that Thomas de Zengotita in his book *Mediated* argued that the speed and information glut creates a kind of 'numbness' (2005: 175). Life moves so fast, he maintains, that the resultant 'numbness' causes us to lose touch with any deeper connections to the world – and to the reality of the economic, political and technological processes that drive us. He goes on to compose a playful piece of writing that seeks to catch the rhythms of this numbness:

> All about time. Crunch time. Time to get a life. Busy, busy, busy being numb. You don't need a Blackberry, you need a chief of staff. Quality time. Down time. Even the food is fast. Real time. She runs marathons too. The end of the day. (2005: 175)

Virilio and Bertman are brief representative examples of a growing concern with speed in the information society. There are other dimensions to this specific perspective, however. For instance, there are those writers who take much of this pathologization as given, and approach the issue of speed from the opposite end. One of those is Carl Honoré, whose book *In Praise of Slowness: Challenging the Cult of Speed* argues that we need to take social acceleration much more seriously and recognize that the 'whole world is time-sick' and that 'we all belong to the same cult of speed' (2004: 3). This time-sickness, he writes, is a new phenomenon, brought on by 'turbocharged capitalism' (5). It is a malady that has its roots in the proliferation of information technologies which bears its fruit – if that is the appropriate metaphor – inside the offices of physicians around the world that are 'swamped with people suffering conditions brought on by stress: insomnia, migraines, hypertension, asthma and gastrointestinal trouble' (5). Honoré has emerged as something of a spokesperson for what is called the 'slow movement'. This is a reaction to the perception of an increase in social acceleration. The movement has its antecedent in Italy in 1986, when a certain Carlo Petrini began to organize people to create an awareness of the inexorable spread of fast-food franchises that were supplanting more traditional ways of producing and consuming food (<slowfoodusa.org>, 2007; see also Schlosser, 2002). In our consumption of food – and in our coping with life in general – speed is creating problems for our society, and Honoré sees this as stemming from a psychological and temporal basis. He sums up this perception when he writes that: 'Perhaps the greatest challenge of the slow movement will be to fix our *neurotic relationship with time* itself' (2004: 44; emphasis added).

By viewing increasing social acceleration as a cause of 'mental concussion' or 'numbness', or as being a 'time-sickness' that makes us 'neurotic', provides us with insights into the effects of social acceleration that many would at least intuitively concur with. Common are the 'stress' of deadlines, of having too much information to digest within a certain (usually short) time frame. This 'time-squeeze' often engenders feelings of 'guilt' because we feel we have not done as good a job as we might have done if given enough time. This can lead to 'anxiety' about what effects our incomplete efforts might have upon our jobs, the relationship with friends, family and so on. Such feelings are now part of everyday life for millions of people. However, these writings, and increasingly others like them, no matter how much of an echo or recognition they may have, are still speculations. What is needed is more empirical evidence that supports the idea of speed having negative psychological effects in the information society.

The connections between speed and social effects, as Hartmut Rosa reminds us, are not easy to make. However, I think that it can be plausibly argued that the rise of *anxiety* in modern societies corresponds with the growing information-alization of the world that began in the 1970s. There is emerging evidence that suggests that as societies become more complex and interconnected, then so too do they become increasingly pathologized – in that more 'sicknesses' are identified and clinical labels for identifying them proliferate. For example, Frank Furedi has researched the upsurge of anxiety-related pathologies that have emerged over the last few decades, as well as the growing number of ways to clinically distinguish them. Furedi sees the rise of a 'therapy culture' that has developed its own 'therapeutic language'. He underscores this prevalence with reference to a survey of instances of certain social-psychological terms that have become general currency in the relatively recent past:

> the term 'syndrome' was entirely absent from the pages of American law journals during the 1950s, 1960s and 1970s. Yet by 1985, the word 'syndrome' appears in 86 articles, in 1998 in 114 articles and by 1990 in 146 articles. In one month alone in 1993, more than 1000 articles in periodicals and newspapers used the term. In Britain, the growth of a therapeutic vocabulary is equally striking. Most people would easily recognize words that were virtually unknown and unheard of by the public in the 1970s . . . Even in the 1980s, people had never heard of terms like generalized anxiety disorder (being worried), social anxiety disorder (being shy), social phobia (being really shy), or free-floating anxiety (not knowing what you are worried about). (2004: 2)

Moreover, Furedi provides evidence that indicates that anxiety and stress are not limited to working-age adults who need to keep up with the pace of change in the speed economy. Children as young as nine or ten, Furedi reports, now express feelings of being 'stressed out' or anxious; and primary school pupils at one institution in Liverpool, England 'are being offered aromatherapy, foot and hand massages, as well as lavender-soaked tissues to help reduce stress and aggression' (2004: 1). The author goes on to note a UK survey that indicated that 53 per cent of university students suffer 'anxiety at a pathological level', whereas another study by the British Association for Counselling and Psychotherapy found that 10 per cent of students seeking professional help are 'already suicidal' (8).

By labelling the problem do we understand anxiety in ways that would empower us and help us deal with it more effectively, to stop its social and cultural spread? To be sure, there has been no want of trying to deal with the problem and 'treat' it at the level of the individual. Since the 1980s, a huge 'anxiety industry' has sprouted in most Western economies. Counselling and counsellors permeate the whole spectrum of government and non-government sectors. The police, army, schools and universities, as well as government departments, all now offer counselling services to staff and students, as do most corporations in the private sector. Yet the 'industry' and the 'problem' continue to burgeon. Writing in the late 1990s, James Nolan observed that 'The monumental increase in the psychologization of modern life is . . . evident in the fact that there are more therapists than librarians, fire-fighters, or mail carriers in the United States, and twice as many thera- pists as dentists or pharmacists' (1998: 8). Counselling has been 'institutionalized' in Britain, Furedi notes, and perme- ates 'all levels of education and the penal system' (2004: 10). The spread and growth of the counselling, therapeutic and also the pharmaceutical industries would seem to indicate that we are no closer to understanding the source of the prob- lem of anxiety as a cultural and social condition, and there- fore no closer to halting its spread as an individual (or individualized) pathology.

As just indicated, it is significant that the growth of anxiety and uncertainty throughout society (and the industries through which to identify and treat them) correlate with the emergence of neoliberalism and the revolution in informa- tion and communication technologies. It has the same tem- poral trajectory, in other words, as the speeding up of society. A primary effect is that the interrelated dynamics of neoliber- alism and ICTs has tended to atomize society into what Ulrich Beck and Elizabeth Beck-Gernsheim (2002: 33) describe as the 'isolation of individuals within homogenized social groups'. The point about the vulnerability of the indi- vidual in such a context is made forcefully by Alberto Melucci who wrote that:

> A society that uses information as its vital resource alters the
> constitutive structure of experience . . . The accelerated pace
> of change, the multiplicity of roles assumed by the individual,
> the deluge of messages that wash over us expand our cogni-
> tive and affective experience to an extent that is unprece-
> dented in human history . . . The self is no longer firmly
> pinned to a stable identity; it wavers, staggers, and may crum-
> ble. (1996: 1–3)

Within this growing privatization of the self, traditional social
support networks become frayed and fragmented as the ideology of individualism strengthens correspondingly. In such a
context, feelings of isolation and powerlessness, together with
the experience of uncertainty and inability to project a recognizable and safe future, can lead to anxieties, to neuroses and
to all the new kinds of social-psychological pathologies that we
have identified and labelled in the last quarter of the twentieth
century.

It is the prevalence of a generalized anxiety, I think, that theorists such as Virilio, Bertman and de Zengotita recognize
when they speculate about the negative effects of speed in the
information society. They also explicitly link these effects to
the industrial way of life, to capitalism and to modernity/
postmodernity more broadly. These are posited as meta-
processes that, as I have tried to show, are predicated upon geographic expansion and temporal acceleration. What these and
similar writers also do, in fact, is to follow an intellectual
trajectory that goes back to the Victorian era, one that links
industrialism/capitalism/modernity with the emergence of
psychological problems. For instance, in the 1860s, physician
and specialist in the treatment of mental disorders, George
Miller Beard, described an effect of the acceleration of life as
'neurasthenia', or nervous exhaustion. Discussing his work in
The Female Malady, Elaine Showalter noted that neurasthenia
was 'originally . . . described as "American nervousness" [by
Beard who] saw a significant correlation between modern social
organization and nervous illness. A deficiency in nervous

energy was the price exacted by industrialized urban societies, competitive business and social environments' (1985: 137).

The list of the negative effects of social acceleration upon the individual and the collective is by no means exhausted. However, for reasons of space I want to concentrate on one more example in this chapter. It is one that is less readily detectable by empirical social science means. Moreover, as I shall show, as the effects become more acute at the level of the individual and at the level of society more generally, the identification of this particular 'pathology' of speed becomes even more difficult to identify. To assess this we need to look at the field of cognitive psychology that studies the effects of the brain (memory, problem-solving and so on) in response to sensory input. The cognitive effect of the speed of information is an area that psychology has been researching over the last few decades. A central question is: what does the increasing acceleration and volume of the data that bombard us in the information society do to our ability to understand and reflect upon this society? James Gleick touches upon this when he makes the point that our cognitive capacity has finite limits, limits within which we are able to take in information at a rate that allows us to at least functionally comprehend it. He cites cognitive theorist Douglas R. Hofstadter who wrote that 'our own intelligence is tied in with our speed of thought' (Gleick, 2000: 100). This leads to the inescapable question: if capitalism aims for optimal 'speed of thought' in its productive processes in the information society, then people are perforce expected to do the same – *but are they able to?*

Well, in a narrow sense, no. Certain corporations, managers and business analysts will concede that the colossal increase of volume and speed of information that people are expected to efficiently manage in the network society is in fact problematic. For instance, in an article written for the business/IT journal *Infoworld* in 2000, journalist Paul Krill quotes a management academic commenting on 'information overload' who pointed out that 'it's worse than ever because we're all on

Internet time. The compressed time for decision-making is putting more demands than ever on our time' (Krill, 2000). The article goes on to make the case that time (or the lack of it) is the central issue, because people need the right amount of time to process information properly, to decide what is helpful and what is not. Krill also quotes a humanities and physics professor at MIT who said that 'high-speed information technologies, while very useful in many ways, have robbed us of our necessary silences of time to reflect on values on who we are and where we're going' (ibid.). As I read this article I imagined that I had finally come across a useful example of business and IT professionals finally getting to the root of the problem. The article ends with a promising subheading ('Ways to beat the overload'), which then rapidly nullifies the promise by articulating a set of homespun banalities that do not address the political-economic fundamentals. What it does is to throw the problem back at the individual. It reads (in speedy and efficient bullet-points):

- Develop an information management strategy that works for you.
- Filter information.
- Accept that not all pertinent data can be examined prior to a decision when data volumes are exceedingly high.
- Attempt to recognize quality data.
- Take control.

(Krill, 2000: website)

Business and IT professionals may see that there is a problem, but they fail to make the connections between the ever-increasing use of ICTs in the context of a neoliberalized economy and the speeding up of every register of social life. Intuitively at least we know that there are limits to our cognitive capacity, the feeling that there is only so much that we are able to 'process' in a given time frame. What is needed is more empirical evidence to back up this assertion. To begin with, the connection between cognitive capacity and information-producing computer systems has long been recognized. For example, as early as 1971, when Daniel Bell was still to publish his book *The Coming of the Information Society*, Herbert Simon, whom I mentioned in the preface, remarked that:

> What information consumes is rather obvious: it consumes the attention of its recipients. Hence, a wealth of information creates a poverty of attention and a need to allocate that attention efficiently among the overabundance of information sources that might consume it. (Simon, 1971: 40–1)

The problem of the speed and volume of information has grown immeasurably since 1971. Nevertheless, there still seems to be a paradox, or blind spot, that makes those believers in the dreams of the information society oblivious to the idea that computers can (even sometimes) be inefficient and psychologically impairing. And so because of this lacuna it falls to the lone individual toiling inside the networked system, as the bullet points above indicate, to adapt to the reality of the technology. She is required to develop strategies that might make her a more 'efficient' user within the restricted parameters of the computer logic itself. What this does, I think, is to *cede control to computers* instead of being able to 'take control' herself, as Krill advocates.

More recent psychology research continues to suggest that our cognitive capacity does have limits as far as our ability to be 'efficient' in our information-filled new economy is concerned. For example, a study in 2006 at UCLA found that the process of learning and cognition in the context of multitasking in the high-speed networked economy 'results in less available memory later on, of the item learned' (Gardner, 2006). The author of the study, Russell Poldrack, goes on to comment that 'If you are learning things under distraction [from multitasking] what you are going to end up learning is going to be different and, in particular, is going to be a lot less flexible.' And, in a quote that represents yet another instance of empirical evidence of the illusion produced by speed, Poldrack goes on to state that 'less flexible' means that the memory 'will be more tied to the specific circumstances of when you learned it'

(Gardner, 2006). In other words, when the context of the 'constant now' changes, as it does continually in the information society, then what we know and what we learn – *what we understand* – is less and less relevant to the new circumstances. What this indicates is that while people may indeed be more 'flexible' in the information society, it is doubtful whether they are efficient as well – and as we have seen 'efficiency' was the whole point of the ICT revolution anyway.

The UCLA study seems to confirm more sociologically based work. Ida Sabelis, for example, conducted interviews with the CEOs of several large corporations in Holland to ascertain the effects of social acceleration in the workplace (2002). Sabelis looks at social acceleration in the CEOs' day-to-day work as one temporal factor among many in this complex study, but nonetheless it does emerge as an important aspect in her findings (2002: 28–9). On her qualitative interviewing of senior managers, she writes that: 'Without exception, managers "have something with time" and usually the relationship to time is expressed as problematic' (79). Quoting one of the CEOs directly, she records that 'I strongly feel that acceleration is a pivotal thing in life for all of us – I can't tell you what causes what, but it is so obvious in notions of how fast things have to be achieved, that everything has become faster' (ibid.). Information technologies and their orientation towards acceleration and totalization are at the core of this 'problematic', according to Sabelis. It emanates from the larger structures of neoliberal globalization and the information technology revolution to produce the time compression and acceleration at the levels of the individual and society. Compression and acceleration, she writes, 'are largely experienced as coming from the outside of the organization, as an effect of the societal flywheel of the industrial world, infusing organizations and not allowing people to ignore it' (139). This compounds the managers' 'problematic' relationship with time, it could be argued, because the *fait accompli* offered in the neoliberal world – together with the commonly held opinion that computers are unequivocally 'efficient' – sits rather awkwardly with the increased time pressure and the growing amounts of information that they are expected to deal with.

If the 'causes' are not always clear, then the effects are usually more recognizable. Here Sabelis quotes another executive on the consequences of time pressure and the need to make decisions quickly: 'Because of time pressure you are supposed to react faster – and this implies faster decision-making and consequently also decision-making based on less consideration than we used to' (83). Competition at the global level of capitalism inflicts this kind of time discipline at the level of the individual. This has consequences not only for the stress levels of the person vainly trying to keep up with greater volumes of information, but also has unintended consequences for the system itself, in terms of its instrumental goal of 'efficiency'. In support of this, Sabelis returns to the theme in an essay from 2004 where she cites another CEO who answered her questions on the coping strategies developed to deal with the deluge of accelerated information: 'The art of leaving things out . . . is the answer to the need or wish for things to happen faster' (2004: 294). 'Leaving things out' means of course that certain things don't get done, or they get partial attention, or they get done badly, or in a way that is rushed. And so, instead of competition driving efficiencies, we can see that it could actually be the cause of inefficiencies when the volume of information and the rate of speed at which it must be processed becomes too much.

We have now considered some empirical evidence that suggests that social acceleration produces social 'pathologies' where medical-psychological factors (such as stress) and cognitive factors (such as the limits humans have in their ability to manage growing amounts of information at faster rates of speed) actually impair the development of the healthy individual and the construction of a stable and adequately functioning society. I want to try to further develop and strengthen this line of argument with a more philosophical speculation upon the processes of speed and its social-psychological effects. The philosophical element is necessary because we are considering our ability to *reflect upon the world* and develop critiques that make it more understandable – and hence changeable.

Once more James Gleick's engaging book, *Faster: The Acceleration of Just About Everything*, is able to offer a chink of insight that may be more deeply explored. This time his musings concern the Internet and the informational ambience it creates through mobile phones, streaming audio and video, and the growing media-rich environments of blogs, news websites, educational software and so on. He writes:

> The American company that promoted the Internet hardest in its early days, Sun Microsystems, conducted research in 1997 into how people read on the Web and concluded simply, 'They don't'. They scan, sampling words and phrases. Why? In part because any one page, on which the fluttering user happens to have lighted momentarily, competes for attention with millions more. (2000: 87)

In other words, the intrinsic nature of the networked computer with speed built into its capacity and design (especially in the move towards mobility and wireless) promotes a kind of restlessness, a 'fluttering' whereupon the user is unable or unwilling to linger for too long. This 'forever searching' and surfing explains much about the success of Internet-based corporations such as Google and applications such as Wikipedia. Users want to get information quickly (or feel that they need to) and so a site like Google is a very much faster alternative to a systematic search for *specific* information. How many times has one used Google to find one piece of information, only to find oneself coming away with something different altogether? Similarly with Wikipedia (wiki, incidentally, is derived from the Hawaiian term *wiki-wiki* which means speed), the attraction is the rapid definition of a term, for which many entries will have additional links to which the user can quickly jump to get a surface grasp of almost any subject in just a few seconds. The success of these applications is by turn mirrored in the failures of others, such as the e-book, a handheld device with which to download novels, news and so on. Attempts to make a commercially acceptable alternative to the traditional book have hit some tricky problems, not only in terms of its 'feel', but also in respect of its suitability for sustained use (Marr, 2007). Close reading requires the holding of one's attention and it has been consistently clear that what novelist E. Annie Proulx (1994) calls the 'twitchy little screen' militates against this.

Issues of literacy are germane here. That is to say, the ways in which people – in the UNESCO definition of literacy – are able 'to identify, understand, interpret, create [and] communicate'. Technology is an important factor in how literacy is achieved, be it through the pen, the tablet, the book, newspaper or any other form. It was through this perspective that Walter Ong (1982) saw the rise of what he termed a 'print culture' and a print-based literacy with the invention of moveable type and the printing press in the sixteenth century. This had replaced the 'oral culture' that held sway for thousands of years previously in a form of human interaction based on the spoken word. Ong argued that the shift from orality to print also evinced a change in our consciousness, a transformation in the ways we see, relate to, and understand the world (Ong, 1982: 78). Oral culture was fluid and based upon communicative interaction between one-to-one, or between one-to-many through public speaking and storytelling (the art of rhetoric). Communication was fixed in time and space (localized) and it was dependent upon and shaped by the proximity of the speakers and listeners, as well as the length of the spoken communication. Print culture itself was based upon communication that was *fixed on the page*. Moreover, the act of reading meant that the individual was 'alone' with the text and this process had its own temporal rhythms, the length of the book (a technology, one might argue, that was functional and amenable to *holding* one's attention and reflecting upon its contents). Spatially, it was a form of mass communication, as books and other printed matter could be widely distributed. Print culture is now being challenged by digitally based technologies that create what has been termed a 'screen culture'. A good definition of this comes from Kathleen Welch in her book *Electric Rhetoric* where she writes that:

> Computer screens and video screens have gradually so infiltrated our habits of being that their presence has become normal for citizens at work and play. . . They have come to constitute, in part, our intersubjectivities, our language interactions with others and within ourselves, including identity formation. (1999: 4)

And so the rise of 'screen culture' suggests another change in our consciousness, one that is less rooted in the fixed or relatively stable times and spaces of print culture. It is a culture that is oriented towards fast-flowing images and screen-based words that are not forever fixed on a paper page, but are 'twitchy' digital representations on an ever-changing screen. The screen does not hold attention in ways that a book does and neither does it encourage concentration and reflection in the way that being 'alone' with a book does. In the virtual times and spaces of the Internet you are never alone. You are liable to 'flutter', to communicate with others who are only a few clicks away. You are liable also to the messages of others (often in the form of automated computer messages) that intrude upon your space and time with email, pop-up adverts, or ICQ messages, or Skype telephone calls or whatever.

Screen-based communication, it seems to me, has serious implications for learning, cognition and understanding if it is predicated on open-ended acceleration. As Ong has argued, such transformations of the 'technologizing of the word', as the subtitle of his book terms it, cannot but have an effect on the ways that we communicate and the forms of consciousness that flow from this. Surveying the evidence from psychologists, from sociology and from the business sector itself seems to indicate that too much information at too fast a rate is debilitating. Our ability to perform tasks involving critical thinking, especially, suffers because to think critically means to reflect and concentrate, and devote *the time necessary* to a particular issue or problem. Of course, people still do this, and philosophers and academics and intellectuals of every kind critically appraise the workings of the world and offer perspectives that may be profound. But the spirit of critique, in order to be effective, must go beyond the rarified realm of systematic philosophical thinking.

The mid-twentieth-century German Frankfurt School philosopher Theodor Adorno argued that 'If philosophy is still necessary, it is so only in the way it has been from time immemorial: as critique, as resistance to the expanding heteronomy' (1998: 10). Adorno himself has often been accused of elitism. However, a way to read this is that the masses of ordinary people, through their schooling, through their working lives, and through their professional and voluntary associations, need to be in an environment of diversity and openness; they need to forge a solid connection with the realities of the world and thus be in a position to make sound judgements about it. Of course this would be the ideal, and the world has never been like this. However, in the information society, the majority of humanity is abstracted more than ever from this optimal democratic environment. The open-ended and increasing speed of networked communication is leading to what I have elsewhere termed 'abbreviated thinking', a form of dealing with information that is necessarily surface-level because of the volume of information we are confronted with and the time constraints social acceleration places upon us (Hassan, 2003: 142–53). In this abbreviated culture where everything has to be fast, 'efficient' and profitable, universities and workplaces alongside sources of news and information have all become speed-oriented and networked, with each node in the network helping to drive the others still faster. As Ida Sabelis's work shows, we tend to develop coping strategies to deal with this: we skim, we multitask, we surf, we develop the barest understanding of problems and issues because there is no time to delve much deeper and because there is always a new priority pushing to assert itself in our altered screen-based consciousness. And, as Sabelis's research confirms, time pressures mean that many things don't get done, or they get partially done, or are badly completed.

I think there is a kind of negative-feedback logic in operation here. That is to say, the more we skim the surface of the information society through information overload, the less we become aware of the deeper economic and political currents that make our surface reality possible. And if I can use a rather depressing analogy to illustrate this pathology of speed, we can see the process as akin to Alzheimer's Disease. The more it develops, then the less we become aware of it through a lack of use. The more it eats into our critical faculties, the more they atrophy. This process is not organic, but *social* and therefore reversible.

On a disagreement over the question of speed

In chapter 1 I described an encounter at a conference with an information technology consultant. He was an American living in Paris who argued, contrary to my position at the meeting, that the increasing pace of life in the information society was a positive thing. After what I've written in this chapter – and in the whole book thus far – it is perhaps time to revisit the issue and consider the questions he posed. These can be summarized as follows. Is the increasing (and open-ended) pace of life simply an aspect of greater 'efficiency', convenience and progress? Are the negative dimensions of speed (some of which I have discussed) simply problems that will be 'sorted out' as computers and networks become yet more capable in their ability to make our lives better? What does one say to the contention that a networked society with no intrinsic speed limit is an unambiguously 'good thing'? How does one counter the argument that says that the trauma of acceleration was felt by an *earlier* generation – by those living at the beginning of the twentieth century – and for whom contact with the telephone, the telegraph, train and automobile constituted contact with technological speed that was *truly* revolutionary and completely transformed what it was to be human? The implication here is that our more mature modernity, by contrast, is able to take 'the acceleration of everything' confidently in its stride.

These are questions, surprisingly, that are not often discussed. Indeed, my American friend expressed an amazement that part of an academic conference was devoted to them, and made his own positive opinion on the speeding up of life known in an intelligent and perceptive way.

The first point to be made might be seen as a rather unfair one, and a case of 'playing the man instead of the ball', to use a football idiom. However, I do think in this case that it needs to be said that it is always risky to generalize from one's own experience. That is to say, it does not necessarily follow that because one person is confident in technological surroundings, and is able to occupy a social and economic position allowing a measure of control to be exerted within it, that this is the case for everyone else. This was my impression from this nonetheless impressive speaker. As we saw from Ida Sabelis's sociological research, even individuals in high-level positions still acutely feel the pressure of acceleration. As many books and studies have shown, time pressure is felt widely and it affects people in all social classes, even when they have the status and power to delegate work to others (see Schor, 1993, for example, or, more recently, Southerton and Shove, 2001).

More substantive, though, is the question of technology itself, and the vital difference between the forms of speed-enhancing technologies. If we look at the impact of the introduction of the railway to remote towns in North America over a hundred years ago, as Jeremy Stein (2001: 106–19) has done, a more nuanced picture emerges. Using historical data of people's experience of the coming of the railway in a Canadian textile town, Stein concluded, contrary to commonly held assumptions, that it would 'be wrong to view [these] experiences . . . as being revolutionary. It is also questionable how widely felt those experiences were' (111). He goes on to add that during this time of relatively fast change in European and North American cities, 'the majority of telegraphic and telephonic communication remained local' (ibid.).

The problem was that these technologies were powerfully *constrained by time and space*. Railways took years to plan and to lay down; telegraphs and telephones similarly relied on infrastructures that took time to build. Partly this was because contemporary machines and technologies of installation (those that did the digging, land clearance, etc.) were slow and cumbersome. To this should be added the even slower rate of work performed by individual workers using picks and shovels and other relatively low-tech tools. The *effects* of the transformation therefore took time to ripple out, to connect with other communications systems in the development of a national network of railways, of telegraphs and telephones.

The grandparents of my American friend no doubt went through a culture shock of change, but the change *must have been incremental*. The fact that the railway, telephone, telegraph and so on were discrete technologies tended to militate against the building of a communications ecology. These were largely *incompatible* as networkable technologies. Apart from running a telephone line in parallel with a railway line, they did not follow a similar logic and had completely different support systems and industries servicing them. Not so with computer technologies. Computers were able in the first instance to hitchhike on existing complex communications networks and city infrastructure that had been decades (or centuries) in the building – and they were able to instantly connect (network) through their common computer language. Moreover, although the railway or telephone could, like the computer, *enhance* a business or a community through commercial change, they could not rapidly *enable* the creation of totally new industries in ways that the computer did. In short, the difference between singular communication technologies and a networked system that functions on a common basis is a profound difference, the consequences of which are only now beginning to be understood through a more critical appreciation of the effects of ICT-driven social acceleration. And the argument is not only applicable to developed countries. Today the transformation of the world view of millions of people in developing countries through the use of a mobile phone, say, cannot be said to be piecemeal or incremental; it is almost instantaneous. Time and space are no longer so difficult to overcome, especially where the communication of information is concerned. Studies are showing that in Africa, for example, transformations in the ways that people live their lives tend to be sudden and comprehensive, as 'old technologies' are being leapfrogged by the use of new information technologies (Scott et. al., 2004).

The most important point to emphasize is that we are not dealing with discrete technologies, such as the telegraph. We are now living in a world of networked systems. Computer networks utilize, connect and extend the infrastructures that have been built up over a hundred years and *digitalize* them. International telephone systems link up with new fibre optic cables, and with old and new wireless and satellite systems, to create a fully compatible Internet, a global communication system that is as fast as new technologies allow, and is one where people, applications, work processes, entertainment, education, commerce and art culture are all drawn into its accelerating orbit. One simply cannot compare this rapid and all-encompassing networking process with the time of Victorian industrialization in terms of the effects of technology on the speed-up of life.

There is a further issue to consider, though, one that goes beyond the pathologies of speed that we have discussed. It is a problem of control. My conference colleague seemed to be, and he believed himself to be, in full control of his life, especially in respect of its technological dimensions. However, this has to be partly an illusion. No individual has full control over his or her destiny. But what about systems? Are they self-organizing and controlling? Or do socially constructed institutions, such as markets and politics, control them for us?

Since the 1970s, societies and polities have increasingly placed their trust in the combined care of computerization and free markets. This has created a globalized world that is, as Anthony Giddens has phrased it, 'a world out of control – a runaway world' (1999: 2). To conclude this book, let us now look at how politics functions in our information society and consider whether computerization serves democracy – or whether democracy has been sacrificed at the altar of computer-driven economic imperatives.

7

Who Rules?: Politics and Control in the Information Society

'You can make money without doing evil'

Who rules? It's not an easy question to answer any more. Once upon a time, not so long ago, the answer was self-evident. It was the state. In the developed democracies it was the government, acting as elected representative of the people, that wielded ultimate and decisive power. For example, as possessors of the only legitimate means of violence, the state was charged, through its military structures, with defending its territory and its political interests. Just as importantly, elected government exercised its legitimate power by taking up its historic responsibilities to its people. A growing function here was to help organize and manage the economy through the creation of the optimal economic conditions to provide jobs and create strong industries. This was achieved in part through the nationalization of key industries and through the protection of economies from overseas competition by means of tariffs and trade restriction. Governments also extended the purview of the state by developing modern social structures that were geared towards the well-being of people, through setting up (in varying degrees) the elements of the welfare state, with the provision of free education, health services and unemployment benefits.

Over the last generation the nature of power and the location of power have changed. War-making – the prime example of state power – has been transformed. The private sector now makes up a growing element of the state's capacity to project power. In the USA, for example, the Blackwater Corporation has its own army, its own barracks – even its own air force with which to transport either its own personnel or 'US Special Operations Command' to conflict zones (Blackwater USA, 2007). Nationalized industries and a government role in the shaping or planning of the national economy are now a thing of the past, and the privatization of education, health and myriad social services have become well-established practices. Moreover, neoliberalism has not meant the augmentation of institutional politics as a primary organizing force in life. Rather, it has led to its partial dissipation into the 'flows' of power that constitute the constantly evolving networks of the information society. As Scott Lash has observed of this new postmodern power configuration: 'power is elsewhere' (2002: 75). But where? Power is still tied to knowledge, as Foucault suggested, and as thinkers such as Daniel Bell took for granted. But, as Lash puts it, in the knowledge society power 'is now largely informational' and tied to the commodity (3). Moreover, what Doreen Massey (1994) calls 'power-geometry' is no longer so clustered around specific (and relatively stable) sites such as government and institutional politics as it was during much of the period of modernity, but linked to the commodity and to the market. Accordingly, in a context where the market and the commodity dominate our postmodernity, power is now a 'thing' that is contestable and flows through the structures of not only the state – but the corporation too.

Google power

The rapid and phenomenal rise of Google is testament to the nature of power in the information society. Google's creators are Larry Page and Sergey Brin. Their names may or may not conjure up immediate recognition, but the company they started as a graduate student research project, at Stanford University in the mid-1990s, will. Google is the search engine that is used daily by hundreds of millions of people. So popular has it become, and so deeply has it been inserted into the online life of a sizeable portion of humanity, that Google can, with a modicum of plausibility, provide a measure of what the information society is thinking. It does this through its Google Zeitgeist website, which categorizes the search traffic using the keywords that people themselves use. Google proclaims this rather loftily as 'a cumulative snapshot of interesting queries people are asking – some over time, some within country domains, and some on Google.com – that perhaps reveal a bit of the human condition' (Google, 2007). Well, perhaps this goes a bit too far – or, given what we have discussed and analysed in this book, perhaps not.

What we can be more certain of is the social and economic *power* of Google, and this is reflected in the *value* that capitalism and governments place upon such a 'weightless' entity. In the English-speaking societies, at least, to 'Google' has become a verb that has slipped into everyday language. We hear it used in instances such as 'why don't you just Google instead of flipping through the phone book?' And moving from the general to the particular, it was publicized that George W. Bush, as president of the USA, and the person who had executive authority over all the satellite and hi-tech communications systems of the US military, used Google Earth, a program that gives access to a photographic map of the whole world, to view his ranch in Crawford, Texas, whenever he felt homesick (Carnevale, 2006). More portentous, perhaps, is the fact that the British prime minister, Gordon Brown, asked Google, alongside other IT behemoths such as Vodafone, to help tackle the problems of development in Africa (Elliot and Boseley, 2007).

Google deals only in information, and its market valuation says something about the centrality of information as a commodity in the information society. When Google floated an Initial Public Offering (IPO) of its shares in 2004, the corporation was valued by the stock market at 23 billion dollars and many of its (then) 270 California-based employees became overnight millionaires (Webb, 2004). Less than three years later, as the Internet boomed on, Google had a stock-market valuation of 155.9 billion dollars and employed 7,942 people across the world, with no doubt a few more millionaires amongst them (<Yahoo.com, 2007>; <Google.com>, 2007).

Compare this with the stock valuation of a corporation such as General Motors (GM). A 2007 Company Report published GM's market capitalization at 17.26 billion (MSN.com, 2007). It was once an article of faith in the age of Fordist production, prior to the age of information, that 'what's good for General Motors is good for America'. No one uses this phrase any longer. Indeed, it would not even make sense to say that 'what is good for Google is good for America'. Google may have a physical HQ in California, but its virtual presence and its virtual effects are global. If it had to it could relocate with the minimum of disruption – a key advantage of being weightless, and a central aspect of the change that the information society has brought, and of the *global power* of the corporations that thrive in this new environment.

I use Google as an example only to make the more general point of the unprecedented power of corporate capitalism in the age of information. Google itself makes a tacit acknowledgement of the power it and other corporations wield in one of its mottos, 'You can make money without doing evil'. The Google website has a list of semi-aphoristic 'Ten Things' that describe its corporate philosophy. The quoted line is number six in what seem to be arranged in no specific order of importance. What this phrase says, in my view, is that corporations have become the new centres of power within neoliberal globalization and that a lot of bad stuff is able to emanate from the boardroom, and traditional political processes are increasingly unable to do much about it. 'We are different' is the Google subtext. Nevertheless, to make such a statement with the word 'evil' in it as part of a corporate philosophy is unusual, if not unheard of. Why do they do it? A clue may lie in two more of Google's 'Ten Things' that we will now consider.

The first is 'Thing' number nine that reads: 'You can be serious without a suit'. On the face of it, this is harmless enough stuff that, as the explanatory text makes clear, lauds the benefits of the casual corporate approach. This is only slightly more offbeat rhetoric than is usual, where open-door communication in a democratic environment is encouraged, where the in-house chef used to cook for the Grateful Dead, and where 'ubiquitous lava lamps and large rubber balls' reflect a kitschy corporate aesthetic. Page and Brin are too young to have been directly involved in the 1960s counter-culture movement, but we can see here distinct traces of what I described in chapter 3 as the 'California ideology' of the early information society, where 'everybody can be both hip and rich'. Google dips into counter-culture ideology as a way to distinguish itself from the mainstream of corporate America, as being a new kind of business entity that knows the 'evil' that 'man' is capable of in the search for profit. Again, there is no harm in this. If Google millionaire employees feel that wearing a suit is uncool, then it should not logically affect the bottom line of what Google does.

The second 'Thing' (number seven) is naturally aligned to the ethos of number nine, but it crosses over into more empirically testable ground. It states crisply and unambiguously that 'The need for information crosses all borders'. Now this is a reasonable, if hackneyed imprecation, something that almost everyone who uses a networked computer and thinks about his or her use of it would readily agree with. It goes on to say that: 'Though Google is headquartered in California, our mission is to facilitate access to information for the entire world'. However, there can be a difference between Google theory and Google practice in the context of neoliberal globalization. And this difference constitutes a symbolic gap that stands for the vacuum at the heart of institutional politics in the world.

It was mentioned briefly in chapter 4 that countries with repressive regimes such as China are continually seeking ways to limit their citizens' exposure to 'subversive' ideas on the Internet. The Chinese government, especially, is on the horns of a particularly acute dilemma here. On the one hand, it is fully committed to the global capitalist system and wants to integrate with the global economy as much as possible to allow it to pursue its ambitious development strategies. This means that the information necessary to connect Chinese development with the wider flows of global capital must 'cross all borders', to allow the optimal environment for economic growth. On the other hand, however, along with the mundane flows of economic information that fuel Chinese growth comes free-thinking *political* information, information that is critical of the Chinese system and the Chinese government. What to do? The Chinese government devotes many resources in its efforts to filter out information it considers dangerous, and attempts to track down those who either read such materials or post their own. To cite just one example, in 2003 a Mr Wang Xiaoning was jailed for ten years for publishing articles the regime considered 'subversive'. Importantly, and the precedent was set here, the government relied on the local Hong Kong branch of Yahoo!, an Internet search company like Google, to supply Mr Wang's email accounts from which they were able to physically locate him (Chosun News, 2007). The Chinese government thus became alerted to the fact that it had 'leverage' over Internet companies – that is to say, they could be made to 'cooperate' if they wanted to continue to do business in their country. And so in 2006 the Chinese government sought and got the help of Google when it requested that the software for its search-engine software be modified (by Google itself) to screen out material that it did not want its citizens to see. Sensitive materials on, say, Tibet, or human rights or democracy, were duly filtered out by the specially tailored software supplied to the Chinese government. It fell to Andrew McLaughlin, Google's senior policy adviser, to make the lame excuse to the media when he stated that: 'In order to operate from China, we have removed some content from the search results available on Google.cn in response to local law, regulation or policy. While removing search results is inconsistent with Google's mission, providing no information is more inconsistent with our mission' (Oates, 2006). The press freedom organization Reporters Without Borders (RWB) rightly pointed at Google's 'hypocrisy' concerning its mission statements and its actions and railed at the company's 'lofty predictions about the future of a free and limitless Internet [whilst] conveniently hid[ing] their unacceptable moral errors' (RWB, 2006).

The point here has not been to show that this or that corporation has been hypocritical – hypocrisy has always been a part of the capitalist system. And the point has not been to show that Google is any worse than other corporations in the neoliberal global economy. The issue is that Google and every other business in the global marketplace follow a strict logic whereby they are compelled to take certain actions or suffer the economic consequences. In parentheses this logic was illuminated once more in 2007 when Google announced the launch of its 'Knol' application (a truncation of the word 'knowledge') as a rival to Wikipedia. From Google's point of view the reasoning is simple: Wikipedia attracts many millions of eyes to what is a commercial free environment. These eyes are potentially a market and potentially a source of revenue if they can be lured away from Wikipedia. If Knol is a raging success and causes Wikipedia to close or become an obscure corner of the Internet, well, 'that's business' as the saying goes, but at a deeper social level a significant (non-economic) cost would be the ethos of collaborative working on the Internet.

Again, this is simply part of the logic of the system, but what is different today in the information society is that corporations are more *overtly political entities* than they have ever been. Corporations have always backed one political party or another (or both at the same time) in whatever country they do business. Governments could change, left-wing for right-wing, and corporations could mostly live with the consequences. Today, however, corporations are themselves the expression of a particular political ideology: neoliberalism, where increasing power resides in the marketplace. The whole rationale of a corporation is now tied into this particular ideology, and their actions (to gain economic and hence political power) must be oriented towards the *preservation of neoliberalism*. In this role, corporations are required to act politically every day.

At the global level institutional politics largely leave business alone in terms of regulating the ways in which they do business. This has meant that political as well as economic power has accreted to capital in ways that are unprecedented. This is what the traces of counter-culture philosophy in Google's mission statement allude to. It says that there are fewer restraints on capitalism than ever before, and more freedom to plunder, to destroy and waste, to make deals with authoritarian regimes, and to consolidate the structures of an increasingly unchallenged power. The reality is that Google's 'California ideology' – rather like the 'just say no' slogan that was part of the futile 'war on drugs' – can only amount to warm and fuzzy mission statements that simply dissolve when confronted by the imperatives of doing business in our 'new age' of neoliberal globalization and networked economy.

To understand this new order of things, what is needed – in place of the acceptance of meaningless platitudes to not do 'evil' – is a solid analysis of the present political and economic context. From this, we are able to form a historical perspective that will give some idea why, in the information society, corporations have become so powerful and the strength of liberal democracy so weak.

The idea of politics

To better comprehend power and politics in the information society, we need first to have an understanding of how political institutions evolved, and of the philosophies that underpinned them. In his critique of neoliberal globalization, Richard Falk pointed out the irony in the fact that 'the Marxist account of the relation between economic and political power seems persuasive only after Marxism has lost its capacity to win adherents to its worldview' (1999: 46). I think that this is right, but I think it also masks a deeper truth that to have a 'materialist' view of economy, history and politics is actually a common perspective, whether the holder of this view is conscious of it or not. It is a perspective held by politicians, economists and CEOs as they try to interpret the world on a daily basis. The ideas do have their genesis in the traditions of Marxism, but they go back further to the writings of eighteenth-century philosophers David Ricardo and Adam Smith. What they do is to put in place a secular theory for understanding the world. This was premised upon the idea that history, its politics and its economic dynamics (the ways in which humans 'create' their social world) operate upon a material and worldly basis. That is to say, it was not the divine 'plan' of God that was unfolding and shaping the affairs of men in an ongoing process of temporal change, but, rather, it was humans and humanly constructed systems, working on the natural world, that propelled change. It was a thesis that of course fitted with the capitalist world view, and saw the production of 'things', the building of cities, of creating networks of trade and so on, as the 'natural' motive powers of the modern world. The idea of 'progress' thus evolved as a measurement of the development of the 'productive forces' of society. These are the economic, organizational and technological processes that make 'acting upon the world' more complex, more 'efficient' and able to extract more 'value' from the natural world. History, then, may be seen in large part as the playing out of the multifarious struggles that take place between classes in the context of these material dynamics. And so instead of history being the effect of the actions of individuals, of 'great men' such as generals and kings and major politicians, instead it was accepted more as a complex of social forces, encompassing the political, economic and technological that was the energy underpinning social life.

How does 'politics' fit into this interaction? We should begin with a definition of what we mean by the term. A serviceable description comes from David Held, who wrote that:

> politics is about power; that is, it is about the *capacity* of social
> agents, agencies and institutions to maintain and transform
> their environment, social or physical. It is about the resources
> that underpin this capacity and about the forces that shape
> and influence its exercise. Accordingly, politics is a phenom-
> enon found in and between all groups, institutions (formal
> and informal) and societies, cutting across public and private
> life. It is expressed in all the activities of co-operation, negoti-
> ation and struggle over the use and distribution of resources.
> It is involved in all the relations, institutions and structures
> which are implicated in the activities of production and repro-
> duction in the life of societies. (1994: 311; emphasis in
> original)

This is of course a wide definition, but we can argue from this
baseline that *certain forms* of politics coalesce and institutional-
ize as society develops. And so, as the modern period of capitalist development began to get under way, the institutions of
an emergent *liberal democracy* began to evolve (in its varying
forms) in Western Europe and North America in the eighteenth and nineteenth centuries (Held, 2006: 70–116).

The political and the economic realms are closely inter-
twined. There existed (and still exists) a definite interaction
(dialectic) between the political and the economic, where one
helps to shape and form the developmental contours of the
other. In this sense Held's emphasis on the term 'capacity' is
insightful. Capacity in this sense connotes a form of power, the
power to change either (or both) the political environment or
the economic realms. This interaction between forms of power
has the effect of creating or limiting agency and choice (Rigby,
1987: 14). Historically, then, the capacity for change within capitalism and institutionalized liberal democracy has for each
been more or less augmented throughout the period of modernity, creating a kind of 'balance' where no one realm dominated
completely. We can see examples of this 'balance' or 'tension'
where the political realm is able to shape the economic through
the passing of laws that 'regulate' how capitalism operates. This
can take the form of laws that mandate the minimum age that

a person can be set to work in a factory, say, or the passing of laws that make the production process safer, cleaner and better remunerated. Alternatively, the economic realm can develop the capacity to drastically reshape the contours of the political process. A good example of this is the emergence of imperialism in the nineteenth century. The increasingly critical need for business to expand and invest, and exploit across an ever-widening physical space, compelled the political class of the developing capitalist countries of Europe to implement ideologies and practical policies that facilitated and legitimated Western imperialism (Hobson, 1965).

It is important to note that in the period of modernity the political process was nationally based. Apart from the extraordinary transnational capacity of political power in the context of imperialism (which began to wane by the early twentieth century for the major imperial powers such as Britain and France), political power has traditionally been territorially delimited. The writ of political power in a given developed country, in other words, ran only as far as its borders, where it came up against another institutionalized and territorialized political power with similar limitations. However, within its legitimate sphere of influence, institutionalized political power in the form of liberal democracy was able to have a sometimes-central role in the shaping of the economy, as we saw in the state's role in the phase of mid-twentieth-century Fordism and the 'managed economy'. Thus constituted, the institutionalized, representative politics occurring in the parliaments and congresses of the Western democratic countries came to be seen, by the mid- to late twentieth century, as the essence of *what politics is*, and as reflective of the 'self-evident truths' of democracy that US President Lincoln had in mind in his famous speech of 1858. However, this perspective connoted a form of timelessness in the institutional political process that neglects the historical tensions between capitalism and democracy, tensions where the power (the capacity) of one may be augmented at the cost of the other.

For much of the period of modernity these tensions waxed and waned to produce the dynamic basis of historical development. However, this dynamic ensures that things never stay the same, and self-evident truths can be eclipsed by new realities. This happened, I will now demonstrate, in the transition from a modernist society – based upon the interactions of capitalism and democracy – to a postmodern society that is still based upon the interaction between the economic and the political, an interaction that is deeply inflected by information technologies.

The message and the medium

A growing vacuum takes over the places that institutional politics used to inhabit. We see the sterile atmosphere of its politics when it tries to use information technologies to 'connect with the people', to keep voters 'in touch' and show itself to be still relevant to the globalized age of information. Establishment politics got in on the act at a relatively early stage of the evolution of the Internet, with President Clinton and Vice President Gore singing its praises during the late 1990s, and rapidly establishing direct email contact between the people and the White House (president@whitehouse.gov). However, some media and social theorists saw the dangers, as well as the promise, of what was termed the 'digital Town Hall' where virtual communities could come together in a virtual *agora*, named after the Greek place where 'the people' gathered. Howard Rheingold, for example, thought that either 'Virtual communities could help citizens revitalize democracy, or they could be luring us into an attractively packaged substitute for democratic discourse' (1993: 220). It is the question of control, I think, that decides Rheingold's conundrum. Does information technology actually empower people to engage in meaningful dialogue with each other and with their elected representatives? Or does it shape the parameters of the communication, to the point where the medium becomes the message, to paraphrase Marshal McLuhan?

David Shenk, writing in his book *Data Smog*, keeps up the optimistic possibilities, especially on the 'grassroots lobbying' front, when he writes that 'Advances in communication have dramatically transformed lobbying from an elite corporate perk into a facet of ordinary citizenship' (1997: 134). At the very least, he suggests, ubiquitous computing has meant that politicians are aware of voter concerns. A million emails from, say, members of the National Rifle Association, over legislation they do not agree with, will no doubt make certain politicians sit up and take notice. High-speed direct communication means that the layers of mediation that separated politician from voter and president from citizen in the past have, in theory at least, been overcome. A few clicks and a few typed-out lines and your representative – from local councillor to Prime Minister – will have a record of your concerns. As Shenk puts it, 'this speedier, purer democracy has been an enormous political boon in several important ways. Faxes, cable television, and modems have rendered the infamous smoke-filled room a thing of the past, transforming . . . America into a thoroughly documented, well-monitored public sphere' (134). It may be wishful thinking that the secret political deal-making culture is coming to an end, but that's not Shenk's primary concern. He is thinking about the reality of *too much information* flowing in the political realm between voters and representatives on every possible subject, to the point where the flows of political information become what Arthur Kroker and Michael Weinstein call 'data trash' (1994). Politics may have moved from those mythical smoke-filled rooms to a distributed and 'many-to-many' broadband-enabled high-speed cyberspace. But what happens to it here? A similar thought occurred to Paul Virilio in his law of 'dromology' when he argued that constant acceleration (of political information, of commodities, of cars on the freeways, etc.) leads not to political transparency or economic efficiencies – but to gridlock (1991: 65). Political gridlock is not very difficult to imagine in the current political scene. It is almost a cliché to say that institutional politics is now a lifeless realm, from where people stay away in droves. For young people especially, the inheritors of the information society, the politics of men in suits are seen to offer nothing. It is disaffection, moreover, that is evidenced at poll after poll in the Western democracies, where voter turnout continues to dwindle precipitously.

Politicians are of course keenly aware of this and of perceptions of their lack of legitimacy. Accordingly, and following the lead of Clinton and Gore in the 1990s, political parties all have their own 'attractively packaged' websites where, in many of them, much expense is devoted to making the party look relevant and connected with voter issues. Moreover, aspiring individual politicians will have their own website, and maybe their own blog too where they can create diaries and put down thoughts on this or that issue and seek voter feedback or 'dialogue'. These media platforms go into overdrive during election time, and, in many of the Western democracies, the period of 'unofficial electioneering' gets longer and longer. As the former Australian Prime Minister John Howard put it, 'perpetual election mode' is fast becoming the default position. There may be the appearance of a vital and progressive party and candidate through all kinds of multimedia tricks and wiki-based interactivity. But what is the political reality in the context of such a surfeit of information, with politicians seemingly so easily within our reach? David Shenk considers this question and forms the opinion that in his own country, at least, 'the increased speed of information has helped throw American democracy into a rut by reducing our leaders to followers' (1997: 135). He argues that the political class now follows the logic of technology in the attempt to make itself as relevant as possible. And in the attempt they, ironically, stall the political process altogether, to the point where political discussion is mostly background noise to the *images* being projected of the politician and the party.

In this, we see a kind of 'network effect' at play where technologies such as the Internet and its various platforms are used primarily because of the powerful logic and ideology that proffers computers and networks as the solution to almost any problem (Roszak, 1986: 51). Instead of a solution, however, there is a further problem that emerges from the information-alizing of the democratic process, and that is the *overdetermination* that the network effect instils. Politicians and the political process turn to computers because they are believed to be 'efficient' in all cases and at all times. Just as the average business now feels it needs to computerize, so too does the politician and the political party. In the case of the political website, or the politician's blog, the network effect compels them to have an online presence when the actual political value of this is far from clear. Take the fact that in 2007 Hillary Clinton, as candidate for the Democratic nomination for the Presidential elections of 2008, decided to announce her run for the nomination first on YouTube. The 'YouTube elections' were how some pundits described the candidates' eagerness to get themselves on to this website so as to 'connect' with as many potential voters as possible. From YouTube appeals for individual support there quickly followed the 'YouTube debates', where the Democratic and Republican candidates for nomination made an en masse party-based appearance to debate questions from interested netizens. Were these 'debates' a form of direct democracy where people could directly question the party candidates? Well, no. The 'YouTube Debates' were actually billed as the 'CNN/YouTube Debates'. Relevancy in the information age is an issue for television companies as well as the political establishment, and a network presence is seen as a way to assure this. CNN organized the YouTube debates, arguably, as a form of marketing its brand with the bloggers and Internet watchers of the world, the ones who are allegedly turning away from the television platform (Markoff, 2004). However, CNN were not prepared to turn this event over to the people, to allow them to ask any questions they liked. As a marketing event (for politicians as well as for CNN), the 'debate' could not be allowed to go wrong in any unanticipated ways, with flaky questions, or questions that the candidates had not prepared for. So CNN editors and journalists selected the questions that would be put to the candidates from the many thousands that had already been submitted. The 'live debate' was a response to carefully selected and recorded questions. There would be no chance of 'unstructured' moments in this highly structured online democracy. Indeed, CNN editor-in-chief David Bohrmann publicly doubted the wisdom of the crowd, by telling *Wired* magazine that leaving it to the people to ask unstructured questions would allow 'troublemakers' to get their inappropriate questions in (Stirland, 2007). In the event, of course, it all went to plan. The 'idea of politics' that we talked about earlier in this chapter, it seems, is not going to find its institutional expression online. What we get is the 'attractively packaged substitute' for politics and for democracy; what Jean Baudrillard (1994) called a 'simulacra' wherein the real and the actual gets buried under multiple electronic re-representations. Under these conditions, politics does not make a real connection with 'the people' as theorists such as Rheingold hoped it might, but the process actually alienates people even further. Through its multiple technological re-representation, and through its dissemination across the sprawling and unstable Internet, the political message in YouTube-type debates, or through the Internet more broadly, is irretrievably lost through hyper-mediation.

Blogging: political diversity or political echo chamber?

What might be called 'online political communication' has always been an aspect of Internet activity. Away from the institutionalized domain that we have just discussed, a growing political activism takes place at the fringes of civil society. Douglas Kellner calls this technopolitics. As a political space, the virtual space of the information society is, as Kellner maintains, a highly 'contested space' where differing ideologies and different agendas clash as much as they intersect. On the plane of anti-globalization politics which constitutes the largest and most significant political struggles outside the institutional realms, Kellner goes on to state that 'Significant political struggles today against globalization are mediated by technopolitics, that is the use of new technologies such as computers and the Internet to advance political goals' (2001: npn). The 'contested space' of cyberspace is an alternative realm where struggles over more traditional questions such as human rights, free speech, gender issues, economic security and political autonomy are now played out every day. Kellner illustrates some of the positive struggles, struggles that are at the same time novel because of the cyberspace underpinnings that incorporate their local-global dynamics. He cites, for example, the 1995 Zapatista Movement in Mexico that used networked computers (emails and list servers, and rudimentary websites) to raise a global consciousness and support for their local cause. He relates also the computer-based campaigns against global multinationals, such as McDonald's or Nike, that have inserted themselves into local communities, or the anti-NAFTA groups that sprang up during the 1990s in an effort to stop a neoliberal free-trade agreement that threatened the jobs of workers in vulnerable manufacturing industries across North America.

The issues and struggles that Kellner describes took place in the last decade of the twentieth century, and already seem like they were eons ago in terms of how politics are conducted in the information society. As information technologies have advanced and become more complex, and as the realm of the information society has massively enlarged, so too have forms of political activism developed and become more multifaceted. We saw evidence of the potential power of a progressive technopolitics in 2003, for example, in the weeks and months leading up to the US invasion of Iraq. It was a form of technopolitics that was deeply embedded in the new media landscape that was forming, and it exploited the opportunities that a public thirst for alternative media made possible. As the expected invasion drew near, across the world, hundreds of thousands of activists began to plan an 'anti-war global day of action' for 15 February (F15). Linked and informed through websites such as Indymedia.org and MoveOn.org, relevant information was created, shared and uploaded. Much of it offered differing opinions on the impending war from that of the institutional media, which for the most part tended to take the allied governments' line at face value (see, for example, FAIR, 2007). Moreover, the populations of these countries were subjected to misinformation – such as 'Operation Mass Appeal' – by state security services such as Britain's counter-intelligence agency MI6, which used media manipulation to lend credence to mainstream media reporting (Pilger, 2006). A global groundswell for the planned day of action grew almost exclusively through the alternative media itself, with newspapers and television giving almost no indication that such an event was building (Hassan, 2004). It was the first 'global demonstration' in history and was made possible – indeed could only have been possible – through networked communication and the creation of an alternative public sphere. The BBC (2003) estimated that between 6 and 8 million people took to the streets on that day, whereas one anti-war document stated that up to 30 million people took part in the worldwide protest – citing a plausible figure of 3 million protesters in Spain alone (Simonson, 2003). Whatever the actual number, it is clear that this 'virtual politics' can have real world effects by putting millions of people on to the streets of the world's major centres of power.

Evolving in tandem with this more complex form of online political activity at the beginning of the new century were more complex technological ways of using the Internet. This was expressed in the rise of user-generated content, made possible by Web 2.0 applications, which in turn allowed the creation of social networking and blogging. In general terms, blogs are usually the result of the work of a self-motivated individual who will post articles of interest to the blog for others – anyone – to comment on. Little technical knowledge is required beyond the mastering of relatively easy-to-use software or 'blogware', such as *Blogger* or *Typepad*. Articles or news items can be joined through a hyperlink that would take you to the source of the article, or they can be archived and preserved for future use and citing through a permalink. Recently, 'moblogs' (mobile blogging) has emerged. This is an even more immediate and media-rich form of blogging where mobile phones and PDAs can be used to upload photos, text or video straight to the Internet. Blogging has become immensely popular. It has been calculated, for example, that the 'blogosphere' is growing by one personal web page every second. By January 2006, there were an estimated 57 million blogs, a 6,000 per cent rise from three years previously, and a phenomenally intricate 1.5 billion links interconnecting them (Technorati, 2006).

Blogs are so simple to create and maintain that, inevitably, they will reflect every whim and obsession that people have. Many blogs are devoted to scouring the Internet for weird and wonderful things: links to pictures, streaming audio and video, stories, new gadgets and so on. This trend might be classified as 'general interest' blogging that people can read, comment on or ignore at their leisure. However, many, if not a majority of blogs would go under the rubric of 'culture, news and politics'. This realm of the blogosphere is even more chaotic and dispersive than that of the emergent global civil society. With thousands upon thousands of blog sites sprouting weekly, political comment, ideas and analysis can range from the first rate to the vacuous, and from the liberal humanist to the neo-Nazi racist. There is no 'ethic' or set of rules that exist to uphold standards – and, if there were, they would be impossible to supervise or enforce. And who would have the right to pronounce on universal principles across a global diversity anyway?

The point is that they are being embraced by millions of people who spend their time creating them, reading them and thinking and acting on what they have created and read. In some ways blogs are having a discernible effect on both the political process and mainstream media whose institutional structures they threaten – or at least are perceived to threaten. Repressive regimes such as those of Iran and China get very uneasy at the thought of free and unregulated communication emanating from within their borders. And with good reason: it was estimated that in 2005 there were about 50,000 bloggers in Iran. One of them, Arash Sigarchi, was jailed for fourteen years for what a BBC report termed 'charges of spying and aiding foreign counter-revolutionaries' (BBC News Online, 2005). Mainland Chinese authorities, for their part, have been busy blocking Blogger- and Typepad-enabled blogs to stop would-be Chinese bloggers from reading overseas blogs or creating their own. Moreover, in addition to using a specially written edition of the Google search engine to censor what its people can see, hear and read on the Internet, it was reported (in a blog) that this blocking capability was supplied to the Chinese government courtesy of US corporation Cisco Systems (RConversation, 2005).

Like the 'beehive' that is Wikipedia, the blogosphere generates its own self-organization. For example, most political blogs have sidebars, or what are termed 'blogrolls', where readers can view links to dozens, sometimes hundreds, of other blogs that share the same interests. At another level of organizational complexity, clusters of like-minded bloggers form in cyberspace to create political pressure groups. One such group is the Paris-based Reporters Sans Frontières, or, in English, Reporters Without Borders (<www.rsf.org>). Their website provides free access to a publication called *Handbook for Bloggers and Cyberdissidents*. This 'manual' gives advice on how wannabe political bloggers can get to work. Information such as 'how to set up and run a blog', 'how to blog anonymously' and 'technical ways to get around censorship' are offered. Julien Pain contributes an essay, 'Bloggers: The New Heralds of Free Expression', to the handbook and in it he writes that:

> Blogs get people excited. Or else they disturb and worry them. Some people distrust them. Others see them as the vanguard of a new information revolution. One thing is for sure: they are rocking the foundations of the media in countries as different as the United States, China and Iran. (2005: 5)

Reporters Without Borders see blogging, naturally enough, as the basis for a potential revolution in journalism. They see it functioning as a kind of journalistic rhizome where honest and truthful reporting has the ability to undermine the corporate media together with the political status quo whose interests it principally serves. As Pain (2005) goes on to argue: 'blogging is a powerful tool of freedom of expression that has enthused millions of ordinary people. Passive consumers of information have become energetic participants in a new kind of journalism'.

It was a kind of journalism that came to the fore during the lead-up to the Iraq War in 2003. In the weeks and months prior to the widely expected US invasion in March of that year, the 'Baghdad Blogger', whose blog name was 'Salam Pax', animated the blogosphere and the wider institutional media with his accounts of daily life in the Iraqi capital, where journalists were unable to operate freely. After the invasion he still kept up his posting to his blog, <dear_raed.blogspot.com>. So popular did his blog become, especially his description of the 'shock and awe' phase of the US bombing, that he was hired by the *Guardian* newspaper to write a fortnightly column (McCarthy, 2003). Much blogging is from a liberal, left-of-centre political perspective. However, there is no shortage of diametrically opposed blogs. Again during the 2003 Iraq War, a blog called <blogsofwar.com> attracted a large following for its alleged revealing of the 'truths' that the left-leaning 'liberal press' would not print about the war.

Blogs can catch politicians lying, they can expose their hypocrisies, they can pick holes in their policies, and they can humiliate them through uploading videos of embarrassing gaffes, through the posting of compromising documents and so on, much to the doubtless amusement and/or disgust of thousands of people across the world. Blogging has an impact, clearly. But, as a new form of politics, what are we to make of the phenomenon? Does blogging represent the flowering of a limitless diversity of political opinion and political choices – and therefore represent a viable alternative to the shallowness of institutionalized politics? A striking fact that one can easily discover is that many blogs simply repeat what is said in other blogs. In other words, if the surface of the blogosphere is scratched, an impression can quickly be formed that political bloggers are a collection of politics nerds who spend their time reading and swapping each other's postings. As the blogosphere expands exponentially, this perceived pattern of political repetition has been seen by some to point to something beyond simple 'information overload' or 'data trash' – as yet another problem for democracy.

In his 2001 book, *Republic.com*, Cass Sunstein makes the point that in the near future technology will have 'greatly increased people's ability to "filter" what they want to read, see, and hear . . . [and] you need not come across topics and views that you have not sought out. Without any difficulty, you are able to see exactly what you want to see, no more and no less' (3). It is a new kind of media use that threatens to make redundant any general interest media that cover a whole range of topics in the one newspaper or magazine. Sunstein has a name for this media consumption. He calls it '*The Daily Me* – a communications package that is personally designed, with each component fully chosen in advance' (7). He notes that this kind of technology was hailed by many as a triumph of individuality, convenience and control. Sunstein sees this as a form of consumer power – the 'growing power of consumers to filter what they see' (8). Ostensibly this does seem like a good thing. You read and see what you want, when you want. No nasty surprises as might happen on old broadcast television, where a graphic vision of, say, a car bomb going off in some far-off city, with many innocents killed and injured, is unexpectedly shown. In this new kind of media consumption, serendipity, or chancing across an interesting article, or hearing a point of view that you were not previously familiar with, becomes increasingly less likely as filtering software becomes more sophisticated. As Sunstein put it, however, such a development is a false kind of social power that puts private control in conflict with public democracy. The shared experiences that help constitute a 'mass society', where people have a similar perspective on the world and fairly similar forms of knowledge through which to inform this common world view, are in danger of degenerating into a kind of social fragmentation within cyberspace (10–13). Through the technological ability to be exposed only to what you want to be exposed to, opinions, views and ideas ring as if in an echo chamber. As Sunstein puts it: 'New technologies, emphatically including the Internet, are dramatically increasing people's ability to hear echoes of their own voices and to wall themselves off from others' (49). Moreover, there is the tendency to listen out only for 'louder echoes of their own voices' (16). This presents a major problem as far as a vibrant and diverse democratic functioning is concerned. Fragmented communication, ghettoized communication, 'niched' communication, leads to a narrowing of opinion. We may feel 'free' and secure within our own digital bubble, but as Sunstein argues:

> Freedom consists not simply in preference satisfaction but also in the chance to have preferences and beliefs formed after exposure to a sufficient amount of information, and also to a wide and diverse range of options. There can be no assurance of freedom in a system committed to the 'Daily Me'. (2001: 50)

There are shades here, I think, of Marshal McLuhan and his thesis on narcissism. In his *Understanding Media*, McLuhan famously characterized technologies as 'extensions' of ourselves. He develops this idea further to suggest that so wholly do they become part of us, that we come to be dependent upon them. For McLuhan this can easily spill over into a technological *obsession*. Indeed, this is something we might recognize in our own time with some people's apparent obsession with mobile phones, Internet surfing and so on. Furthermore, as these technologies are in a sense 'part' of us, acting as 'extensions' of ourselves, this obsession can lead to an *obsession with ourselves*, what McLuhan calls a 'Narcissus fixation' (1964: 19). Here, immersed in our own technologized media world, what McLuhan terms the 'private point of view' forms part of this fixation and the individual becomes 'quite shut off' and 'ceases to be sensitive to the diverse and discontinuous life' (ibid.).

Writing in the 1960s, McLuhan could not foresee how his 'global village' thesis would come to pass so dramatically through economic globalization and the information society. Sunstein, however, did prefigure by a couple of years the rise of the blog. He did not use the term in *Republic.com* because in 2001 the term had not yet been coined – but forms of blogging were beginning to make themselves salient. He identified websites where 'news and views' could be personalized, and the user could get a digest of the kinds of things that he or she was interested in, then could share these with like-minded others through email. The term he used for this process was 'collaborative filtering', where people, as well as sophisticated websites like Amazon.com, are able to pander to your private opinions and tastes (25).

'Collaborative filtering' can be seen as another pre-blogging term for blogging, and is something Sunstein took up in 2007 in an updated *Republic.com 2.0*, where he devotes a whole chapter to the subject. He writes that political blogging is but a small percentage of the vast and growing total, but nonetheless they 'seem to be having a real influence on people's beliefs and judgements' (2007: 138). According to Sunstein, there are genuine benefits to be had from blogging in the political realm. For example, thousands of keen-eyed bloggers can act as fact-checkers (a bit like the Wikipedia community) on the claims of politicians or the media. Political bloggers are also able to highlight issues and force them on to the institutional agenda, issues that might otherwise have been forgotten or buried in an ocean of information. However, as yet, the evidence of the blogosphere's ability to influence the agendas of the public stage is, Sunstein concludes, 'all too little' (146). He believes that the wiki-based technologies of blogging simply make the echo-chamber effect much more efficient. Political bloggers, he observes, are 'primarily interested in cherry-picking items of opinion or information that reinforce their preexisting views' (143). Recall here my description of 'blogrolls' where like-minded bloggers advertise each other's sites.

Sunstein's main point is that as a forum for 'deliberative democracy' the blogosphere does not work. The echo-chamber effect, he argues, fragments the public sphere and polarizes political opinion. To strengthen his case, he cites the 'Colorado Experiment' from 2005, whereby in a controlled laboratory situation the polarization of political opinion within selected groups became strongly evident. The experiment consisted of ten groups of six American citizens, with each group consisting of people with either 'liberal' or 'conservative' opinions. They were asked to discuss between them three of the most contentious issues of the time: same-sex marriage, affirmative action and whether the USA should sign the Kyoto climate-change agreement. Participants were asked their opinion after fifteen minutes of deliberation, and then asked to try to reach a public verdict prior to the final anonymous statement. The results indicated that in 'almost every group, members ended up with more extreme positions after they spoke with each other' (60–1). So, not only was the polarization effect strengthened, but also the opinions within the polarized groups tended to become more radical. Sunstein suggests that 'it is entirely reasonable to think that something of this kind finds itself replicated in the blogosphere every day' (145). He cites further evidence that suggests that the blogosphere is indeed comprised of discrete political ghettoes: a study conducted during the 2004 US elections found that out of the 1,400 blogs surveyed, fully 91 per cent of the links (the 'blogrolls') were to like-minded sites (Sunstein, 2007: 149).

Blogging, or general online communication, can put millions of people on to the street, as we saw in the positive perspective – or, conversely, it can become a highly efficient echo chamber where opinions, ideas and strategies for political action are discussed in an increasingly narrow context, and where the tendency is towards ever more polarized and extreme opinion. As technological expressions of politics, or 'technopolitics', what can we take from this positive–negative summary? Unfortunately, it is not possible to give definitive answers or clear-cut predictions. Why? Because it is in the nature of the media – and in the nature of society – to militate against such a neat packaging of postmodern political reality. This is even more the case in the context of social/technological acceleration. For example, Wikipedia tells us that although blogging was fairly widespread from 2001, it did not become mainstream until 2004, when easy access to wiki software created the explosion in user-generated content. In the space of just a few years it has made an impact, intellectually and practically, as we have seen. However, this rapid acceleration should tell us something. The information society is still evolving. It is evolving in ways that we cannot predict because the logic of the information society, the rationale that drives it, is anarchic and based upon the disorder of competition. Blogging (political and otherwise) rose rapidly to become global phenomena. But if no one had conceived of it a decade ago, who's to say that it won't rapidly fall into abeyance over the next few years, when the new 'killer app' sweeps the planet as the latest techno-fad? Who, indeed, can argue against the *strong likelihood* of this happening? Change is a constant within capitalism, but capitalist change, or what Joseph Schumpeter called 'creative destruction', has become digitalized, and is expressed in the information that flows through the network at speeds that increase with every new microprocessor that is the latest 'system benchmark'.

Economy and politics are about social power, and power is now attached to the bits and bytes that comprise the network traffic. As Castells puts it, 'relentless adaptation' and the 'multiple strategies (individual, cultural, political) deployed by various actors' are what constitute the question for dominance in the information society (Castells, 1999). Power moves and stops, dissipates and concentrates, but in the context of a constantly moving dynamic where nothing stands still for very long. We discussed the power of Google at the beginning of this chapter. Google is presently top of the globalization/ICT heap with shares worth over $700 apiece and rising; it is the current darling of Wall Street. It is also the current favourite at the highest political levels, as we saw with the British government initiative to have Google involved with solutions for poverty in Africa. It has come a long way in a few short years. But Google could easily fall prey to the power flows of an uncertain and volatile economic/political system. 'Confidence' in the Google business model could evaporate in the wake of a political decision or technological development. Who knows? As for the institutional political realm itself, there is precious little sign that it has fallen out of love with a free market, or with globalization based on a free-market premise. This means that its self-marginalization from the loci of economic (and hence social/political) power will remain – and probably increase. Global and local political institutions still invest inordinate power in both the market and information technologies as the solutions for societies' ills. They do this in the face of very little supporting evidence, and do it at the expense of democracy, negating society itself, through its elected representatives, taking responsibility for humanity and its future. For example, global warming is possibly the most important challenge that faces us. But it is not to be tackled through the application of science and the mobilization of political will to prioritize action and to take the rational and logical measures necessary. Instead, humanity is to confront this impending catastrophe through the application of a market in carbon trading. In other words, we are entrusting our collective future to the irrational and illogical dynamics of capitalist competition (Monbiot, 2007).

Evidence of our unreflective faith in information technology as a social panacea was demonstrated in the Australian election of late 2007. A central policy platform of the opposition Labor Party was to launch an 'education revolution' if elected. The basis of this 'revolution' was to hand a laptop computer to every high school student in the country, which they could connect to a (proposed) 'high-speed broadband network [that would] ensure our global competitiveness in business and education' (Australian Labor Party, 2007). Exactly what (and on what evidence) a laptop and broadband connection would do to revolutionize education was not explained, only asserted. Nonetheless, Labor was elected on a landslide.

The question begs: what keeps society (global and local) together? *Fear* might be a reason. Fear of the pace of change (and so we tend not to challenge it, even as it accelerates); fear of our economy collapsing (so we don't question 'the experts'); and fear that our politicians don't really know what they are doing any more (Giddens's observation that we live in a 'runaway world'). In an information society governed by the volatility of market competition and driven by the hyperspeed of networked computers, and in the absence of an effective politics at the local or global level, the 'fear factor' makes some sense. Consider the opinion of Tony Judt (2007), writing on the logic of contemporary capitalism in the *New York Review of Books*:

> Fear is re-emerging as an active ingredient of political life in Western democracies. Fear of terrorism, of course; but also, and perhaps more insidiously, fear of the uncontrollable speed of change, fear of the loss of employment, fear of losing ground to others in an increasingly unequal distribution of resources, fear of losing control of the circumstances and routines of one's daily life. And, perhaps above all, fear that it is not just we who can no longer shape our lives but that those in authority have lost control as well, to forces beyond their reach.

And fear is at the centre of the supposed solutions for the crises of Western democracy: neoliberal globalization and information technologies. For example, the fear engendered by the Cold War is at the core of the computing logic that helped create the Internet. And fear of the threat of rising interest rates, of rising inflation, of rising prices for a barrel of oil, of a return to the generalized crises of the 1970s and so on, is the gel that binds globalization; not promise, or progress or hope. This baleful scene is a far cry from the rather more positive visions of someone such as Daniel Bell who foresaw the possibility of progress carrying the information society forward through knowledge workers and expert systems that were 'managed politically' in the context of a functioning and committed democratic polity (1973: 18–19). It is a scene that is also in stark contrast to those boosters of the information society for whom all kinds of social, material and democratic benefits would flow. They see the information society fundamentally in terms of pure technological progress. None of those we have discussed – and they are salient and typical of the tendency – view the information society as the offspring of a particular political/economic system. I have tried to propose another reality, one that is constructed through a political economy prism. It presents us with a reality quite different from the 'dreams' of progress and efficiency. We see their opposites.

Some conclusions

In this book I have attributed a specific logic (its causes and its effects) to the phenomenon we call the information society. This comes from the inevitable realization (for me) that the information society did not simply 'evolve' as some ineluctable process – or did not suddenly 'appear' due to the revolutionary invention of, say, the microprocessor that allowed the development of the desktop computer in the early 1980s. It, of course, has a pre-history comprising a whole set of human-made decisions, institutional transformations and political and economic imperatives that created the necessary context for the insertion of this particular logic and the creation of our current society.

And it is a logic, as we saw, that stems from the conjunction of neoliberal globalization and the revolution in the development and application of computer-based technologies. This has been the key point. These interrelated processes are two sides of the same coin, and have developed rapidly to become indispensable to each other. There would have been no neoliberal globalization without the amazing transformation in our relationship with computer technologies – and the ubiquity of computers and our dependency upon them would be at a relatively low level today without the massive ideological boost given by the rise of neoliberal economics. Notwithstanding the polished and seemingly ideologically neutral surface of the information society, with its wondrous applications and gadgets, it is nonetheless deeply inscribed by the logic of neoliberalism and the free market. Consequently these are, first and foremost, applications and gadgets developed not for human need, but as commodities for sale in a marketplace. Usefulness and saleability are therefore not necessarily mutually compatible considerations in the development of a computer-based product.

A reply to this might be: so what? This is a capitalist system and a neoliberal world. This is just how things are, you might be tempted to say. And indeed, many do, and they see, or are tutored to see, the information society as an essentially natural way of making a natural system more 'efficient', 'productive' and more 'flexible' to the point where we will all eventually have easier lives. Such a common response has its own possible explanations, as the preceding chapters have tried to show. First, as an *ideology*, neoliberalism has become so powerful that it has indeed become more or less naturalized as the normal and inevitable state of human affairs (Harvey, 2005: 19–31). That the organization of life through increasingly arbitrary market competition is largely accepted as the optimal form is given a veneer of credence by the fact that there are now no systemic challenges to neoliberalism. Socialism and communism have been mouldering in history's dustbin since the fall of the

Berlin Wall in 1989. Even the moderate social democracy of the kind articulated by labour and workers' parties around the world since 1945 has either withered on the vine of continual marginality, or the parties have simply transformed themselves into neoliberal parties. The British 'New Labour' transmogrification over the 1990s is the signal example.

Second, the information society itself reinforces the neoliberal world view. What Jeremy Rifkin (2000: 22) terms the 'economy of speed' made possible through computerization ensures that not only are productive processes accelerated, but that society is also. The world moves so fast, and is propelled by ever-increasing volumes of information, that we tend not to see the past any more as a guide to the present and the future, or see the future as the effects of acts in both the past and the present. We live more and more in the present itself. We spend our time, increasingly, in 'multitasking mode' where all we are capable of thinking about, or concentrating on, are the task(s) that are immediately to hand. And so the damage, cognitive and social, political and economic, wrought by what Simon (1971: 40–1) termed the 'poverty of attention', is only now coming to be recognized through a closer focus on the temporal dimension of the information society.

Having our attention diverted by the multifarious choices that the information society lays before us every day, at work or at home or at play, means in the first instance that we become necessarily less reflective. We simply have less time to devote to doing nothing other than thinking through a problem or an issue with the attention it deserves. So we have a less than 'full' picture of, say, how the global economy works, what the stock market is for, why fuel prices and interest rates are so volatile – and we are less able to usefully consider what might be done about it. The effect is that we are not only less reflective, but also less critical. To be less critical, to be less able to deliver a critique of an issue – or the world that surrounds us – makes us necessarily less politically powerful; it drains us of political agency, of the intellectual ability to see the concrete economic and social reality of the world, and be able to individually and collectively propose better ways and better solutions to problems that confront us.

The value of the political economy approach that this book has taken is that two primary features of the information society and its neoliberal undergirding are revealed behind the ideological mask. The first is negative and the second positive. On the negative side of the ledger is the fact that neoliberal capitalism and the information society are increasingly devoid of any institutional political control, leaving the market to decide how society is comprised. The more positive idea emerging from our analysis is that this free-market version of capitalism, notwithstanding a complete lack of any serious rivals, is not a natural or inevitable or permanent state.

Lack of political control, as we saw, was a conscious application of neoliberal ideology. Arguments made by political philosophers such as von Hayek, and implemented by professional politicians such as Ronald Reagan and Margaret Thatcher, to 'let the market decide' how society is organized, away from the allegedly corrupting, bureaucratic, slow-moving and inept hands of government were a response to the crises of the post-war regime of worldwide Fordism. Having begun in the 1970s, the process of neoliberalization has become universal today. In the USA, for example, the most advanced capitalist country on earth, Naomi Klein observed in 2007 that 'the state has lost the ability to perform its core functions' (417). As to the government of the day in the USA, Klein goes on to write that 'the state still has all the trappings of a government – the impressive buildings, presidential press briefings, policy battles – but it no more does the actual work of governing than the employees at Nike's Beaverton campus stitch running shoes' (418). This is Giddens's undemocratic 'runaway world', the world we all now inhabit under neoliberal globalization. Volatile and chaotic imperatives shape this reality, and it is a reality that touches all of us through the ubiquity of networked information technologies. With every passing day and month and year we pass through uncharted waters with no one at the helm, with no political leadership to shape the market and globalization to the forms of human need and a sustainable future. This is the reality of the information society.

The fact that this need not necessarily be so should be obvious through the political economy perspective. What it has shown us is that the questions of the information society, and the negative effects of speed, are essentially political and therefore must have, at least in the first instance, political solutions. Politics has not gone away, notwithstanding the withdrawal of political institutions from actively participating in the democratic shaping of the global economy; it simply reappears in other forms such as in the World Social Forum, or the growing activity of NGOs, and the ongoing vibrancy of what Douglas Kellner terms 'technopolitics'. And so the question posed in chapter 7, '"Who rules?" the market or democratic institutions?', will increasingly arise in these early years of the twenty-first century, as disaffection with neoliberal globalization mounts (Klein, 2007). If political institutions willingly abrogated much of their power in favour of the supposed 'laws' of competition, the solution therefore must be to take at least some of this power back and return it to the only really legitimate place – to the parliaments and congresses of representative democracies. But how?

The perspective shown here reveals no easy answers, only pathways of possibility. We can begin the journey by thinking about the information society more reflexively, as I have tried to do through comparing its boosters with its critics. To see the fundamental flaws in the ideas of those who embrace market-driven information technologies does not mean that we reject computers and try to live our lives without them. Already, for most of humanity, this would be an impossible task anyway. It means being yet more reflective and analytical, in spite of the imperatives of 'social acceleration', and it means a conscious effort to be intellectually aware of the deep and abiding links between the information society, as it is presently constructed, and neoliberal globalization. This then becomes *a critique* that focuses on the nature of neoliberal globalization, with its manifest propensity towards inequality, volatility and the undermining of the basis for social cohesiveness. We can add to this what I see as a major and in many ways unprecedented effect of the network society, that is, the social acceleration that has evolved due to the nature of capitalist competition and the 'need for speed' generated by it. Information technologies have been found by business to be ideally suited to speeding up almost every realm of life, from education, to work, to our family and private life. We need to realize that this conjunction of computer-based technology and free-market economics has created a networked society, but it is a society that is going nowhere in respect of human ideals of progress and sustainability. This does not mean that computers per se are to blame. It is the random and chaotic 'laws' of the market that are. However, we can reflect upon this more deeply to realize that in fact computerization may be one of the greatest technological resources that humans have ever developed. It's just that we don't control their use democratically or develop their potential towards social needs. As a result, the immense potential of computers is unrealized.

The information society today is political insofar as it functions in a democratic vacuum. Until the vacuum is filled by a politics that is oriented towards controlling this society we will continue to accelerate towards destinations unknown, to an existential emptiness, where the past and its lessons rapidly disappear and the future is a permanently dark horizon. It is inside here that the loop of reasoning always returns us again and again to the political question. And so we have an intellectual and political responsibility to think it through once more, looking for insights and for cracks in the edifice of current reality – to seek more positive spaces where we envision different ones.

Glossary

(My thanks to the Wikipedia community for many of the following definitions.)

assembly line   An assembly line is a manufacturing process in which interchangeable parts are added to a product in a sequential manner, using optimally planned logistics to create a finished product much faster than with handcrafting-type methods. The best-known form of the assembly line, the moving assembly line, was realized in practice by Ford Motor Company between 1908 and 1913, and made famous in the following decade by the social ramifications of mass production, such as the affordability of the Ford Model T.

blog   A blog (a portmanteau of web log) is a website where entries are commonly displayed in reverse chronological order. 'Blog' can also be used as a verb, meaning *to maintain or add content to a blog*. Many blogs provide commentary or news on a particular subject; others function as more personal online diaries. A typical blog combines text, images and links to other blogs, web pages and other media related to its topic. The ability for readers to leave comments in an interactive format is an important part of many blogs. Most blogs are primarily textual, although some focus on art (artlog), photographs (photoblog), sketchblog, videos (vlog), music (MP3 blog) or audio (podcasting), which are part of a wider network of social media.

broadband   Refers to telecommunication in which a wide band of frequencies is available to transmit information. Because a wide band of frequencies is available, information can be multiplexed and sent on many different frequencies or channels within the band concurrently, allowing more information to be transmitted in a given amount of time.

browser   A web browser is a software application that enables a user to display and interact with text, images, videos, music and other information typically located on a web page at a website on the World Wide Web. Text and images on a web page can contain hyperlinks to other web pages at the same or a different website. Web browsers allow a user to quickly and easily access information provided on many web pages at many websites by traversing these links.

civil society   In the modern sense, civil society connotes those areas of culture, politics, private life, the economy, media and so on that are outside or apart from the power of the state and its bureaucracies.

commodification In Marxist political economy, commodification takes place when economic value is assigned to something not previously considered in economic terms; for example, an idea, identity or gender. So commodification refers to the expansion of market trade to previously non-market areas, and to the treatment of things as if they were a tradeable commodity.

cyberspace A term coined by science-fiction writer William Gibson to describe his computer-generated virtual reality in which the information wealth of a future corporate society is represented as an abstract space. The word has come to be used as a very generalized term to cover any sense of digitally created 'space', from the Internet to virtual reality.

dark fibre Dark fibre is optical fibre infrastructure (cabling and repeaters) that is currently in place but is not being used. It is referred to as 'dark' fibre because optical fibre conveys information in the form of light pulses, so when unused they are dark.

dialectical/dialectics The word 'interaction' is sometimes used as a synonym for dialectic and this captures the dynamic of dialectic – but there is more. The word 'dialectic' is derived from the Greek word for open-ended dialogue or debate. A debate begins with a proposition (thesis), then the examination of a contrary view (antithesis), and then arrives at a new view that incorporates elements of both sides (synthesis). In the Marxist tradition this basic philosophical framework was developed, passing through Hegel's more spiritual meaning, into what was called 'dialectical materialism' (the application of this reasoning to real-world criteria). For Marx, this was in the dialectic of history that was being played out in the struggle between the bourgeoisie and the proletariat that would eventually be resolved in the 'synthesis' of communism. In cultural studies, the dialectic has been imbued with a critical element, or the arrival at synthesis through critical reflection, or what Fredric Jameson called 'stereoscopic thinking' – the ability to think through both sides of the argument (1992: 28).

digital divide
Stems from critique of the nexus between neoliberalism and the ICT revolution, and argues that free-market-based distribution of the fruits of information technologies will always leave behind those with the inability to pay. As information technologies spread across much of society, those who cannot afford them are increasingly disadvantaged.

dot-com bubble
The 'dot-com bubble' was a speculative bubble covering roughly 1995–2001 (with a climax in 2000), during which stock markets in Western nations saw their value increase rapidly due to

growth in the new Internet sector and related fields. The period was marked by the founding (and, in many cases, spectacular failure) of a group of new Internet-based companies, commonly referred to as dot-coms. A combination of rapidly increasing stock prices, individual speculation in stocks and widely available venture capital created an exuberant environment in which many of these businesses dismissed standard business models, focusing on increasing market share at the expense of the bottom line. The bursting of the dot-com bubble marked the beginning of a relatively mild yet rather lengthy early 2000s recession.

Fordism   A stage in the development of twentieth-century capitalism characterized by mass factory-based production for mass consumption in a mass market. Also characterized in the 'high Fordism' phase (1945–73) as the operation of the 'social contract' between capital, labour and government. In this 'managed economy' phase the 'strategic heights' of the economy such as shipbuilding, steel, heavy engineering and so on were planned and regulated to a high degree.

Frankfurt School   Group of German philosophers and sociologists who moved to the USA to escape Nazi repression in the 1930s. Its leading theorists, such as Theodor Adorno, Max Horkheimer and, more peripherally, Walter Benjamin, pioneered theories on the nature of cultural production in industrial society.

global civil society   Loose worldwide coalition of diverse groups, including NGOs, social movements, trade unions, political parties, religious groups and so on, that arose to confront neoliberal globalization and effects on their local constituencies.

globalization   In its economic context it is closely linked to the idea of the New Economy. Globalization is characterized by the opening up of markets and borders to economic competition, and the drastic deregulation of economies more generally, making them susceptible to 'market forces'.

hegemonic   Describes the process of domination of subordinate classes and groups through the elaboration and penetration of ideology (ideas and assumptions) into the common sense and everyday practice of those subordinate classes and groups (see Gitlin, 1981: 253).

historical materialism   Historical materialism is the methodological approach to the study of society, economics and history that was first articulated by Karl Marx (1818–83). Historical materialism looks for the causes of developments and changes in human societies in the way in which humans collectively make the means to live, thus giving an emphasis, through economic analysis, to everything that coexists with the economic base of society (e.g. social classes, political structures, ideologies).

human–computer interaction Human–computer interaction (HCI), alternatively man–machine interaction (MMI) or computer–human interaction (CHI), is the study of interaction between people (users) and computers. It is often regarded as the intersection of computer science, behavioural sciences, design and several other fields of study. Interaction between users and computers occurs at the user interface (or simply interface), which includes both software and hardware, for example, general-purpose computer peripherals and large-scale mechanical systems, such as aircraft and power plants.

ICTs Information and Communication Technologies. Literally, any device or application, hardware or software, such as a PC, mobile phone, scanner or personal digital assistant (PDA) that is connectable, in theory or in practice, to the network of networks that comprise the contemporary high-tech information society.

ideology An ideology is an organized collection of ideas. Count Antoine Destutt de Tracy coined the word in the late eighteenth century to define a 'science of ideas'. An ideology can be thought of as a comprehensive vision, as a way of looking at things as in 'common sense' and several philosophical tendencies, or a set of ideas proposed by the dominant class of a society to all members of this society. The main purpose behind an ideology is to offer change in society through a normative thought process. Ideologies are systems of abstract thought (as opposed to mere ideation) applied to public matters and thus make this concept central to politics. Implicitly every political tendency entails an ideology whether or not it is propounded as an explicit system of thought.

laissez-faire   A French phrase literally meaning 'let happen', or 'let do'. From the French diction first used by the eighteenth-century physiocrats as an injunction against government interference with trade, it became used as a synonym for strict free-market economics during the early and mid-nineteenth century. It is generally understood to be a doctrine that maintains that private initiative and production are best allowed to roam free, opposing economic interventionism and taxation by the state beyond that which is perceived to be necessary to maintain individual liberty, peace, security and property rights.

Luddism   The Luddites were a social movement of British textile artisans in the early nineteenth century who protested – often by destroying mechanized looms

	– against the changes produced by the Industrial Revolution, which they felt threatened their livelihood.
MIT Media Lab	Institution founded by Nicholas Negroponte and Jerome Wiesner in 1985. Funded through corporate sponsorship, the Media Lab conducts research that aims to integrate ICTs into many realms of culture, economy and society.
mode of production	In the writings of Karl Marx and the Marxist theory of historical materialism, a mode of production (in German: *Produktionsweise*, meaning 'the way of producing') is a specific combination of:

- *Productive forces:* these include human labour power and the means of production (e.g. tools, equipment, buildings and technologies, materials, and improved land), and desire.
- *Social and technical relations of production:* these include the property, power and control relations governing society's productive assets, often codified in law, cooperative work relations and forms of association, relations between people and the objects of their work, and the relations between social classes.

MP3	Motion Picture Export Group Layer 3. Digital format for encoding sound, widely used for sharing music files over the Internet.

NASDAQ	National Association of Securities Dealers Automated Quotation. It is a virtual, computer-driven equities trading system for over 3,600 communications, biotechnology, financial services and media companies. It began trading in the USA in 1971.
neoliberalism	Ideology that argues the innate superiority of the 'free market' as the principal means for organizing economic life. Arose as a re-reading (or misreading) of Adam Smith's *Wealth of Nations* (1776), which argued that the hidden hand of market forces would bring an economy into an 'equilibrium' of supply and demand. Contra Smith, however, neoliberal fundamentalists aim to bring the logic of the market to every realm of society. Neoliberalism underpins both globalization and the New Economy.
network society	A historical trend whereby the dominant functions of society, that is to say, its economic, cultural and media processes, are increasingly organized around networks. ICT-based networks have become, as Castells puts it, 'the new social morphologies [organizing structures] of our societies' (1996: 469).
podcast	A podcast is a collection of digital media files that is distributed over the Internet, often using syndication feeds, for playback on portable media players

and personal computers. The term 'podcast' is a portmanteau of the acronym 'Pod' – standing for 'Portable on Demand' – and 'broadcast'.

political economy   Originally the term for studying production, buying and selling, and their relations with law, custom and government. Political economy originated in moral philosophy and developed in the eighteenth century as the study of the economies of states. In the late nineteenth century, the term came to be replaced by the term 'economics', and was used by those seeking to place the study of economy upon mathematical and axiomatic bases, rather than the structural relationships of production and consumption.

post-Fordism   The term for the mode of production and associated socio-economic system theorized to be found in most industrialized countries today. It can be contrasted with Fordism, the productive method and socio-economic system typified by Henry Ford's car plants, in which workers work on a production line, performing specialized tasks repetitively. Post-Fordism can be applied in a wider context to describe a whole system of modern social processes. Because post-Fordism describes the world as it is today, various thinkers have different views of its form and implications. As the theory continues to evolve, it is commonly divided into three schools of thought: Flexible Specialization, Neo-Schumpeterianism and the Regulation School.

Regulation theory Regulation theory discusses historical change using two central concepts: Regimes of Accumulation (ROA) and Modes of Regulation (MOR). ROAs are particular forms in which capital organizes and expands for a period of time, exhibiting some degree of stability. A key example of an ROA from the work of the Regulation theorists is 'Fordism'. MORs are those constructs of law, customs, forms of state, policy paradigms and other institutional practices which provide the context of the ROA's operation. Generally speaking, MORs support ROAs by providing a conducive and supportive environment. But sometimes there is tension between the two, and this means that something must give. The change to and from Fordism is explained by the School in these terms.

social capital The term has been around since at least Bourdieu (1983) but brought to prominence by Robert Putnam (2000). It refers to features of social organization such as networks, norms and social trust that facilitate coordination and cooperation for mutual benefit.

social democracy Social democracy is a political ideology that emerged in the late nineteenth

	century out of the socialist movement. Modern social democracy is unlike socialism in the traditional sense which aims to end the predominance of the capitalist system, or in the Marxist sense which aims to replace it entirely; instead, social democrats aim to reform capitalism democratically through state regulation and the creation of state-sponsored programmes and organizations which work to ameliorate or remove injustices inflicted by the capitalist market system. The term itself is also used to refer to the particular kind of society that social democrats advocate. While some consider social democracy a moderate type of socialism, others, defining socialism in the traditional or Marxist sense, reject that designation.
technopolitics	Used here to refer to the politics of the 'global civil society movement', whose organization and communications are based around ICTs.
Wi-fi	Abbreviation for **wireless** fidelity.
World Social Forum	The World Social Forum (WSF) is an annual meeting held by members of the anti-globalization (using the term 'globalization' in a doctrinal sense, not a literal one) or 'alter-globalization' movement to coordinate world campaigns, share and refine organizing strategies, and inform each other about movements from around the world and their issues.

References

Abramson, Ronna (2005) 'Linux Looms Larger Than Thought', <http://www.thestreet.com/_yahoo/tech/ronnaabramson/10199089.html>.

Adam, Barbara (2004) *Time*, Cambridge: Polity.

Adorno, Theodor W. (1998) 'Why Still Philosophy?', in *Critical Models: Interventions and Catchwords*, translated by Henry W. Pickford, New York: Columbia University Press, p. 10.

AFL-CIO (2005) <http://www.aflcio.org/corporatewatch/paywatch/pay/index.cfm>.

Aglietta, Michel (1979) *A Theory of Capitalist Regulation*, London: New Left Books.

Anderson, Perry (2007) 'Jottings on the Conjuncture', *New Left Review* 48 (December): 6.

Angell, Marcia (2004) *The Truth About the Drug Companies: How They Deceive Us and What to Do About It*, New York: Random House.

Armstrong, Rebecca (2007) 'Who Wants To Be a Virtual Millionaire?', *The Independent*, 24 March, <http://news.independent.co.uk/world/science_technology/article2387853.ece>.

Arthur, Charles (2007) 'Do Social Network Sites Genuinely Care about Privacy?', *The Guardian Online*, <http://www.guardian.co.uk/technology/2007/sep/13/guardianweeklytechnologysection.news1>.

Australian Labor Party (2007) <http://www.alp.org.au/action/broadband.php?task=submit_form>.

Aviation News (2007) <http://www.aviationnews.us/articles.php?art_id=1449&start=1> (accessed 22 February 2007).

Bachelard, Gaston (1994) *The Poetics of Space*, New York: Orion Press.

Bangeman, Eric (2006) 'Apple, Creative Settle Lawsuits', *ArsTechnica*, <http://arstechnica.com/news.ars/post/20060823-7575.html>.

Barton, John H., Goldstein, Judith L., Josling, Timothy E. and Steinberg, Richard H. (2006) *The Evolution of the Trade Regime: Politics, Law, and Economics of the GATT and the WTO*, Princeton, NJ: Princeton University Press.

Bates, Tony (2004) 'The Promise and the Myths of e-learning in Post-secondary Education', in *The Network Society: A Cross-cultural*

Perspective, Manuel Castells (ed.), Cheltenham: Edward Elgar Publishing, pp. 23–53.

Battino, David and Richards, Kelli (2005) *The Art of Digital Music*, New York: Backbeat Books.

Baudrillard, Jean (1994) *Simulacra and Simulation*, trans. Sheila Faria Glaser, Ann Arbor: University of Michigan Press.

BBC News Online (2003) 'Millions Join Anti-War Protest', <http://news.bbc.co.uk/2/hi/europe/2765215.stm>.

BBC News Online (2005) <http://news.bbc.co.uk/2/hi/technology/4072704.stm>.

BBC News Online (2007) 'Facebook Costs Businesses Dear', <http://news.bbc.co.uk/1/hi/technology/6989100.stm>.

Beck, Ulrich and Beck-Gernsheim, Elizabeth (2002) *Individualization: Institutionalized Individualism and Its Social and Political Consequences*, Thousand Oaks, Calif.: Sage.

Bell, Daniel (1973) *The Coming of the Post-Industrial Society*, New York: Basic Books.

Bergstein, Adrian (2007) 'Tech Researchers Calculate Digital Info', *Wired Magazine* (16 March), <http://www.foxnews.com/wires/2007Mar06/0,4670,InformationExplosion,00.html> (accessed 17 March 2007).

Berman, Marshall (1981) *All That is Solid Melts into Air: The Experience of Modernity*, New York: Verso.

Bertman, Steven (1998) *Hyperculture: The Human Cost of Speed*, Westport, Conn.: Praeger.

Bhat, Devika (2007) 'JJB Sports Faces Legal Action over Price-fixing', *Times Online*, <http://business.timesonline.co.uk/tol/business/law/article1353424.ece> (accessed 4 April 2007).

Blackburn, Robin (2006) 'Finance and the Fourth Dimension', *New Left Review* 39 (May–June): 39–70.

Blackwater USA (2007) <http://www.blackwaterusa.com/>.

Borsook, Paulina (1993) 'Release', *Wired* 1.05 (November), <http://www.wired.com/wired/archive//1.05/dyson.html?person=esther_dyson&topic_set=wiredpeople>.

Bourdieu, P. (1983) 'Forms of Capital', in J. C. Richards (ed.), *Handbook of Theory and Research for the Sociology of Education*, New York: Greenwood Press, pp. 241–58.

Boyer, Robert (2000) 'Is a Finance-led Growth Regime a Viable Alternative to Fordism? A Preliminary Analysis', *Economy and Society* 1: 29.

British General Election (2001) <http://www.historylearningsite.co.uk/2001_british_general_election.htm>.

Branstetter, Lee and Lardy, Nicholas (2006) 'China's Embrace of Globalization', Working Paper 12373, National Bureau of Economic Research, July, <http://www.nber.org/papers/w12373> (accessed 12 March 2007).

Brenner, Robert (1998) 'Uneven Development and the Long Downturn: The Advanced Capitalist Economies from Boom to Stagnation, 1950–1998', *New Left Review* 229 (May–June): 1–265.

Brenner, Robert (2003) 'Towards the Precipice', *London Review of Books* 25/3 (February), <http://www.lrb.co.uk/v25/n03/breno1_.html>.

Cairncross, Frances (1997) *The Death of Distance*, Boston: Harvard Business School Press.

Cairncross, Frances (2001) *The Death of Distance 2.0*, Boston: Harvard Business School Press.

Campbell-Kelly, Martin and Aspray, William (1996) *Computer: A History of the Information Machine*, New York: Basic Books.

Carnevale, Mary Lu (2006) 'Googler-in-Chief', *Wall Street Journal Online*, <http://blogs.wsj.com/washwire/2006/10/23/googler-in-chief/> (accessed 4 June 2007).

Cassidy, John (2002) *Dot-con: How America Lost Its Mind and Its Money in the Internet Era*, New York: Harper Collins.

Castells, Manuel (1989) *The Informational City*, Oxford: Blackwell.

Castells, Manuel (1996) *The Rise of the Network Society*, vol. 1, *The Information Age: Economy, Society and Culture*, Oxford: Blackwell.

Castells, Manuel (1997) *The Information Society*, vol. 2, *The Power of Identity*, Oxford: Blackwell.

Castells, Manuel (1999) 'Information Technology, Globalization and Social Development', United Nations Research Institute for Social Development, Discussion Paper Number 114 (September).

Castells, Manuel (2001) *The Internet Galaxy*, Oxford: Oxford University Press.

CBA (Center for Bits and Atoms) (2007) <http://www.cba.mit.edu/about/index.html>.

China Daily Online (2005) <http://www.chinadaily.com.cn/english/doc/2005-06/08/content_449600.htm>.

China Development Brief (2006) 'Bank Report Highlights Asphyxiating Drive towards Urban Gridlock', <http://www.chinadevelopmentbrief.com/node/662> (accessed 12 March 2007).

Chmielewski, Dawn (2004) 'Sony to Launch iPod Counterattack', <http://www.ecommercetimes.com/story/34945.html> (accessed 1 May 2007).

Chomsky, Noam (1999) 'Who Runs America?', <http://www.chomsky.info/interviews/19990401.htm>.

Chosun News (2007) 'Wife of Cyberdissident to Sue Yahoo', <http://english.chosun.com/w21data/html/news/200703/200703080003.html> (accessed 5 June 2007).

CIS (Center for the Internet and Society) (2007) <http://cyberlaw.stanford.edu/about>.

Conn, David (2006) 'How the Geordie Nation Turned into a Cash Cow', *The Guardian Online*, <http://football.guardian.co.uk/News_Story/0,,1704798,00.html> (accessed 4 April 2007).

Copeland, Douglas (1991) *Generation X: Tales for an Accelerated Culture*, London: St Martin's Griffin.

Currie, Jan (1998) 'Introduction', in Jan Currie and Janice Newson (eds), *Universities and Globalization: Critical Perspectives*, London: Sage, pp. 1–14.

Davies, Kevin (2007) 'Computing the Genome; Conversation with Charles DeLisi', *BIO-IT World* (September), <http://www.bioitworld.com/archive/091604/horizons_genome.html?page:int=-1>.

Davis, Mike (2006) *Planet of Slums*, London: Verso.

Delanty, Gerard (2001) *Challenging Knowledge: The University in the Knowledge Society*, Buckingham: Open University Press.

Dell Corporation (2007) 'Dell PCs Featuring Ubuntu', <http://www.dell.com/content/topics/segtopic.aspx/linux_3x?c=us&cs=19&l=en&s=dhs>.

Denise, Malcolm L. (1962) 'Automation and Unemployment: A Management Viewpoint', in *Automation, The Annals of the American Academy of Political and Social Science*, vol. 340, pp. 90–9.

de Sola Pool, Ithiel (1983) *Technologies of Freedom*, Cambridge, Mass.: Harvard University Press.

Deutsche Bank (2007) 'Global Economic Outlook 2007 – Longest Ever Recovery about to End?', <http://www.dbresearch.com/PROD/DBR_INTERNET_EN-PROD/PROD0000000000205476.PDF> (accessed 8 March 2007).

de Zengotita, Thomas (2005) *Mediated: How the Media Shape Your World*, London: Bloomsbury.

Dillon, Sam (2004) 'What Corporate America Can't Build: A Sentence', <http://www.nytimes.com/learning/teachers/featured_articles/2004 1210friday.html?8bl> (accessed 25 February 2007).

Dodgson, Kath (2001) 'Electronic Monitoring of Released Prisoners: An Evaluation of the Home Detention Curfew Home Office Research Study 222', available at: <http://www.crimereduction.gov.uk/workingoffenders/workingoffenders25.htm>.

DO-IT (1995) 'NII Award Winners Highlighted at Telecommunications Bill Signing Ceremony', <http://www.washington.edu/doit/Award/nii.html>.

Drucker, Peter F. (1993) *Post-capitalist Society*, Oxford: Heinemann.

Dyson, Esther (1997) *Release 2.0: A Design for Living in the Digital Age*, New York: Broadway Books.

Dyson, Esther (1998) *Release 2.1: A Design for Living in the Digital Age*, New York: Broadway Books.

Economist, The (1994) 64/7 (July): 44.

Edwards, Paul N. (1996) *The Closed World: Computers and the Politics of Discourse in Cold War America*, Cambridge, Mass: MIT Press.

Eisenhower, Dwight, D. (1961) 'The Military-Industrial Complex Speech', <http://coursesa.matrix.msu.edu/~hst306/documents/indust.html>.

Elliot, Larry and Boseley, Sarah (2007) 'Brown Calls on Google to Help World's Poor', the *Guardian* (10 December), <http://www.guardian.co.uk/society/2007/dec/10/internationalaidanddevelopment.google>.

Ellul, Jacques (1980) *The Technological System*, trans. from the French by Joachim Neugroschel, New York: Continuum.

Ellul, Jacques (1990) *The Technological Bluff*, trans. by Geoffrey W. Bromiley, Grand Rapids, Michigan: William B. Eerdmans Publishing.

Engels, Friedrich (1987) *The Condition of the Working Class in England*, London: Penguin Classics.

FAIR (Fairness and Accuracy in Reporting) (2007) 'Iraq and the Media: A Critical Timeline', <http://www.fair.org/index.php?page=3062>.

Falk, Richard (1999) *Predatory Globalization: A Critique*, Cambridge: Polity.

Fastcompany.com (2007) 'Facebook by the Numbers', <http://www.fastcompany.com/magazine/115/open_features-hacker-dropout-ceo-facebook-numbers.html>.

Faunce, William A., Hardin, Einar, and Jacobson, Eugene H. (1962) 'Automation and the Employee', *Annals of the American Academy of Political and Social Science*, vol. 340, *Automation* (March), pp. 60–8.

Flannery, Tim (2006) *The Weather Makers*, New York: Atlantic Monthly Press.

Flew, Terry (2003) *New Media: An Introduction*, Melbourne: Oxford University Press.

Foucault, Michel (1980) 'Truth and Power', in *Power/Knowledge: Selected Interviews and Other Writings 1972–1977*, ed. Colin Gordon, New York: Pantheon Books, pp. 109–33.

Fox, Loren (2003) *Enron: The Rise and Fall*, New York: John Wiley & Sons.

Fraim, John (2005) 'Symbolism of Control'. *foamy custard* blog, <http://www.indigogroup.co.uk/foamycustard/fc050.htm> (accessed 23 May 2007).

Frank, Thomas (2001) *One Market Under God: Extreme Capitalism, Market Populism and the End of Market Democracy*, New York: Secker & Warburg.

Froud, Julie and Williams, Karel (2003) 'Enron: A Case Study in Financialization', in *Critical Perspectives on Accounting* 14: 83–115.

Furedi, Frank (2004) *Therapy Culture: Cultivating Vulnerability in an Anxious Age*, London: Routledge.

Gardner, Amanda (2006) 'Hectic Days Leave Fleeting Memories', *HealthDay*, <http://www.nlm.nih.gov/medlineplus/news/fullstory_36573.html>.

Gare, Arran (1996) *Nihilism Inc*, Sydney: Eco-Logical Press.

Gates, Bill (1995) *The Road Ahead*, New York: Penguin Books.

Gates, Bill (2000) *Business @ the Speed of Thought*, New York: Warner Business Books.

Giddens, Anthony (1990) *The Consequences of Modernity*, Stanford: Stanford University Press.

Giddens, Anthony (1999) *Runaway World: How Globalisation is Shaping Our Lives*, London: Profile Books.

Gilder, George (1992) *Life after Television*, New York: W. W. Norton.

Gilder, George (1999) *Gilder Report*, in Thomas Frank (2001), *One Market Under God: Extreme Capitalism, Market Populism and the End of Market Democracy*, New York: Secker & Warburg, p. 355.

Gitlin, T. (1981) *The Whole World is Watching*, Berkeley: University of California Press.

Gleick, James (2000) *Faster: The Acceleration of Just About Everything*, New York: Abacus.

Glyn, Andrew (2006) 'Marx's Reserve Army of Labour is about to Go Global', *The Guardian Online*, 5 April, <http://www.guardian.co.uk/comment/story/0,,1746818,00.html> (accessed 13 March 2007).

Goldberg, Arthur J. (1962) 'The Role of Government', in *The Annals of the American Academy of Political and Social Science*, Automation 340: 1, 10–16.

Google.com (2007) Corporation Website, <http://www.google.com/intl/en/corporate/facts.html> (accessed 4 June 2007).

Gore, Al (1993) The National Information Infrastructure: Agenda for Action (Executive Summary), <http://www.ibiblio.org/nii/NII-Executive-Summary.html>.

Gore, Al (1994) 'Speech to Royce Hall', UCLA Los Angeles, California, 11 January, <http://www.clintonfoundation.org/legacy/011194-remarks-by-the-vp-on-television.htm>.

Greene, Rachael (2004) *Internet Art*, London: Thames and Hudson.

Grossman, Lev (2004) 'Ten Questions for Bill Gates', *Time Magazine Online*, <http://www.time.com/time/magazine/article/0,9171,993537-1,00.html>.

Hale, Briony (2003) 'Beckham's Brand Power', BBC News, <http://news.bbc.co.uk/1/hi/business/2980562.stm> (accessed 4 April 2007).

Harvey, David (1983) *The Limits to Capital*, Oxford: Blackwell.

Harvey, David (1989) *The Condition of Postmodernity*, Oxford: Blackwell.

Harvey, David (2005) *A Brief History of Neoliberalism*, Oxford: Oxford University Press.

Hassan, Robert (2003) *The Chronoscopic Society*, New York: Lang.

Hassan, Robert (2004) *Media, Politics and the Network Society*, Maidenhead: Open University Press.

Hassan, Robert (2008) *Empires of Speed* (forthcoming), Champaign, Ill.: University of Illinois Press.

Hayek, von Friedrich (1978) *The Constitution of Liberty*, Chicago: University of Chicago Press.

Heath, Joseph and Potter, Andrew (2004) *The Rebel Sell: Why the Culture Can't Be Jammed*, Toronto: Harper Collins.

Heim, Michael (1993) *The Metaphysics of Virtual Reality*, New York: Oxford University Press.

Held, David (1994) 'What Should Democracy Mean Today?', *The Polity Reader in Social Theory*, Cambridge: Polity.

Held, David (2006) *Models of Democracy*, Stanford: Stanford University Press.

Henwood, Doug (1995) 'Info Fetishism', in James Brook and Iain Boal (eds), *Resisting the Virtual Life: The Culture and Politics of Information*, San Francisco: City Lights Publishers, pp. 163–71.

Hesseldahl, Arik (2004) 'The Wont-be iPod Killer', *Forbes.com*, <http://www.forbes.com/technology/feeds/wireless/2004/06/14/wireless01087222502107-20040614-004600.html> (accessed 1 May 2007).

Hewitt de Alcántara, Cynthia (2001) 'The Development Divide in a Digital Age', United Nations Research Institute for Social Development, Paper Number 4 (August).

Hobsbawm, Eric (1996) *The Age of Empire*, London: Weidenfeld & Nicholson.

Hobson, J. A. (1965/1902) *Imperialism, A Study*, Ann Arbor: University of Michigan Press.

Honoré, Carl (2004) *In Praise of Slowness: Challenging the Cult of Speed*, London: Orion.

Hughes, Thomas P. (2004) *American Genesis: A Century of Invention and Technological Enthusiasm, 1870–1970*, Chicago: Chicago University Press.

Human Genome Project (2007) Information Website, <http://www.ornl.gov/sci/techresources/Human_Genome/home.shtml> (accessed 10 May 2007).

ILO Report (2006) <http://www-ilo-mirror.cornell.edu/public/english/employment/strat/download/getbo6en.pdf> (accessed 15 February 2007).

Jameson, Fredric (1991) *Postmodernism or, the Cultural Logic of Late Capitalism*, London: Verso.

Jameson, Fredric (2001) 'September 11', *London Review of Books* (4 October), <http://www.lrb.co.uk/v23/n19/multo1_.html>.

Jenkins, Peter (1989) *Mrs Thatcher's Revolution: The End of the Socialist Era*, London: Pan.

Johnson, Bobbie (2007) 'Bloggers Silenced as Curbs Bring Internet Blackout', *Guardian Unlimited*, <http://www.guardian.co.uk/burma/story/0,,2180905,00.html>.

Joseph, Emma (2005) *Analysis*, BBC World Service, 'Video Games', broadcast 5 June.

Judt, Tony (2007) 'The Wrecking Ball of Innovation', *New York Review of Books Online* 54/19 (6 December), <http://www.nybooks.com/articles/20853>.

Kellner, Doug (2001) 'Globalization and Technopolitics', <http://www.gseis.ucla.edu/courses/ed253a/kellner/globtech.html> (accessed 28 June 2007).

Kelly, Kevin (1998) 'The Computational Metaphor', *Whole Earth* (winter), <http://www.wholeearth.com/ArticleBin/201.html>.

Kenyon, Susan (2008) 'Internet Use and Time Use', *Time and Society* 17/2–3: 85–103.

Kingwell, Mark (1998) 'Fast Forward: Our High-speed Chase to Nowhere', *Harpers Magazine* (May).

Klein, Naomi (2000) *No Logo*, London: Flamingo.

Klein, Naomi (2002) *Fences and Windows: Dispatches from the Front Lines of the Globalization Debate*, London: Flamingo.

Klein, Naomi (2007) *The Shock Doctrine: The Rise of Disaster Capitalism*, London: Allen Lane.

Kling, Rob (1998) 'Technological and Social Access to Computing, Information and Communication Technologies', *White Paper for Presidential Advisory Committee on High-Performance Computing and*

Communications, Information Technology, and the Next Generation
Internet, <http://rkcsi.indiana.edu/archive/kling/pubs/NGI.htm>.

Kolko, Joyce (1988) Restructuring the World Economy, New York:
Pantheon Books.

Krill, Paul (2000) 'Overcoming Information Overload', Infoworld,
<http://www.infoworld.com/articles/ca/xml/00/01/10/000110ca
overload.html> (accessed 23 May 2007).

Kroker, Arthur and Weinstein, Michael (1994) Data Trash: The Theory of
Virtual Class, London: Palgrave Macmillan.

Krotosi, Aleks (2006) 'Korea Shows Where the Avatars are Leading
Us', Guardian Unlimited, <http://technology.guardian.co.uk/games/
story/0,,1876808,00.html> (accessed 4 July 2007).

Kumar, Krishan (1995) From Post-industrial to Post-modern Society: New
Theories of the Contemporary World, Oxford; Cambridge, Mass.:
Blackwell.

Kurzweil, Ray (2001) 'The Law of Accelerating Returns', <http://
www.kurzweilai.net/articles/art0134.html?printable=1>.

Laing, R. D. (1967) The Politics of Experience, London: Harmondsworth;
quotes available online at: <http://www.worldofquotes.com/topic/
Change/index.html>.

Lanchester, John (2007) 'Warmer, Warmer', London Review of Books,
29/6: 23.

Lasch, Christopher (1979) The Culture of Narcissism, New York: W. W.
Norton.

Lash, Scott (2002) Critique of Information, London: Sage.

Lash, Scott and Urry, John (1987) The End of Organized Capitalism,
Cambridge: Polity.

Legend of Mir (2007) <http://www.legendofmir.net/>.

Lessig, Lawrence (2000) Code and Other Laws of Cyberspace, New York:
Basic Books.

Lessig, Lawrence (2002) The Future of Ideas: The Fate of the Commons in
a Connected World, New York: Random House.

Lessig, Lawrence (2004) Free Culture: How Big Media Uses Technology
and the Law to Lock Down Culture and Control Creativity, New York:
Penguin Books.

Licklider, J. C. R. (1960) 'Man–Computer Symbiosis', in IRE Transactions
on Human Factors in Electronics, vol. HFE-1 (March), pp. 4–11.

Loader, Brian (2002) 'A Paper for Community and Information
Technology: The Big Questions' (16 October), Melbourne, Australia:
Monash University, <http://ccnr.net/searchconf/loader.htm>.

Lyon, David (1988) The Information Society: Issues and Illusions,
Cambridge: Polity.

Lyon, David (2001) *The Surveillance Society: Monitoring Everyday Life*, Buckingham: Open University Press.

Lyons, Daniel (2005) 'Linux Rules Supercomputers', <http://www.forbes.com/home/enterprisetech/2005/03/15/cz_dl_0315linux.html>.

Lyotard, Jean-François (1979) *The Postmodern Condition: A Report on Knowledge*, Manchester: Manchester University Press.

Machlup, Fritz (1962) *The Production and Distribution of Knowledge in the United States*, Princeton, NJ: Princeton University Press.

McCarthy, Rory (2003) 'Salam's Story', the *Guardian* (30 May), <http://www.guardian.co.uk/world/2003/may/30/iraq.digitalmedia>.

Mackenzie, Donald (2006) *An Engine, Not a Camera: How Financial Models Shape Markets*, Cambridge, Mass.: MIT Press.

McLuhan, Marshal (1964) *Understanding Media*, London: Abacus.

Madlin, Nancy (1999) 'MIT Media Lab: Birthplace of Ideas', *Photo District News* 19/2: 35.

Manovich, Lev and Kratky, Andrea (2005) *Soft Cinema: Navigating the Database*, Cambridge, Mass.: MIT Press.

Markoff, John (2004) 'Internet Use Said to Cut into TV Viewing and Socializing', *New York Times* (30 December), <http://www.nytimes.com/2004/12/30/technology/30Internet.html>.

Marr, Andrew (2007) 'Curling up with a Good Rebook', *Guardian Unlimited*, <http://technology.guardian.co.uk/news/story/0,,2077278,00.html> (11 May; accessed 1 June 2007).

Marx, Karl (1973) *The Grundrisse*, London: Penguin.

Marx, Karl (1975) *Selected Works*, Moscow: Progress Publishers.

Marx, Karl (1982) *Capital*, vol. 1, London: Penguin.

Massey, Doreen (1994) *Space, Place and Gender*, Cambridge: Polity.

Melucci, Alberto (1996) *The Playing Self*, Cambridge: Cambridge University Press.

Merrill Lynch (2005) 'High-Net-Worth Wealth Grows Strongly at Over 8 Percent, Surpassing $30 Trillion in 2004, According to Merrill Lynch and Capgemini', <http://www.ml.com/index.asp?id=7695_7696_8149_46028_48149_48228>.

Microsoft (2006) <http://advertising.msn.co.uk/MSNSites/SiteDetail.aspx?siteid=43>.

Mills, C. Wright ([1956] 1970) *The Power Elite*, London: Oxford University Press.

MIT Media Lab (2007) 'Lab Overview', <http://www.media.mit.edu/about/retro.html>.

MIT Media Lab (2007a) 'Sponsor List', <http://www.media.mit.edu/sponsors/sponsors.html>.

MIT Media Lab Research, <http://www.media.mit.edu/research/ResearchPubWeb.pl?ID=31>.

Mitchell, William (1996) *City of Bits*, Cambridge, Mass.: MIT Press.

Monbiot, George (2006) *Heat*, London: Penguin.

Monbiot, George (2006a) 'Selling Indulgences', Monbiot.com, <http://www.monbiot.com/archives/2006/10/19/selling-indulgences/> (accessed 17 March 2007).

Monbiot, George (2007) 'Another Species of Denial', Monbiot.com, <http://www.monbiot.com/archives/2007/01/30/another-species-of-denial/>.

Morris, Sue (2004) 'Co-creative Media: Online Multiplayer Computer Games Culture', *Scan Journal* 1/1 (January), <http://scan.net.au/scan/journal/display.php?journal_id=16)>.

Mosco, Vincent (1988) 'Information in the Pay-per Society', in Vincent Mosco and Janet Wasko (eds), *The Political Economy of Information*, Madison: University of Wisconsin Press, pp. 3–27.

MSN.com (2007) <http://moneycentral.msn.com/companyreport?Symbol=GM> (accessed 4 June 2007).

MSNBC (2007) 'Microsoft Invests 240 Million in Facebook', <http://www.msnbc.msn.com/id/21458486/>.

Mumford, Lewis ([1934] 1967) *Technics and Civilization*, London: Routledge & Kegan Paul.

Negroponte, Nicholas (1995) *Being Digital*, Rydalmere, NSW: Hodder and Stoughton.

Neubauer, Deane (2004) 'Mixed Blessing of the Megacities', Yale Global Online, <http://yaleglobal.yale.edu/display.article?id=4573> (accessed 13 March 2007).

Noble, David F. (1998) 'Digital Diploma Mills: The Automation of Higher Education', *First Monday* 3/1, <http://www.firstmonday.org/issues/issue3_1/noble/#d3>.

Noble, Richard (1999) *Thrust: The Remarkable Story of One Man's Quest for Speed*, London: Bantam.

Nolan, James (1998) *The Therapeutic State*, New York: New York University Press.

Nowotny, Helga (1994) *Time: The Modern and Postmodern Experience*, trans. Neville Plaice, Cambridge: Polity.

Oates, John (2006) 'Google Kowtows to China', *The Register* (25 January; accessed 5 June 2007), <http://www.theregister.co.uk/2006/01/25/google_censors_chinese_results/>.

Olson, Mancur (1984) *The Rise and Decline of Nations: Economic Growth, Stagflation, and Social Rigidities*, New Haven, Conn.: Yale University Press.

Ong, Walter (1982) *Orality and Literacy: The Technologizing of the Word*, London: Methuen and Co.

O'Shaughnessy, Michael and Stadler, Jane (2003) *Media and Society: An Introduction*, Oxford: Oxford University Press.

Pain, Julien (2005) 'Bloggers: The New Heralds of Free Expression', <http://www.rsf.org/article.php3?id_article=14998> (accessed 2 July 2007).

Pilger, John (2006) 'The Real First Casualty of War', *New Statesman Online*, <http://www.newstatesman.com/200604240013>.

Poe, Marshall (2006) 'The Hive', <http://www.theatlantic.com/doc/200609/wikipedia>.

Poster, Mark (1990) *The Mode of Information: Poststructuralism and Social Context*, Cambridge: Polity.

Poster, Mark (2006) *Culture and Politics in a Digital Age*, Durham, NC: Duke University Press.

Postman, Neil (1993) *Technopoly: The Surrender of Culture to Technology*, New York: Vintage.

Proulx, Annie E. (1994) 'Books on Top', *New York Times* (26 May), p. A23.

Purser, Ron (2000) 'The Coming Crisis in Real-Time Environments: A Dromological Analysis', <http://online.sfsu.edu/~rpurser/revised/pages/DROMOLOGY.htm>.

Putnam, Robert D. (2000) *Bowling Alone: The Collapse and Revival of American Community*, New York: Simon & Schuster.

PWC (2005) *The Outlook for Video Games 2003–2007: A Global Overview*, <http://www.pwcglobal.com/extweb/newcolth.nsf/docid/152B12C8 21D261FE85256E28007668C9>.

RConversation Blog (2005) <http://rconversation.blogs.com/rconversation/2005/06/confirmed_all_t.html> (accessed 2 July 2007).

Reuters (2006) 'Service Sector Stumble in September', <http://money.cnn.com/2006/10/04/news/economy/ism_service.reut/index.htm?postversion=2006100410>.

Reuters (2006a) '60 Billion Emails Sent each Day', <http://news.cnet.co.uk/software/0,39029694,49265163,00.htm> (accessed 25 February 2007).

Rheingold, Howard (1993) *The Virtual Community*, Reading, Mass.: Addison-Wesley.

Rheingold, Howard (2002) *Smart Mobs: The Next Social Revolution*, Cambridge, Mass.: Perseus Publishing.

Rifkin, Jeremy (2000) *The Age of Access*, London: Penguin.

Rigby, S. H. (1987) *Marxism and History*, Manchester: Manchester University Press.

Robins, K. and Webster, F. (1988) 'Cybernetic Capitalism: Information, Technology, Everyday Life', in V. Mosco and J. Wasko (eds), *The Political Economy of Information*, Madison: University of Wisconsin Press.

Robins, K. and Webster, F. (1999) *Times of the Technoculture: From the Information Society to the Virtual Life*, London: Routledge.

Rochlin, Gene L. (1997) *Trapped in the Net: The Unanticipated Consequence of Computerization*, Princeton, NJ: Princeton University Press.

Rosa, Hartmut (2003) 'Social Acceleration: Ethical and Political Consequences of a Desynchronized High-Speed Society', *Constellations* 10/1: 3–33.

Rossetto, Louis (1998) 'Change is Good', *Wired* 6.01 (January), <http://www.wired.com/wired/archive/6.01/toc.html>.

Roszak, Theodore (1986) *The Cult of Information*, Berkeley, Calif.: University of California Press.

RWB (2006) 'Google Launches Censored Version of its Search-engine', <http://www.rsf.org/article.php3?id_article=16262> (accessed 5 June 2007).

Sabel, C. (1989) 'Flexible Specialization and the Reemergence of Regional Economies', in P. Hirst and J. Zeitlin (eds), *Reversing Industrial Decline?*, New York: St Martin's Press, pp. 17–70.

Sabelis, Ida (2002) *Managers' Times*, Amsterdam: Bee's Books.

Sabelis, Ida (2004) 'Global Speed: A Time View on Transnationality', *Culture and Organization* 10/4: 291–301.

Salon.com (2000) 'Esther Dyson', <http://www.salon.com/audio/ 2000/10/05/dyson/index.html>.

Schiller, Dan (2000) *Digital Capitalism*, Cambridge, Mass.: MIT Press.

Schiller, Dan (2007) *How to Think About Information*, Champaign, Ill.: University of Illinois Press.

Schlosser, Eric (2002) *Fast Food Nation*, New York: Perennial.

Schor, Juliet (1993) *The Overworked American*, New York: Basic Books.

Scott, Nigel, Batchelor, Simon, Ridley, Jonathon and Jorgensen, Britt (2004) 'The Impact of Mobile Phones in Africa', paper prepared for the Commission for Africa, <http://www.commissionforafrica.org/ french/report/background/scott_et_al_background.pdf>.

SecondLife.com (2008) <http://secondlife.com/>.

Sennett, Richard (1998) *The Corrosion of Character: The Personal Consequences of Work in the New Capitalism*, New York: W. W. Norton and Company.

Shenk, David (1997) *Data Smog*, New York: Abacus.

Shukman, David (2006) 'Addressing China's Climate Challenge', <http://news.bbc.co.uk/2/hi/science/nature/6111528.stm> (accessed 6 July 2007).

Showalter, Elaine (1985) *The Female Malady: Women, Madness, and English Culture, 1830–1980*, New York: Pantheon.

Simon, Herbert (1971) *Computers, Communications and the Public Interest*, ed. Martin Greenberger, Baltimore, Md.: Johns Hopkins University Press.

Simonson, Karin (March 2003) 'The Anti-War Movements – Waging Peace on the Brink of War' (document cited and accessible through Wikipedia), <http://en.wikipedia.org/wiki/February_15,_2003_anti-war_protest#_note-Millions> (accessed 28 June 2007).

Slater, Don and Kwami, Janet (2005) 'Embeddedness and Escape: Internet and Mobile Use as Poverty Reduction Strategies in Ghana', Information Society Research Group (ISRG) Working Paper Series, <http://www.isrg.info/ISRGWorkingPaper4.pdf> (accessed 13 March 2007).

Slaughter, Sheila and Leslie, Larry L. (1997) *Academic Capitalism*, Baltimore, Md.: Johns Hopkins University Press.

Slowfoodusa.org (2007) website accessed 21 May 2007.

Smith, Adam ([1776] 1965) *An Inquiry into the Nature and Causes of the Wealth of Nations*, New York: Modern Library.

Southerton, D., Shove, E. and Warde, A. (2001) '"Harried and Hurried": Time Shortage and the Co-ordination of Everyday Life', *CRIC Discussion Paper No. 47*, University of Manchester and UMIST, Warwick: CRIC.

Stallman, Richard (1985) *The GNU Manifesto*, <http://www.gnu.org/gnu/manifesto.html>.

Stallman, Richard (1999) 'The Free Universal Encyclopedia and Learning Resource', <http://www.gnu.org/encyclopedia/free-encyclopedia.html>.

The Stanford Encyclopaedia of Philosophy 'Globalization', <http://plato.stanford.edu/entries/globalization/>.

Stein, Jeremy (2001) 'Reflections on Time, Time-space-compression and Technology in the Nineteenth Century', in Jon May and Nigel Thrift (eds), *Timespace*, London: Routledge, pp. 106–19.

Stiglitz, Joseph E. (2002) *Globalization and Its Discontents*, London: Allen Lane.

Stirland, Sarah Lai (2007) 'CNN-YouTube Debate Producer Doubts the Wisdom of the Crowd', *Wired* (27 November), <http://www.wired.com/politics/onlinerights/news/2007/11/cnn_debate>.

Stone, Brad (2007) 'In Facebook, Investing in a Theory', *New York Times*, <http://www.nytimes.com/2007/10/04/technology/04facebook.html?ex=1349496000&en=dccd3bc016ab95a7&ei=5088&partner=rssnyt&emc=rss>.

Strange, Susan (1986) *Casino Capitalism*, Oxford: Blackwell.

Sunstein, Cass (2001) *Republic.com*, Princeton, NJ: Princeton University Press.

Sunstein, Cass (2007) *Republic.com 2.0*, Princeton, NJ: Princeton University Press.

Tait, Robert (2007) 'Iran Shuts Down Website Critical of President', *The Guardian Online*, <http://www.guardian.co.uk/iran/story/0,,2016552,00.html> (accessed 28 February 2007).

Taylor, Fredrick W. (1911) *The Principles of Scientific Management*, New York and London: Harper & Brothers.

Technorati (2006) <http://technorati.com/blog/2006/11/161.html> (accessed 2 July 2007).

Terdiman, Daniel (2005) C/Net News.com, <http://www.news.com/2100-1038_3-5997332.html>.

Thompson, Tony (2005) 'They Play Games for 10 Hours – and Earn £2.80 in a "Virtual Sweatshop"', *Observer Online* (13 March), <http://observer.guardian.co.uk/international/story/0,6903,1436411,00.html>.

Time Magazine (1992) 'How Sam Walton Got Rich', 15 June, <http://www.time.com/time/time100/builder/profile/walton2.html>.

Toffler, Alvin (1970) *Future Shock*, New York: Random House.

Trades Union Congress (TUC) (2005) Report, '2020 Vision for Skills', *Skills in the UK: The Long term Challenge*, Interim Report of the Leitch Review of Skills (December).

University of Northampton Website (2007) <http://www.northampton.ac.uk/courses/undergraduate/twoyear/#what>.

Utsumi, Yoshio (2005) 'Calls on World Leaders to Bring Benefits of Information to All', <http://www.itu.int/wsis/geneva/newsroom/press_releases/wsisopen.html> (accessed 8 March 2007).

Virilio, Paul (1991) *La Vitesse*, Paris: Éditions Flammarion.

Virilio, Paul (1995) 'Speed and Information: Cyberspace Alarm!', *Ctheory*, <http://www.ctheory.net/articles.aspx?id=72>.

Warschauer, Mark (2003) *Technology and Social Inclusion: Rethinking the Digital Divide*, Cambridge, Mass.: MIT Press.

Webb, Cynthia (2004) 'Google's IPO: Great Expectations', <http://www.washingtonpost.com/wp-dyn/articles/A14939-2004Aug19.html> (accessed 4 June 2007).

Webster, Frank (2002) *Theories of the Information Society*, London: Routledge.

Weiser, Mark and Seely Brown, John (1996) 'The Coming Age of Calm Technology', <http://www.ubiq.com/hypertext/weiser/acmfuture2endnote.htm>.

Weiser, Mark and Seely Brown, John (1997) 'The Coming Age of Calm Technology', in Peter J. Denning and Robert M. Metcalfe (eds), *Beyond Calculation: The Next Fifty Years of Computing*, New York: Copernicus, pp. 75–86.

Welch, Jack (2001) *Jack Welch Speaks: Wisdom from the World's Greatest Business Leader*, New York: Wiley.

Welch, Kathleen E. (1999) *Electric Rhetoric: Classical Rhetoric, Oralism, and a New Literacy*, Cambridge, Mass.: MIT Press.

Whitaker, Brian (2005) 'Politicians Least Trusted People', *Guardian Weekly* (23–9 September): 75–86.

White House Press Release (2000) 'President Clinton Announces the Completion of the First Survey of the Entire Human Genome', <http://www.ornl.gov/sci/techresources/Human_Genome/project/clinton1.shtml>.

Winokur, Mark (2003) 'The Ambiguous Panopticon', ctheory.net, <http://www.ctheory.net/text_file.asp?pick=371>.

Wittel, Andreas (2001) 'Toward a Network Sociality', *Theory, Culture & Society* 18/6: 51–76.

WSF (2007) <http://wsf2007.org>.

Yahoo.com (2007) <http://finance.yahoo.com/q?s=Goog> (accessed 4 June 2007).

Žižek, Slavoj (2001) 'Have Michael Hardt and Antonio Negri Rewritten the Communist Manifesto for the Twenty-First Century?', *Rethinking Marxism* 13/3: 190–8.

Index